a Manifesto for EARLY CHILDHOOD

a Manifesto for EARLY CHILDHOOD

edited by

AARON BRADBURY, RUTH SWAILES & PHILIPPA THOMPSON

Sage

1 Oliver's Yard
55 City Road
London EC1Y 1SP

2455 Teller Road
Thousand Oaks
California 91320

Unit No 323-333, Third Floor, F-Block
International Trade Tower
Nehru Place, New Delhi – 110 019

8 Marina View Suite 43-053
Asia Square Tower 1
Singapore 018960

Editor: Amy Thornton
Senior project editor: Chris Marke
Cover design: Wendy Scott
Typeset by: C&M Digitals (P) Ltd, Chennai, India
Printed in the UK

Editorial arrangement © Aaron Bradbury, Ruth Swailes and Philippa Thompson 2025.

Chapter 1 Dr Helen Simmons and Emma Twigg; Chapter 2 Dr Diane Boyd, Kerrie Lee and Dr Angela Scollan; Chapter 3 Dr Pat Day and Delya Lane; Chapter 4 Dr Jackie Musgrave; Chapter 5 Professor Verity Campbell-Barr, Dr Katherine Evans and Sasha Tregenza; Chapter 6 Philippa Thompson; Chapter 7 Dr Donna Gaywood, Professor Tony Bertram and Professor Chris Pascal; Chapter 8 Dr Aaron Bradbury; Chapter 9 Dr Nathan Archer and Dr Jo Albin-Clark; Chapter 10 Dr Lorna Arnott and Professor Rosie Flewitt; Chapter 11 Ruth Swailes; Chapter 12 Dr Sharon Colilles; Chapter 13 Professor Eunice Lumsden; Chapter 14 Gary Coffey and Lynsey Wigfull.

Apart from any fair dealing for the purposes of research or private study, or criticism or review, as permitted under the Copyright, Designs and Patents Act 1988, this publication may be reproduced, stored or transmitted in any form, or by any means, only with the prior permission in writing of the publishers, or in the case of reprographic reproduction, in accordance with the terms of licences issued by the Copyright Licensing Agency. Enquiries concerning reproduction outside those terms should be sent to the publishers.

Library of Congress Control Number: 2024950306

British Library Cataloguing in Publication data

A catalogue record for this book is available from the British Library

ISBN 978-1-0362-0602-4
ISBN 978-1-0362-0601-7 (pbk)

CONTENTS

About the authors   vii

Introduction   1

1 Early Childhood Policy: Advocating for Change   9
  Dr Helen Simmons and Emma Twigg

2 Early Childhood Sustainable Pedagogy into and Beyond the 21st Century   23
  Dr Diane Boyd, Kerrie Lee and Dr Angela Scollan

3 Transforming the Role of the School Nurse to Meet the Needs
  of Young Children   38
  Dr Pat Day and Delya Lane

4 Babies and Children's Health and Wellbeing   48
  Dr Jackie Musgrave

5 Early Childhood Curriculum   61
  Professor Verity Campbell-Barr, Dr Katherine Evans and Sasha Tregenza

6 Partnership or Coproduction with Parents?   72
  Philippa Thompson

7 Global Dynamics of Early Childhood: Welcoming Practices
  to Support Belonging in Early Childhood Education and Care (ECEC)   83
  Dr Donna Gaywood, Professor Tony Bertram and Professor Chris Pascal

8 Early Childhood Workforce Development   94
  Dr Aaron Bradbury

9 Children's Rights and Participation   107
  Dr Nathan Archer and Dr Jo Albin-Clark

10 Harnessing the Potential of Digital Devices in Early Childhood   118
  Dr Lorna Arnott and Professor Rosie Flewitt

11	Early Childhood Play and Pedagogy *Ruth Swailes*	129
12	Social Contexts of Early Childhood *Dr Sharon Colilles*	141
13	Keeping Children Safe in a Changing World *Professor Eunice Lumsden*	153
14	Inclusion, Special Educational Needs and Disabilities Gary Coffey and Lynsey Wigfull	164

Index   177

ABOUT THE AUTHORS

Dr Nathan Archer is a researcher at Leeds Beckett University. He has a professional background as a Montessori teacher and has worked in early childhood education for 25 years in practice, policy and research. Nathan completed a PhD at the University of Sheffield in 2020 exploring the agency and activism of early childhood educators in England. Since then, he has undertaken research with Sutton Trust, Nuffield Foundation and the University of Leeds.

Dr Lorna Arnott is a Reader in Early Childhood Education at the Strathclyde Institute of Education. Her work focuses on young children's lived experiences, primarily play around technologies, social experiences and creativity. She also has an interest in children's voice and creative approaches to participatory research with children in the Early Years. Arnott is currently a Co-I on a study across the UK, funded by the Economic and Social Research Council (ESRC), investigating birth to three-year-old children's language and literacy play with digital media at home in diverse communities.

Professor Verity Campbell-Barr is a Professor of Early Childhood Education at the University of Plymouth. Verity has over 20 years of experience researching early childhood education and care services, particularly the quality of early childhood services, the professional knowledge and skills of early childhood professionals and the meaning of child-centred practice.

Professor Tony Bertram is Director of the Centre for Research in Early Childhood (CREC). He is co-founder and trustee of the European Early Childhood Education Research Association (EECERA) and was its elected president from 1992–2007. He is currently Editor-in-Chief of the *European Early Childhood Education Research Journal*.

Dr Diane Boyd's experience is varied, with over 40 years of education teaching with a range of children from three to 11 years as an Early Years, infant and primary teacher. She has worked in higher education for the last 18 years supporting students in understanding child development and teaching experiences with a strong education for sustainability focus, challenging students to become climate activists and give agency to young children. She was involved with the DfE leading up to COP 26 and was personally invited to the launch of the DfE Sustainability and Climate Change Strategy. She was asked by the DfE to write a supporting document – *Sustainability Matters in Early Childhood* – which is situated as an exemplar on the government website. She has just contributed to a European Commission (EC) report (2024) highlighting the role of early childhood and also to a United Nations (UN) report (2024), again showcasing early childhood sustainable pedagogy. Diane has written and developed an early childhood resource that celebrates all 17 Sustainable Development Goals to support the EYFS, as well as the Northern Ireland curriculum and the Australian Early Years curriculum. She is currently promoting early childhood sustainability through the DfE Stronger Hub for the Northwest of England.

Dr Aaron Bradbury is the Principal Lecturer for Early Years and Childhood and Early Childhood Studies at Nottingham Trent University. Aaron is a member of the Coalition for the Early Years on the Birth to 5 Matters Non-Statutory Guidance for the EYFS and chaired and wrote the Equalities and Inclusion section with colleagues in the sector. Aaron is a published author on early childhood theories and child development. He sits on many national and early childhood groups and is also a consultant on many aspects of Early Years and child development. Aaron has spoken as a keynote speaker both nationally and internationally on contemporary issues within the early childhood sector. Aaron has a passion for making the voice of the child, nurturing through a diverse lens and pioneers of early childhood, the foreground of practice.

Dr Jo Albin-Clark is a lecturer and researcher in early childhood education at Edge Hill University. Following a teaching career in schools, Jo has undertaken roles in advising and research. She co-leads the Edge Hill University Research Network Children's Agency and Rights in Education (CARE). Her research interests include documentation practices and methodological collaboration and research-creation through feminist materialisms, posthuman and hauntological theories. Throughout her work, embodied senses of resistances and subversions to dominant discourses have been a central thread.

Gary Coffey is the Executive Headteacher at a federation of special schools and a special college in Birmingham. Gary has previously worked as a teacher within the Early Years and primary sector, within both mainstream and special educational needs. He has 12 years of experience as a senior leader within special schools. Gary has also supported the development of a special educational needs strategy with the Department of Education and Knowledge in Abu Dhabi. He is passionate about ensuring that every child has access to a meaningful and inclusive education, which supports their wider development. He is a Makaton regional tutor and uses his knowledge of communication to support his work in providing inclusive practice for all children.

ABOUT THE AUTHORS

Dr Sharon Colilles is a Senior Lecturer within Early Childhood Studies. Sharon is a trustee on the Froebel Trust Council as well as a member of their Education Research sub-committee and a vice chair on the Executive of the Early Childhood Studies Degrees Network (ECSDN). Other professional responsibilities include being an associate trainer for Early Education, a national charity supporting practitioners with training, resources and networks, and campaigning for quality education for the youngest children. She has a diverse career background, working initially in the Department for Work and Pensions (DWP) as a policy manager, owning a private day nursery, assessor for the award of EYPs, participating in the review of the Teacher Standards and, more recently, working as project assistant for the development of Birth to 5 Matters Non-Statutory Guidance. Sharon's research interests are particularly concerned with play-based participatory pedagogies and its part in developing children's mixed ethnic identity and cultural learning and development – especially learning and development informed by child-led perspectives. She also has a deep interest and engages in work that develops anti-oppressive and anti-discriminatory practice.

Dr Pat Day is a School Nurse and a Specialist Nurse Practitioner in young people's sexual health. She is passionate about making a difference to the outcomes of children and young people. She has worked in the community since 1995. Her interests are children and young people's mental health, sexual health promotion, safeguarding children and behaviour change. She teaches on the Public Health Nursing programme at Sheffield Hallam and has been part of the team since 2004. Her main priority is teaching and supporting public health nursing students in working with families to improve their health. She has remained a practitioner and works as a school nurse in Sheffield.

Dr Katherine Evans is a Lecturer in Education at the University of Plymouth, specialising in early childhood studies and Early Years/primary initial teacher education. Katherine's research interests include early childhood education and Early Years teacher education, with a particular focus on discourses of readiness and transition in the educational experience of children and practitioners.

Professor Rosie Flewitt is Professor of Early Childhood Communication at Manchester Metropolitan University. Her work focuses on how young children communicate through embodied, sensory modes as well as through language and with material artefacts, including digital technologies. Flewitt is currently leading a study across the UK, funded by the Economic and Social Research Council (ESRC), investigating 0–36-month-old children's language and literacy play with digital media at home across diverse communities.

Dr Donna Gaywood is a Senior Lecturer at the University of Gloucestershire, teaching on the Children, Young People and Families course. She is a co-convener for the European Early

Childhood Education Research Association (EECERA) Special Interest Group for Children from Refugee and Migrant Backgrounds.

Delya Lane is a Children's Nurse and Qualified School Nurse, having worked within the field of school nursing since 1995. She is passionate about making a difference to improve the health and wellbeing of young people. Having worked in areas of high deprivation, she feels that ensuring care is accessible to all is key to improving health outcomes.

Kerrie Lee is a Director of Student Experience and a Lecturer in Early Childhood Studies and Education at the University of Hull. She has over 27 years of Early Years practice, research and further/higher education teaching experience working from Level 3 to Level 7. Kerrie is a qualified Forest School leader leading Level 1 to Level 3 training sessions for the School of Education students and colleagues. Kerrie has developed both a Foundation Degree and BA (hons) Top-Up Degree to support early childhood practitioners in gaining qualifications while continuing to work, reflecting the journey she took herself. Over the last seven years Kerrie has worked with a local art gallery in developing an intergenerational space and has been co-lead on research projects with a local theatre group on productions aimed at birth to two and two- to five-year-olds who face social and economic barriers to the arts. Kerrie is Co-Chair of the ECSDN Sustainability Group alongside Dr Angela Scollan and she is working with her co-authors of the chapter to highlight sustainable pedagogy as a critical element of early childhood education.

Professor Eunice Lumsden is Professor of Child Advocacy at the University of Northampton. She is a Route Panel Member for the Institute of Apprenticeships and Technical Education and has advised the government on Early Years qualifications and health inequalities. She led the development of the Early Childhood Graduate Competencies and has contributed to workforce development internationally. Her research interests include the professionalisation of the children's workforce, child maltreatment, social justice, poverty and adoption.

Dr Jackie Musgrave is Associate Head of School with responsibility for Learning and Teaching in the School of Education, Childhood, Youth and Sport (ECYS) in the Faculty of Wellbeing, Education and Language Studies at the Open University. She leads on Academic Conduct in the School and co-chairs the Faculty-wide Academic Integrity Implementation group. She is a Principal Fellow of Advance HE. Jackie completed her MA in Early Childhood Education and Doctor of Education at the University of Sheffield. Jackie's research explores issues relating to the health of babies and children, reflecting her previous professional experience as a general as well as paediatric nurse. Her research has explored how Early Years practitioners support the health of young children in Early Years settings. She is a member of the Executive for the Early Childhood Studies Degrees Network for the Research and Knowledge Exchange and was a contributor to the development of the ECGPCs.

ABOUT THE AUTHORS

Professor Chris Pascal OBE is Director of Centre for Research in Early Childhood (CREC), based at the St Thomas Children's Centre in Birmingham. She is a co-founder and President of the European Early Childhood Education Research Association and a Vice President of Early Education.

Dr Angela Scollan is Associate Professor in Early Childhood Studies and Education at Middlesex University, where she is a member of the Centre for Educational Research and Scholarship. Her numerous peer-reviewed publications demonstrate Angela's leading role as an international researcher and scholar in children's rights, self-determination, reflective professional development, sustainable pedagogy, ethical research with and for young children and dialogic pedagogies. Her philosophy focuses on the 'child first' principle, which transpires in her numerous publications, where children's self-determination is approached as a resource for children, as well as for adults' learning. Angela has contributed to two large-scale European projects: Erasmus+ SHARMED (www.sharmed.eu/uk-international/home) and Horizon 2020 CHILD-UP (www.child-up.eu/). Both projects worked directly to promote integration of children with migrant backgrounds and refugees in the classroom through the facilitation of their active participation and agency. Angela combines her research and scholarly profile with 35 years of practice and teaching experience in early childhood, working with children, and then students across all academic levels up to doctoral studies.

Dr Helen Simmons is a Senior Lecturer in Education (Childhood, Youth and Families) at the University of Northampton, Vice Chair for Policy, Lobbying and Advocacy for the Early Childhood studies Degrees Network (ECSDN), a Trustee Board Member for the Association of Infant Mental Health (AiHM) and a Doctor of Education. Her teaching, research and publications centre on early childhood and infant and family mental health and wellbeing, with a particular focus on the sociology of childhood and parenting, and the promotion of a critically reflective early childhood workforce.

Ruth Swailes has over 30 years' experience in education. She has taught every year group in primary school from Nursery to Year 6. She has held a range of senior leadership roles including primary headship. Ruth has worked as a School Improvement Advisor, Inspector, Early Years Advisor, strategic lead and consultant in several local authorities. Ruth's passion is working with children in the 0-7 range and she currently works with settings, providers, MATs, LAs, Hubs and schools nationally and internationally providing training and support. Ruth is the lead author and trainer for the Oxford University Press International Early Years Curriculum for children aged 2-6. She was named Nursery World Trainer of the Year in 2021 and recognised by ISC research as a leading influencer in International Education in 2022.

Philippa Thompson is a Senior Lecturer in Early Childhood Studies at Nottingham Trent University. Philippa is Vice Chair of the Early Childhood Studies Degrees Network and Chair of the QAA ECS Subject Benchmark Statement review. Among her 14 years of practice experience, Philippa worked in many Early Years roles including senior leadership, international outdoor education and community partnership within Sure Start. Philippa also has nearly 20 years of higher education experience with research interests centred around the hidden voices of parents and families, rights and participation, wellbeing, food allergies and anaphylaxis.

Sasha Tregenza is a Sessional Lecturer at Truro College, Cornwall, and Doctoral Teaching and Research Assistant at the University of Plymouth. Sasha's research focuses on how young children's views of learning may enhance early childhood practice and understandings of quality.

Emma Twigg is a Senior Lecturer and Programme Leader for the Early Childhood Studies degree at the University of Derby. She is also a Vice Chair for the Policy, Lobbying and Advocacy strategy group for the ECSDN. She is in the process of completing her PhD looking at early childhood practitioners' representations of children who have experienced domestic abuse. Her teaching responsibilities include child protection and the tensions between legislation and policy.

Lynsey Wigfull is the Strategic School Improvement Lead for the James Montgomery Academy Trust, where she supports schools across a large trust of South Yorkshire primary schools drawing on 25 years of experience in primary and Early Years education. She has been a teacher across EYFS, KS1 and KS2, a SENCO, inclusion lead, headteacher, advisor for three local authorities, an Ofsted inspector, governor and chair of a children's centre cluster. She spent time as a Senior Lecturer in Primary and Early Years Education at Sheffield Hallam University and was also Course Leader for the SENCO Award there.

INTRODUCTION

The purpose of this book is to provide early childhood professionals, policy-makers, practitioners, parents and academics with an insight into how we can support a future based around child-centred outcomes. The book focuses on how early childhood policy changes need to concentrate on the needs of the child in the key areas of education, health and children's rights. Additionally, it suggests how professionals can improve the services available to children and families in modern Britain. The book addresses the needs of children in the 21st century. In an era of political change for children and families, this manifesto book considers where current policy-makers should focus from the perspective of experienced early childhood experts.

Rather than working against each other, this book explores the importance of inclusive early childhood policy. Policy-makers, academics and early childhood professionals are encouraged to engage in policy development and understanding by using current research and initiatives. In addition, we should speak out for our youngest citizens, emphasising the importance of inclusive, respectful initiatives that support families. High expectations in early childhood are underpinned by the importance of an early childhood graduate-led workforce (Bonetti and Blanden, 2020; Richardson et al., 2021). Our manifesto is built on the belief that quality provision will lead to the best start in life for our youngest children. As early childhood professionals, we must support each other in our advocacy role for children and their families. By influencing policy-makers and subsequent legislation, we can improve the lives of children and families.

To set the stage for change, the book begins with an overview of the policy landscape. The Child Poverty Action Group (CPAG) (2023) states that the Department for Work and Pensions (DWP) statistics in 2021–2 reported 4.2 million children were in poverty and the numbers are rising. Getting policies right for children from conception to age eight has never been more important. It can be suggested that policy could provide an opportunity for advocacy if research were considered from the discipline of early childhood. Professionals also play a complex role that requires knowledge and understanding of the environment in which they work including an understanding of how policy is developed.

There are several government departments that have quite different priorities in early childhood, according to Hasan (2007). All of these have their own difficulties and funding challenges, including education, health, social care and work and pensions. There is one thing they have in common: they all affect the quality of life of children and their families (Thompson, 2023; Bollinger et al., 2006). Knowing what has happened in the past is also important to our understanding. Table 0.1 is important to provide a context that dates from an historical change in government (to Labour, under Tony Blair) in 1997 which saw a strong focus on the importance of early childhood as part of society. With a ten-year strategy, the new government prioritised early childhood, including an emphasis on childcare. The election of 2010 saw 14 years of Conservative administration. As this book is written, we have a new (Labour) government that suggests moving the Family Hub agenda forward. We will need to wait and see how this is proposed.

Table 0.1 Key policy milestones

Date	Policy	Implications
1998	National Childcare Strategy (DFEE)	Sure Start development, Early Excellence Centres and Neighbourhood Nurseries all increased provision for childcare and nursery education.
2003	Green Paper – Every Child Matters (DfES)	Expansion of Early Years services which included a stronger emphasis on families.
2004	Choice for Parents, the Best Start for Children (HM Treasury)	A ten-year childcare strategy. The term 'good-quality affordable childcare' involved support for parents financially, increase in paid maternity time, hours were increased to 15 hours per week for free nursery education. A continued confusion between childcare and education.
2006	Childcare Act	Previous services were brought together as approximately 3,000 children's centres were developed, and the local authorities were deemed responsible for securing adequate provision of childcare for working parents. The emphasis is again on childcare.
2008	Introduction of the Early Years Foundation Stage (EYFS) (DfES)	This has since been revised in 2012, 2014, 2017 and 2021.
2010	Free Nursery education for two-year-olds introduced.	This created a clash of emphasis on quantity versus quality. The idea of affordable childcare against the qualifications of the workforce providing more than simply childcare.
2011	Early Intervention: The Next Steps – Allen Report	Heavy emphasis on early intervention with a suggestion that this would support the economy long term. There was a positioning of parents as hard to reach and vulnerable. A recommendation is included that pre-schools should be graduate or postgraduate led. Positive interventions such as a continuation of the Family Nurse Partnership were highlighted and a proposal that the Healthy Start Initiative and the EYFS should be more streamlined.

Date	Policy	Implications
2013	More Affordable Childcare	This included a new tax-free childcare scheme for working families.
2013	More Great Childcare: Raising quality and giving parents more choice	Introduction of Early Years teacher status and Early Years educator qualifications. Was deemed as a response to the Nutbrown review.
2015	*Building Great Britons,* published by the All-Party Parliamentary Group for Conception to Age 2 – The First 1001 Days.	This highlights a significant role for children's centres, antenatal and perinatal support and early intervention.
2018	Evidence-based Early Years Intervention. The Science and Technology Select Committee.	Makes the link with adverse childhood experiences and later life usage of health and social care services.
2019	Tackling Disadvantage in the Early Years. The Education Select Committee.	This cross-party report criticises government policy on Early Years. Recommendations are balanced on the premise that to reduce disadvantage children need quality Early Years provision and a quality home environment.
2019	First 1000 Days of Life. The Health and Social Care Select Committee.	The Healthy Child Programme is at the heart of this, with strong mention of the role of the family, the number of health visitor visits and continuity of care past 1,000 days.
2020	Ipsos MORI (2020). *State of the Nation: Understanding Public Attitudes to the Early Years.*	Report by the Royal Foundation with a key focus on positive encouragement of the role of parents with under-fives.
2021	The Best Start for Life: A Vision for the 1,001 Critical Days. The Early Years Healthy Development Review Report. HM Government.	This report formed part of the Early Years healthy development review. Six areas for action were outlined to support the improvement of all babies in England.

(Thompson, 2023, p. 90)

OVERVIEW OF CHAPTERS

CHAPTER 1: EARLY CHILDHOOD POLICY: ADVOCATING FOR CHANGE

This chapter explores the importance of inclusive early childhood policy and how, working together rather than against each other, policy could be a force for good. Using current research and initiatives, the chapter considers how policy-makers, academics and early childhood professionals can be engaged in policy development and understanding. This includes speaking up for our youngest citizens, highlighting the importance of respectful and inclusive initiatives that support families.

CHAPTER 2: EARLY CHILDHOOD SUSTAINABLE PEDAGOGY INTO AND BEYOND THE 21ST CENTURY

This chapter investigates levels of sustainability awareness and early childhood professionals' confidence to engage with Sustainable Development Goals (SDGs) in practice. It explores how understanding and knowledge of education for sustainable development (ESD) in early childhood practice has been left wanting, therefore confidence to embrace and embed it requires attention. Further, in this chapter the authors explore the historical and contemporary impact of sustainability in early childhood while also discussing the ways forward, including an emphasis on the need to develop a *sustainable pedagogy* (Scollan et al., 2024).

CHAPTER 3: TRANSFORMING THE ROLE OF THE SCHOOL NURSE TO MEET THE NEEDS OF YOUNG CHILDREN

This chapter advocates transformation of the role of the school nurse to meet the health needs of young children. The authors of this chapter are experienced school nurses who have worked in many different Early Years settings within the city of Sheffield. The chapter explores how the actions of well-meaning policy and systems can result in disengaged parents, hostility from parents, children being taken into care, poor academic achievements and emotional wellbeing issues. The authors believe that the time is right for significant resources to be allocated to the wellbeing of young children through upstream interventions.

CHAPTER 4: BABIES AND CHILDREN'S HEALTH AND WELLBEING

This chapter outlines a manifesto for improving the health of babies and young children and foregrounds the role of early childhood professionals in achieving this goal. The content outlines the author's motivation for wanting to encourage all of us to be aware of what we can do individually, within society as well as including key messages for government.

CHAPTER 5: EARLY CHILDHOOD CURRICULUM

This chapter begins with considering what is *curriculum* and who and what determines this, recognising the social-historical dimension of the epistemological framing of curriculum. The authors then consider the historical perspective in detail to ascertain what has shaped and influenced current perspectives on curriculum, but also recognising that these are often debated and contentious ideas. The chapter continues with a consideration of curriculum as something based in children's rights and respectful of early childhood professionals' professional knowledge and agency.

CHAPTER 6: PARTNERSHIP OR COPRODUCTION WITH PARENTS?

This chapter explores and challenges current approaches to 'partnership' in early childhood with a focus on all services that connect across health, education and social care. As the title suggests, the idea of coproduction is considered as a way of engaging in a reciprocal way and listening to those who have lived experiences of the services they receive. The chapter will focus on a manifesto idea of community which disrupts the often-proposed idea of engagement with parents where they are positioned from a deficit perspective and as one homogeneous group.

CHAPTER 7: GLOBAL DYNAMICS OF EARLY CHILDHOOD: WELCOMING PRACTICES TO SUPPORT BELONGING IN EARLY CHILDHOOD EDUCATION AND CARE (ECEC)

This chapter will be drawing on the PhD study: 'The post migration lived experiences of Syrian refugee children in early childhood education and care in England: four children's stories' (Gaywood, 2023). It will also be drawing on research conducted by the European Early Childhood Education Research Association (EECERA) Special Interest Group: *Inclusive Education for Refugee and Migrant Children: A Toolkit for Early Childhood Education and Care Settings* (2022). The chapter aims to support early educators to think about the impact of forced displacement on children and reflect on their own practice as a powerful tool to enable the children to develop a new sense of belonging.

CHAPTER 8: EARLY CHILDHOOD WORKFORCE DEVELOPMENT

This chapter is not suggesting that it has all the answers; it aims to build the vision needed for the sector to become sustainable for children and families. Change is inevitable, and now is the time to start that change. In recent years, it has become increasingly evident that skilled and well-qualified early childhood and education practitioners contribute significantly to the quality of early childhood education and care. It explores how, over the past decade, qualifications in the early childhood sector have been continually scrutinised and evaluated, but little has changed in the scope and recognition for our early childhood professionals.

CHAPTER 9: CHILDREN'S RIGHTS AND PARTICIPATION

In this chapter, the authors explore the concepts of (and relationships between) young children's rights, voices, participation and agency in early childhood education and care. Historically, childhood was seen as an early biological/physiological stage of life, marked by widely accepted stages of growth and development. Pre-sociological perspectives considered childhood as a time where innocence needed protection and where children needed discipline as they were an adult in the making. More recently, post-sociological perspectives on childhood reflect ideas that children are human beings in their own right, and that their development is shaped by the dynamic contexts in which they live and are cared for.

CHAPTER 10: HARNESSING THE POTENTIAL OF DIGITAL DEVICES IN EARLY CHILDHOOD

In this chapter, the authors offer alternatives to negative narratives about childhood and technology and suggest the need to support educators and children to evaluate the creative and critical potential of digital technologies for young children's learning, development and enjoyment. It provides opportunities to support professionals to move gradually towards all young children being enabled to flourish as they grow up in a digital world, where they can learn to make thoughtful and carefully crafted decisions about their own digital lives under the mentorship of informed and confident educators in a post-digital world.

CHAPTER 11: EARLY CHILDHOOD PLAY AND PEDAGOGY

The author explores early childhood play and pedagogy, positioning this at the heart of young children's learning and development. They argue that it would be impossible to envisage an early childhood education without play. Yet when we seek to define what we mean when we talk about play our definitions and understandings are very much affected by the lens through which we view the world.

CHAPTER 12: SOCIAL CONTEXTS OF EARLY CHILDHOOD

This chapter attempts to take as the focus social contexts that may serve to reshape attitudes surrounding child development, learning and ways of behaviour for 21st-century Britain. It recognises that sociology is a complex area as it is a subject that studies human societies. The chapter encourages the development of understanding that children are unique individuals, which is perhaps the most important principle to grasp when thinking about the social contexts in which they develop. Besides physical and psychological differences, the chapter explores that every one of us brings together our own individual combination of ethnic, cultural and social background.

CHAPTER 13: KEEPING CHILDREN SAFE IN A CHANGING WORLD

This chapter explores the challenges and threats to safeguarding children from harm which are more complex and multifaceted than ever before. In addition to the ongoing issues of child abuse, trauma and adverse experiences, children's safety is further compromised by digital technology, shifting social norms, economic fluctuations and environmental changes. Three key themes are explored, providing a framework for understanding the challenges and approaches to promote change.

CHAPTER 14: INCLUSION, SPECIAL EDUCATIONAL NEEDS AND DISABILITIES

In this chapter, the authors consider what inclusion is and how this relates to our work with children. It explores the links between inclusive practice and early childhood and the way in which each supports the other, along with the significant role that adults can play in reducing and removing barriers. Controversially, perhaps, it also suggests that true inclusion might not ever be possible and what might influence successful inclusion.

REFERENCES

Bollinger, M. E., Dahlquist, L. M., Mudd, K., Sonntag, C., Dillinger, L. and McKenna, K. (2006). The impact of food allergy on the daily activities of children and their families. *Annals of Allergy, Asthma and Immunology*, 62(3), 415–21.

Bonetti, S. and Blanden, J. (2020). The Early Years Foundation Stage: Impact on children's cognitive development. *Educational Research*, 62(3), 325–46.

Child Poverty Action Group (CPAG) (2023). *Official Child Poverty Statistics: 350,000 More Children in Poverty and Numbers Will Rise*. Available at: https://cpag.org.uk/news/official-child-poverty-statistics-350000-more-children-poverty-and-numbers-will-rise#:~:text=The%20DWP's%20figures%20show%204.2,to%20social%20security%20are%20felt. Accessed 8 October 2024.

EECERA Special Interest Group: Children from refugee and migrant backgrounds (2022). Inclusive Education for Refugee and Migrant Children: A Toolkit for Early Childhood

Education and Care Settings. Available at: https://refugee-early-years.org/. Accessed 11 October 2024.

Gaywood, D. (2023). The post migration lived experiences of Syrian refugee children in early childhood education and care in England: four children's stories. Doctoral dissertation, Birmingham City University. Available at: www.open-access.bcu.ac.uk/14739/1/Donna%20Gaywood%20PhD%20Thesis%20published_Final%20version_Submitted%20Sept%202022_Final%20Award%20Jul%202023.pdf. Accessed 11 October 2024.

Hasan, A. (2007). Public policy in early childhood education and care. *International Journal of Childcare and Education Policy*, *1*, 1–10.

Richardson, T., Wall S. and Brogaard-Clausen, S. (2021). *Exploring Practitioner, Academics and Student Perspectives of Early Childhood Studies Degrees Graduate Practitioner Competencies (Pilot) in Building Professional Identities and Relationships?* Early Childhood Studies Degrees Network (ECSDN) funded research update presentation, Research Conference, April (ecsdn.org).

Scollan, A., Boyd, D. and Lee, K. (2024). Exploring UNITY underpinning early childhood sustainable pedagogy in the 21st century [manuscript submitted for publication].

Thompson P. (2023). Partnership with parents and caregivers: competency seven. In A. Bradbury, J. Musgrave and H. Perkins (eds), *A Practical Guide to Early Childhood Studies Graduate Practitioner Competencies*. London: Learning Matters, pp. 87–96.

1

EARLY CHILDHOOD POLICY: ADVOCATING FOR CHANGE

Dr Helen Simmons and Emma Twigg

> **KEY DEFINITIONS**
>
> **Advocacy:** Activity that aims to influence policy and subsequent legislation which will positively impact the lives of children and families.
>
> **Lobbying:** Active dissemination of key messages regarding the early childhood workforce. This includes speaking up for a well-valued graduate-led workforce for children and families.
>
> **Policy:** A set of principles, guidelines, or rules established by governments or organisations to address specific issues or achieve certain goals
>
> **Local policy:** Specific regulations, guidelines, or directives implemented at the local or community level in early childhood.
>
> **Government policy:** Principles, objectives and strategies set by national or state governments to guide decision-making.
>
> *(Continued)*

> **Early childhood setting policy:** Guidelines written to inform early childhood practitioners on how to work to best practice guidelines.
>
> **Agency:** Being able to be independent and make decisions and choices that will enable an individual to live to their full potential.
>
> **Neoliberalism:** A political and economic ideology advocating for free markets, deregulation, privatisation, reduced government spending and individual responsibility.

INTRODUCTION

This chapter explores the importance of inclusive early childhood policy and how, working together rather than against each other, policy could be a force for good. Using current research and initiatives, the chapter considers how policy-makers, academics and early childhood professionals can be engaged in policy development and understanding. This includes speaking up for our youngest citizens, highlighting the importance of respectful and inclusive initiatives that support families. Underpinning the discussion on policy are high expectations in early childhood reinforced by the importance of having an early childhood graduate-led workforce (Bonetti and Blanden, 2020; Richardson et al., 2021) – a manifesto built on the belief that this will give our youngest children the best start in life through quality provision. Every early childhood professional must be supported to take on the role of advocacy when working with children and their families. This can ensure that the lives of children and families are improved through the influencing of policy-makers and subsequent legislation.

The chapter begins with an overview of the policy landscape to set the scene for change. Since 1997, government policy has had a keen focus on free early years group provision (Sylva and Eisenstadt, 2024) to lift the 4.3 million children across the UK out of poverty (Jarvie et al., 2023). The potential of research and policy to have this impact is emphasised throughout. Finally, the role of the early childhood professional in policy development leads to five key takeaways forming the basis for manifesto development. The professional's role is complex and requires knowledge and understanding of the landscape within which we work. The following section provides a starting point for those who want to begin to understand and advocate for quality and change.

A BRIEF POLICY OVERVIEW

Policy in early childhood is extremely complex (Archer, 2024), encompassing a range of government departments, each with its own priorities. These include education, health, social care and work and pensions, all with their own difficulties and funding challenges.

What they do have in common is that they all have an influence on children's quality of life and the experiences of their families (Thompson, 2023). As part of a manifesto, it is crucial to begin by calling for policy to be more streamlined. We know that this time in a child's life is so important, yet it is also a time of changes when the range of carers may expand from immediate family to include those outside the home environment. This transition needs to be supported by policy across departments that support a high-quality graduate-led workforce with a deep understanding of the range of needs of children and families. A homogeneous approach to policy is not a requirement as we should remember the unique child has a unique family, but policy that understands socio-cultural dynamics is essential.

As part of our understanding, it is also important to know what has happened previously. Table 1.1 highlights some key challenges to policy via select committees and all-party parliamentary groups. These mechanisms are in place to scrutinise policy and listen to those advocates from across the sector who want to have an influence. As of 2024 we have a new government that suggests it will prioritise early childhood once again. The hope is that this will mobilise the sector and its organisations to advocate for children and families.

Table 1.1 Policy milestones over the last decade

Date	Policy	Implications
2015	*Building Great Britons*, published by the All-Party Parliamentary Group for Conception to Age 2 – The First 1001 Days.	This highlights a significant role for Children's Centres, antenatal and perinatal support and early intervention.
2018	Evidence-based Early Years Intervention. The Science and Technology Select Committee.	Makes the link with adverse childhood experiences and later life usage of health and social care services.
2019	Tackling Disadvantage in the Early Years. The Education Select Committee.	This cross-party report criticises government policy on early years. Recommendations are balanced on the premise that to reduce disadvantage children need quality Early Years provision and a quality home environment.
2019	First 1000 Days of Life. The Health and Social Care Select Committee.	The Healthy Child Programme is at the heart of this, with strong mention of the role of the family, the number of health visitor visits and continuity of care past 1,000 days.
2020	Ipsos MORI (2020). *State of the Nation: Understanding Public Attitudes to the Early Years.*	Report by the Royal Foundation with a key focus on positive encouragement of the role of parents with under-fives.
2021	The Best Start for Life: A Vision for the 1,001 Critical Days. The Early Years Healthy Development Review Report. HM Government.	This report formed part of the Early Years healthy development review. Six areas for action were outlined to support the improvement of all babies in England.

(Thompson, 2023, p. 90)

> **REFLECTION 1.1**
>
> Consider Table 1.1 and reflect on the following:
>
> - How do you think the policies below reflect the transdisciplinary nature of early childhood?
> - How do you think select committees can advocate for early childhood in a positive way?

EARLY CHILDHOOD FUTURE FOCUS: RECENT RESPONSES TO A CHILD-CENTRED APPROACH

The following demonstrate the current trends in regard to policy documents and thinking. *A Manifesto for Babies* (Parent Infant Foundation, 2024), *The Power of Play: Building a Creative Britain* (Children's Alliance, 2024) and *Early Childhood Manifesto* (ECSDN, 2024) are crucial contemporary documents advocating for holistic and integrated approaches to early childhood. These documents emphasise the importance of nurturing all aspects of a child's development, advocating for support for families and for the practitioners that work alongside families and communities.

THE POWER OF PLAY: BUILDING A CREATIVE BRITAIN

Drawing on interdisciplinary approaches, the Children's Alliance report (https://childrensalliance.org.uk/wp-content/uploads/2024/05/Play-Policy-18Apr2024-Childrens-Alliance.pdf) advocates for the importance of play across childhood, across the lifespan and, indeed, play is seen as central to lifelong, life-wide learning, with a particular focus on this not only being a right of children but also integral to the future-facing development of creativity and innovation in our changing society and economy. The working group developed ten key recommendations to enable this:

1. recognise play as a fundamental right
2. integrate play into education policies
3. investment in play provision
4. prioritise play through cross-sector collaboration

5. prioritise lifelong learning and over coordinated and dedicated training programmes for staff working in schools, Early Years settings, family hubs and children's centres
6. promote parental engagement in play
7. update policies to reflect changing needs
8. address disparities in play opportunities
9. support children facing adversity
10. support children's community initiatives.

A MANIFESTO FOR BABIES

The Parent Infant Foundation report (https://parentinfantfoundation.org.uk/1001-days/manifesto/) recognises that the first 1,001 days of life – from pregnancy through the first two years of a baby's life – is a crucial period. The manifesto outlines five recommendations to address this:

1. an ambitious cross-government strategy to support babies' healthy development
2. more investment in prevention
3. tackling health inequalities so that all babies have a good start in life
4. developing a workforce plan for children's social care and the early years
5. a rapid review of the tax and benefits system for parents and carers of under-twos.

EARLY CHILDHOOD MANIFESTO

The Early Childhood Studies Degrees Network (ECSDN) (https://www.ecsdn.org/) has outlined five recommendations. It calls for:

1. the consistent use of the term 'Early Childhood' across research and practice
2. assurance of and promotion for the sustainability of a graduate workforce
3. quality research from academics and government bodies to support evidence-based practice
4. a streamlining of the training and workforce available in Early Childhood so that all stakeholders and parents have a clear and deep understanding of progression and provision
5. Early Childhood graduates to form part of a trans disciplinary Family Hubs leadership team.

A Manifesto for Babies highlights children's fundamental rights to high-quality care and provision, serving as a guiding document for child-centred policies and practice. *The Power of Play* shines a light on the critical role of play in children's development, enhancing creativity, innovation and social interactions. The ECSDN *Early Childhood Manifesto* supports the recognition of a highly valued and well-qualified early childhood workforce, promoting collaboration among disciplines, and encouraging research, lobbying and advocacy that informs the sector.

To focus on early childhood as being transdisciplinary, we can develop the collaborative approaches highlighted in these documents which facilitate an enhanced sense of shared professional identity for those working in health, education and social care. Key messages in these reports also reflect the importance of policy-makers and local government actively listening and responding to the views of families in the building of family and community provision. As stated by Eisenstadt (2024), this is an essential part of 'striking the balance: what seems to be needed versus what parents want'.

By advocating for inclusive practices, play-based learning, coproduction in family support and strong community networks, these manifestos support a unified approach to early childhood development, leading to a better future for our children.

REFLECTION 1.2

Based on the themes and principles of *A Baby Manifesto*, *The Power of Play* and the ECSDN *Early Childhood Manifesto*, consider the following reflective questions:

1. How can we better incorporate report and manifesto recommendations such as these into daily practices within early childhood?
2. What role does play have in creating an inclusive learning environment and how can we ensure a more play-focused approach?
3. How can we ensure cultural sensitivity, inclusivity and coproduction in community and family engagement initiatives?

THE POTENTIAL OF RESEARCH

Research is fundamental to our ability to secure better outcomes and experiences in early childhood. By providing reliable and timely evidence, we can better assess the needs of children and families and make better decisions on how to improve outcomes based on what works.

Royal Foundation, Centre for Early Childhood (2024)

As outlined in the above quotation from the Royal Foundation, it is important for all engaged in early childhood policy and practice to continually be engaged with research. This can be difficult for professionals on the ground working directly with children and their families, but it is important to find ways for academics and practitioners to come together as one early childhood voice and engage in a critical perspective of policy. Currently, the scenario is confusing for so many. There is no shared language as a starting point and although there is beginning to be agreement, it is still conflicted between Early Years, early childhood and early childhood education and care (ECEC). This book takes the position of early childhood as an academic discipline and defines the age range from conception to eight years old. This academic discipline is clear about its transdisciplinary nature rather than the government-determined label of Early Years which only considers those from birth to five years and has a heavy focus on education. ECEC is a common term in research and stretches beyond the UK to a wider European audience.

Research provides ways to communicate important messages that need to be shared with early childhood policy-makers. If professionals working with children can be given a voice through this research, it can become even more powerful. Sharing examples of activities that respond to current policy-based initiatives, research and reports across early childhood networks provides opportunities for understanding and potential policy development. These responses may come from a position of demonstrating support and the alignment of core shared values. On other occasions, this may come from a more critical position, asking important questions, and calling for more clarity or consideration on specific points. Both approaches are important ways of being heard by both local and national politicians and provide opportunities for further discussion and debate, aiming to influence the policy that impacts the lives of children and families. The example below is of a professional response to a current report (Carneiro et al., 2024) looking into the short- and medium-term impacts of the Sure Start initiative.

THE SHORT- AND MEDIUM-TERM IMPACTS OF SURE START ON EDUCATIONAL OUTCOMES

To follow is a study of the impacts of Sure Start.

BACKGROUND TO THE REPORT

'Introduced in 1999, Sure Start was the first large government initiative to provide holistic support to families with children under the age of 5 in England' (Carneiro et al., 2024, p. 4).

The Sure Start initiative was a groundbreaking Labour initiative which sought to improve the educational outcomes of children. It was initially targeted to those in the most disadvantaged areas of England and then rolled out to become a universal service for all. While the initiative has begun to be reinvented by family hubs, further research would have supported the suggestions and the potential allocation of funds. This report, therefore, highlights some of the findings.

KEY FINDINGS

1. Access to a Sure Start centre between the ages of 0 and 5 significantly improved the educational achievement of children, with benefits lasting at least until GCSEs.
2. There were much larger impacts for those from the poorest backgrounds and those from non-white backgrounds.
3. Access to a centre increased the likelihood of children being recorded as having a SEND (Special Educational Needs and Disabilities) at age 5.
4. Positive impacts are entirely driven by children who lived near the earlier centres.
5. The benefits of using a Sure Start centre are around three times as large as the average impact on all children in the area.
6. Although total spending was £2.5 billion this far outweighs the cost of SEND support.
7. These key findings demonstrate further the importance of intervening early through a holistic family approach.

(Carneiro et al., 2024, pp. 5–6)

SUGGESTED PROFESSIONAL RESPONSE AND NEXT STEPS

This report provides key evidence of the importance of such initiatives and early intervention programmes for our youngest children. It is encouraging to see the importance of early intervention programmes highlighted in this report, especially programmes that focus on children supported through a holistic family approach.

The report's findings highlight the continued inequalities in our society and support early childhood graduates to work towards supporting better outcomes for all children. It is encouraging to see outcomes improved for children living in the poorest backgrounds and those children from non-white backgrounds.

Using the outline of the Sure Start report (https://ifs.org.uk/sites/default/files/2024-04/SS_NPD_Report.pdf) and the reflections on the professional response and next steps, consider the following reflective questions.

- How can this report influence your setting's policies?
- How can this report influence your practice?
- How would you share the report findings with colleagues you work with?
- What are the benefits of sharing such research?

ACADEMICS AND RESEARCH

A call for a graduate profession from the academic discipline of early childhood studies could be considered best placed to support and advocate for all children and families, particularly when accessing early intervention programmes. Through their studies, graduates engage in research-informed teaching and understand the valuable role that advocacy plays in the support of our youngest children and families. Supporting an understanding of how policy is developed locally and nationally, while students are studying early childhood through the range of routes available, is an essential part of linking policy and practice together to have impact. This, of course, is not an easy route for policy-makers to take as it incurs costs to encourage a higher level of education and pay accordingly. However, it is proposed that the cost savings later for society in terms of health care, crime, social care and education would be considerable.

It is also useful to explore how academics are engaging in debate and ongoing discussion regarding key aspects of the early childhood education system. This is not always an easy task as, potentially, conflicting with current government policy can lead to quick dismissal by politicians. Moss and Cameron (2020), for example, published *Transforming Early Childhood Education in England: Towards a Democratic Education*. Important messages within this text consider 'policy neglect' while also offering insight into 'possibilities and hope, about how it might be possible, even at this late stage, to alter course and create an inclusive, coherent and democratic system of early childhood service' (p. 2). This text has provided much discussion between academics and students, but it could be argued that it has not had much influence on policy. This can create frustration within the sector as research that reflects their knowledge and understanding appears not to be heard. Vandenbroeck et al. (2023) have also produced a global exploration of how processes of neoliberalism, including marketisation and privatisation in early childhood education and care, have impacted our understanding of childhood and the way we support children and families in practice. In their exploration, they provide valuable examples for alternative understanding, which can be used within policy and practice. However, while Vandenbroeck et al. (2023) offer examples of global resistance to neoliberalism within the early childhood sector, they are equally challenging current political and economic ideology. They reflect the views of a considerable amount of early childhood research, with three key areas for consideration:

- resisting children as human capital
- resisting the consumentality of parents
- resisting the alienation of the workforce

REFLECTION 1.3

- Why do you think these are highlighted as important considerations for future policy development in early childhood?
- How do you think this research could be heard by current policy-makers?

CAN POLICY PROVIDE AN OPPORTUNITY TO ADVOCATE?

There are many professional networks across the four nations and the early childhood sector. While this could be seen as positive enthusiasm, it could also be considered as highly problematic when attempting to advocate for the professionals, children and families in policy development. The sector has been marketised as a way to provide more childcare and this approach has not been aligned to one political party. However, this has created rifts as 'affordable childcare' has become the government rhetoric to support parents back to work and has influenced policy, keeping professionals' wages suppressed for profit and therefore a reluctance from some business owners to engage with a graduate workforce to improve quality. However, the early childhood sector continues to be passionate and driven to provide the best-quality services it can at a time when funding and support following the Covid-19 pandemic and long-term austerity feels lacking.

In 2021, 16 organisations came together and formed the Early Years Coalition. This coalition was remarkable as it brought together differing views and perspectives for the common good and had significant impact on the sector and policy-makers' responses. The preface to the *Birth to 5 Matters* document is interesting to consider as a starting point to understand the position in challenging current education policy directives:

We came together because we wanted to create a resource which pooled our members' considerable expertise and experience and kept alive multiple possibilities for the future of early childhood education. The document is intended to work with members' many values, principles and aspirations. As a coalition we encompass a range of early years traditions and approaches and reflect the diversity of experiences and views of our members. We hope this guidance does justice to the collaborations and rich discussions that took place as part of its development. We have sought to reach points of consensus and support diversity of practice and interpretation. This guidance is a reference point for practitioners developing their practice, not a 'how to' manual or a tick-list. We want Birth to 5 Matters *to support practitioners to implement the Statutory Framework for the Early Years Foundation Stage (EYFS) in a pedagogically sound, principled and evidence-based way. Practitioners can then use their professional judgement based on their knowledge of the children in their setting and their wider context including family, community and the setting itself to construct an appropriate curriculum.*

(Early Years Coalition, 2021, p. 5)

The document was a sector response to a more formal non-statutory document, *Development Matters*, released by the Department for Education (DfE) in 2021. It was also a response to the continuing datafication and schoolification (Ovington, 2023) of Early Years education. Here is an example of how policy and practice can be changed when expertise is brought together from research and practice and is driven by a passion to do the right thing for young children and their families. *Birth to 5 Matters* (Early Years Coalition, 2021) was never intended to cause conflict with a government department (DfE), but to provide an alternative for those working daily with families who felt a sense of restriction with neoliberalist targets that it could be argued were not always fit for purpose.

Professionals working with young children are also advocates and agents of change and need to be trusted to know what is best for those they support. What is interesting in comparing the documents is that both suggest that the early childhood professionals are best placed to make decisions for those they are working in partnership with. It is also important to state that the sector did not reject one document in place of another but rather used both together. This strongly suggests that if the policy-makers had come together with the coalition, one document could have been created with a coproductive approach to policy development.

REFLECTION 1.4

- What lessons can be learnt by both policy developers and sector organisations for future policy development?

THE ROLE OF THE EARLY CHILDHOOD PROFESSIONAL

As we look forward to a changing landscape for children, practitioners and settings can consider how their role and strategies can be developed through actions outlined by Sir Al Aynsley-Green (2019, p. 224) when he asked, what is needed from professional staff?

- *Understand childhood today.*
- *Understand the local and national context and situation for children, young people, and families.*
- *Learn from a global perspective.*
- *Put the child and family's needs at the centre of your services and design services around competencies to meet needs.*
- *Reach out, be prepared for, celebrate and exploit crises – they are opportunities for 'unfreezing' attitudes and practices especially when coupled with sensible suggestions for improvement.*
- *Identify early potential leaders of the future and give them inspiration and toolkits to become effective advocates for children.*

The points demonstrate that any action, big or small, can provide the space for change. As we move forward into a new phase of early childhood policy development, these examples illustrate that, whether it be by engaging and developing your knowledge, remaining open to new perspectives, or engaging in larger-scale implementations for improvement, the key is to continue to learn from the past as we move forward into the future.

> **FIVE KEY TAKEAWAYS**
>
> 1. Ensure that early childhood professionals are highly valued and at the centre of policy reform.
> 2. Continue to work towards one early childhood voice in support of children, families and the development of local and national policy. Through connections and networking, organisations can support one another and share their common aims and values.
> 3. Research-informed policy is essential. The recognition of early childhood as a transdisciplinary research discipline can enhance both strategy and policy at local and national level.
> 4. Recognition of the role of the early childhood professional as an expert and advocate in the discipline preconception to eight years.
> 5. Policy-makers to consider the range of voices required as a collective to improve the range of services for young children and their families. The voices of the child and their families are key, supported by graduate early childhood professionals.

CONCLUSION

This chapter has explored the importance of understanding and engaging with early childhood policy. Working together is the only way that we will move towards positive change in early childhood. Collaboration can develop creativity, motivation and positive change as explored in this chapter. The early childhood sector is full of amazing creative, ethical and innovative activity, and now is the time to stand up for all children, families and a workforce that deserves the absolute best.

REFERENCES

Archer, N. (2024). Uncovering the discursive 'borders' of professional identities in English early childhood workforce reform policy. *Policy Futures in Education*, *22*(2), 187–206.

Aynsley-Green, A. (2019). *The British Betrayal of Childhood: Challenging Uncomfortable Truths and Bringing About Change*. London: Routledge.

Bonetti, S. and Blanden, J. (2020). *Early Years Workforce Qualifications and Children's Outcomes*. Education Policy Institute and Nuffield Foundation. Available at: https://epi.org.uk/publications-and-research/early-years-qualifications-and-outcomes/. Accessed 2 July 2024.

Carneiro, P., Cattan, S. and Ridpath, N. (2024). *The Short- and Medium-Term Impacts of Sure Start on Educational Outcomes*. London: Institute of Fiscal Studies. Available at: https://ifs.org.uk/publications/short-and-medium-term-impacts-sure-start-educational-outcomes. Accessed 17 June 2024.

Children's Alliance (2024). *The Power of Play: Building a Creative Britain*. Available at: https://childrensalliance.org.uk/wp-content/uploads/2024/04/Play-Policy-05Apr2024-Childrens-Alliance.pdf. Accessed 23 July 2024.

Department for Education (DfE) (2021). *Development Matters: Non-Statutory Curriculum Guidance for the Early Years Foundation Stage*. Available at: https://assets.publishing.service.gov.uk/media/64e6002a20ae890014f26cbc/DfE_Development_Matters_Report_Sep2023.pdf. Accessed 9 October 2024.

Early Childhood Studies Degrees Network (ECSDN) (2024). *Early Childhood Manifesto*. Available at: www.ecsdn.org/tag/manifesto/. Accessed 23 July 2024.

Early Years Coalition (2021). *Birth to 5 Matters: Non-Statutory Guidance for the Early Years Foundation Stage*. Available at: https://birthto5matters.org.uk/wp-content/uploads/2021/04/Birthto5Matters-download.pdf. Accessed 9 October 2024.

Eisenstadt, E. (2024). *Investing in Early Years Family Support: Four Lessons from the Sure Start Programme*. International Inequalities Institute. Available at: https://blogs.lse.ac.uk/inequalities/2024/05/22/investing-in-early-years-lessons-from-sure-start/. Accessed 23 July 2024.

Jarvie, M., Ollerearnshaw, R. and Goddard, E. (2023). *Tackling Disadvantage Through Childcare*. London: Coram Institute, Joseph Rowntree Foundation.

Moss, P. and Cameron, C. (2020). *Transforming Early Childhood Education in England: Towards a Democratic Education*. London: UCL Press, pp. 1–18.

Ovington, J. A. (2023). The 'unruly' snowflake: (re)imagining school readiness for two-year-old children. *Cultural and Pedagogical Inquiry*, 14(2), 61–73.

Parent Infant Foundation (2024). *A Manifesto for Babies*. Available at: https://parentinfantfoundation.org.uk/wp-content/uploads/2024/03/F1001D-Manifesto-for-Babies-FINAL.pdf. Accessed 23 July 2024.

Richardson, T., Wall S. and Brogaard-Clausen, S. (2021). *Exploring Practitioner, Academics and Student Perspectives of Early Childhood Studies Degrees Graduate Practitioner Competencies (Pilot) in Building Professional Identities and Relationships?* Early Childhood Studies Degrees Network (ECSDN) funded research update presentation, Research Conference, April (ecsdn.org).

Royal Foundation, Centre for Early Childhood (2024). *Early Childhood: The Role of Public Research*. Available at: https://centreforearlychildhood.org/latest-learnings/essays/early-childhood-the-role-of-public-research/. Accessed 8 June 2024.

Sylva, K. and Eisenstadt, N. (2024). *Transforming Early Childhood: Narrowing the Gap between Children from Lower- and Higher-Income Families*. Available at: https://media.nesta.org.uk/documents/Transforming_Early_Childhood_-_narrowing_the_gap_between_lower-_and_higher-income_families.pdf. Accessed 9 October 2024.

Thompson P. (2023). Partnership with parents and caregivers: competency seven. In A. Bradbury, J. Musgrave and H. Perkins (eds), *A Practical Guide to Early Childhood Studies Graduate Practitioner Competencies*. London: Learning Matters, pp. 87–96.

Vandenbroeck, M., Lehrer, J. and Mitchell, L. (2023). *The Decommodification of Early Childhood Education and Care: Resisting Neoliberalism*. London: Routledge.

2
EARLY CHILDHOOD SUSTAINABLE PEDAGOGY INTO AND BEYOND THE 21ST CENTURY

Dr Diane Boyd, Kerrie Lee and Dr Angela Scollan

KEY DEFINITIONS

Sustainable pedagogy: A holistic, interconnected pedagogical approach that draws on all aspects of sustainability, experiential learning and the co-construction of knowledge and research (Scollan et al., 2024).

Wisdom shepherd: Nurturer and protector of their ecological world and knowledge acquired to co-exist.

Rights-based pedagogy: A recognition of the equality, agency and balance of both human and non-human realities.

Sustainable Development Goals: 17 global goals adopted by all United Nations member states. Designed to help the world move towards a more sustainable future.

(Continued)

> **Three pillars of sustainability:** Outlined by the Bruntland report in (1987), published by the UN World Commission on Environment and Development, the three pillars of sustainability (social, environmental, economic) offer a foundation for building a sustainable future.

INTRODUCTION

The Sustainable Development Goals (SDGs) (UNESCO, 2015) have been seen to present challenges for early childhood education in creating a path to support how young children see the world and themselves (Chapman and O'Gorman, 2022). The goals are:

1. no poverty
2. zero hunger
3. good health and wellbeing
4. quality education
5. gender equality
6. clean water and sanitation
7. affordable and clean energy
8. decent work and economic growth
9. industry, innovation and infrastructure
10. reduced inequalities
11. sustainable cities and communities
12. responsible consumption and production
13. climate action
14. life below water
15. life on land
16. peace, justice and strong institutions
17. partnerships for the goals.

In this chapter we will investigate levels of sustainability awareness and adult confidence levels to engage with SDGs in practice. But how can we embrace this challenge to ensure that early childhood education survives and flourishes into the 21st century and beyond? The call for education for sustainable development (ESD) (UNESCO, 2020) and the *Sustainability and Climate Change Strategy* (DfE, 2023) highlight the need for children and adults to be active in becoming more sustainable, to challenge and be agents for all ecological participants. However, understanding and knowledge of ESD in early childhood practice has been left wanting, therefore confidence to embrace and embed it requires attention.

In the following chapter we will explore the historical and contemporary impact of sustainability in early childhood while also discussing the ways forward, including an emphasis on the need to develop a *sustainable pedagogy* (Scollan et al., 2024).

EARLY CHILDHOOD AND THE RELEVANCE OF EDUCATIONAL SUSTAINABLE DEVELOPMENT

The original concept of sustainability was introduced in the Brundtland report as a 'development that meets the needs of the present without compromising the ability of future generations to meet their own needs' (WCED, 1987, p. 47). As a result of this report, three pillars were designed to demonstrate the interconnected nature of sustainability beyond just environmental. The original three pillars were social, economic and environmental, but each must not be viewed in isolation as it weakens the concept of sustainability. Relating sustainability to early childhood, there is an urgency around awareness of the wider social, economic and environmental influences that impact on quality rights-based (human and non-human) early childhood practice.

Current political, societal and economic climates harshly capture the need for sustainability more than ever. Technical, pedagogical, systematic and sustainable acts and skills in practice are only the tip of the iceberg when the concept of sustainability is deconstructed, both in and for early childhood practice. ESD aims at developing competencies that empower individuals to reflect on their own actions, considering their current and future social, economic and environmental impacts from a local and a global perspective. Empowerment of individuals to act in a sustainable manner may require them to strike out in new directions; and to participate in socio-political processes, supporting the movement of societies towards sustainable development (UNESCO, 2015).

The Early Years Foundation Stage (EYFS) (DfE, 2024, p. 12) suggests that children should 'respond to what they hear with relevant questions', but what does *relevant* mean to the individual child in comparison to the individual adult? There is a broad agreement that to become sustainable citizens, one must possess key competencies for sustainability. UNESCO (2017b) describes key components for sustainability as (a) systems thinking, (b) anticipatory, (c) normative, (d) strategic, (e) collaboration, (f) critical thinking, (g) self-awareness and (h) integrated problem-solving competencies.

FOUNDATIONS OF SUSTAINABILITY: THEORISTS AND PIONEERS

The historical foundations of sustainability can be understood through educational pioneers and theorists supporting early childhood practice (Boyd, 2018a). For example, Froebel's principles encourage inclusivity and eco-perspective of community and collaboration (Liebschner, 1992) rather than ego-perspective of neoliberalism (Moss, 2017). Neoliberal perspectives see children as being vulnerable, needing protection from the world and the questions that arise. This is in direct contrast to Steiner, Malaguzzi and Montessori. These pioneers saw children as active agents of their own learning, driven by innate curiosity, creativity, awe, wonder and playfulness. Playfulness is a child's right to decode their world (UNCRC, 1989) and problem-solve the lived realities that they are actively involved in. Dewey recognised all learning occurs in social experiences and children's own cultural context (Donaldson, 1978). The social and cultural context of child development was explored by Bronfenbrenner's ecological systems theory (1979) which argued that child development is a process of reciprocal relationships between the developing child and the world around them. However, Davis and Elliott (2024) note that although Bronfenbrenner's theory is pervasive, it fails to consider the Earth's bio-systems; they therefore developed 'a revised module of a child's biosystem' (p. 17). Considering the urgency of climate change and the role of sustainability today, it is apparent that these bio-systems are bi-relational and affecting children's health and wellbeing and therefore need to be explored, acknowledged and understood in early childhood.

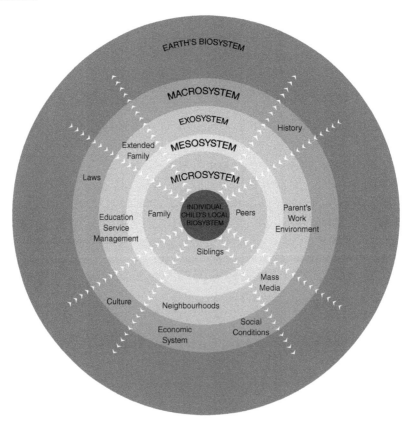

Figure 2.1 A revised module of a child's bio-system (Davis and Elliot, 2024, p. 17)

EARLY CHILDHOOD AGENCY

Social sustainability can be defined by many terms including 'agency', 'participation', 'self-determination', 'activism', 'decision-making' and 'voice'. Children constantly transition in and out of choice-making moments where their self-determined expressions are influenced by reflections, engagements and environments (Farini and Scollan, 2019). Sustainable pedagogy (Scollan et al., 2024) is underpinned with a rights-based lens meaning that those engaging with self-determined children need to be aware of their own expectations, responses and interpretations. To be inclusive is to be aware of our own bias, tradition and expectations. Why? Because if children are agentic and make choices that do not *fit* with adult, routines or agenda, the child may inherit a negative response or label from those who do not *hear* or understand the child's choice. This does not mean every decision a child makes must be followed; rather it means that those of us working with or for children need to consciously engage with our listening filters (Scollan and McNeil, 2019) so we are able to hear what children are telling us.

Sustainability Matters in Early Childhood (Boyd et al., 2022) highlights the importance of children having agency in climate action, resonating with the DfE's 2023 strategy on sustainability. When positioning children as activists it is important to remember a child's sense of agency goes beyond purely providing them with choices led by adults and society. Agency is owned by children and empowers them to feel in control. For instance, when children are being agentic, their understanding of the world and people around them evolves. However, historically, little attention has been paid to this by researchers and educators (Borg and Samuelsson, 2022) and society as a whole. Is there a lack of awareness by adults of social sustainability when considering agency in practice and beyond?

While the Graduate Practitioners Competencies (GPC) (ECSDN, 2019) acknowledge children's agency, like the EYFS (DfE, 2024) they do not explicitly have any direct links to either the SDGs or ESD. In September 2023, the United Nations reacted to children's concerns about climate action and, as a result, General Comment No 26.2 was incorporated into the UNCRC (1989) emphasising 'the obligations of States to address environmental harm and climate change' (UNCRC, 2023, summary). It can therefore be argued that, if sustainability is not seen as mandatory in policies, we should question how we expect them to appear in training, qualifications and practice.

IS SUSTAINABILITY ALL POLITICAL TALK AND NO ACTION?

The Paris Agreement (UNESCO, 2015) has been signed by 194 states and is seen as being essential in the achievement of the SDGs and the *2030 Agenda*. By signing the legally binding international treaty states have agreed to all 17 SDGs and to implement them into policy. A key aspect of the *2030 Agenda* (UNESCO, 2015) is SDG 4, Quality education, which positions pre-school as an important precursor to primary, leading all lifelong learners to acquire the knowledge and skills to promote sustainable development. What is interesting, though, is the indicator for SDG 12.8 (Responsible consumption and production) explicitly states that all aspects of education for sustainable development must be 'mainstreamed in (a) national education policies; (b) curricula; (c) teacher education; and (d) student assessment' (12.8.1, UNESCO, 2015).

Considering that the UK was one of the signatories at the Paris Agreement little appears to have been achieved in England. Wales (Welsh Government, 2022) and Scotland (Scottish Government, 2020) have embedded learning through sustainability in curriculums and, in Scotland, it is explicitly embedded in the Professional Standards for Teachers, therefore meaning that it is being disseminated.

The question that has to be asked now is: why not in England?

An opportunity was missed when the government published its *Sustainability and Climate Change Strategy* (DfE, 2023), which only focused on SDG 13: Climate action. Focusing on one SDG at a macro level (Bronfenbrenner, 1979) reduces the effectiveness of sustainability as a policy and, therefore, practice. As UNESCO (2015) reminds us, the SDGs are meant to be interconnected and holistic throughout the child's bio-system (Davis and Elliott, 2024). Additionally, Scotland and Wales have made sustainability engagement mandatory, whereas in England it is voluntary, which impacts on both awareness and confidence to implement and engage with. This, therefore, calls into question the DfE (2023) target that by 2025 all settings and schools must have a nominated sustainability lead and have put a climate action plan in place.

If the Political agenda (big P) in England is not meeting *The 2030 Agenda for Sustainable Development* (UNESCO, 2015), the emphasis must return to a bottom-up approach (little p) and focus on early childhood qualifications, training, children's services and initial teacher training (ITT), including the need to recognise that: 'Integral to the degrees is holistic knowledge and understanding of the ecology of child development in the context of the family, community and wider socio-political context' (ECSDN, 2019, p. 4).

EARLY CHILDHOOD INTO THE FUTURE: SUSTAINABLE PEDAGOGY AND WISDOM SHEPHERDS

When reflecting upon the three key points it is clearly apparent that there is a disconnection between expectations from the Paris Agreement (UNESCO, 2015), actual policy into practice, practitioners' understanding of sustainability and their confidence to implement it. It is also important to emphasise that sustainability is not *just* environmental; there are two equally supporting and interdependent pillars. Current beliefs and understanding around sustainability indicate a lack of authentic clarification in the early childhood landscape.

So, how do we move forward into the 21st century and become more sustainable interconnecting early childhood with all pillars and SDGs?

In early childhood we always start with a baseline – so let us start with what we do well, what we know and do excellently. Quality education expects practitioners and students to be tuned into children, through listening and knowing them, through relationships that encourage empowerment and positivity. This is *social sustainability*, which is the bedrock of early childhood pioneering giants' philosophies – all of whom promoted social justice, empowerment, agency and children as active participants in their own learning. By recognising and interconnecting social sustainability, practitioners will be able to build upon what they already do, to extend and enhance sustainable pedagogy (Scollan et al., 2024). This holistic, interconnected approach draws on all aspects of sustainability, experiential learning and the co-construction of knowledge and research. Sustainable pedagogy is essential to critical thinking, being self-determined and empowered as agents for change (Farini and Scollan, 2019). In September 2023, the UNCRC (1989) was updated to include General Comment No 26. The United Nations (UNCRC, 2023, paragraph 1) recognised the urgency of children's own anxieties and questions about their future, focusing on climate change, stating 'the efforts of children to draw attention to environmental crises created the motivation and were the momentum behind this general comment'. As Arlemalm-Hagser and Elliott (2020) advocate, children should have opportunities to enact their agency and advocacy for broad concepts of sustainability and social justice. General Comment No 26 (UNCRC, 2023) clearly demonstrates this ability of children to make change and be listened to; do we need to question why we adopt a certain approach in early childhood?

It was widely recognised that social sustainability could not be fully achieved without the inclusion of culture (Agenda 21, United Cities and Local Governments, 2010), evolving as the socio-cultural pillar, because culture is integral to all aspects of our identity, heritage and community values. The importance of culture was included in the UNESCO (2015) 2030 Agenda; as UNESCO (2017a) states 'Culture is who we are and what shapes our identity', demonstrating the importance of heritage and community. When you consider the diversity of the UK and the multiple cultural communities and traditions (Boyd, 2018b), it makes sense that in terms of early childhood, culture must be considered at the forefront of quality education (SDG 4) (UNESCO, 2015). To move early childhood education for sustainability forward into the 21st century, practitioners need to tune in and listen to the ecological and bio-system (Davis and Elliott, 2024) community that surrounds the children and their families. We can learn from *other* perspectives by reflecting on *otherness* rather than just repeating the same stories of practice, and by listening to these alternative cultural and social narratives we can break the disconnect. As Moss (2006, p. 37) states, we must be 'open to the other, striving to listen without grasping the other and making the other the same'. The 'Global education monitoring report' (UNESCO, 2016) highlighted the need to consider new approaches in education and changes in daily practice, including creativity, critical reflection and consideration of different perspectives.

When considering the discussion above it is necessary to re-vision early childhood to articulate how the SDGs, the three pillars and children's agency are integrated holistically. Therefore, there is a need to develop, reflect and engage with sustainable pedagogy (Scollan et al., 2024). The three pillars (WCED, 1987) and the SDGs (UNESCO, 2015) are entangled and, while entanglement is part and parcel of early childhood practice, we argue that each pillar of sustainability needs to be untangled. By identifying each pillar in its own right and reconnecting to the curriculums it becomes relevant and contextualised to early childhood. Sustainable pedagogy aims to support practitioners to gain confidence and engage with *all* aspects of sustainability. When we say *all* aspects of sustainability, we do not only mean a human-centric rights perspective, but children also need to develop empathy and care for the *other* – in this case, the non-human world.

Focusing on the environmental pillar of sustainability it is important to recognise a key element of Indigenous ways of being, in particular the *wisdom keepers*, who 'lived closely and in tune with the Earth' (Ritchie, 2012, p. 63) recognising the importance of the non-human rights which must be protected. Wisdom keepers are a crucial intergenerational and cultural element, bringing transformative knowledge (Boyd, 2018b) to share as part of sustainable pedagogy (Scollan et al., 2024). But we need children to do more than just learn from wisdom keepers; we need them to develop their own nurturing element for the Earth too. When we consider the term 'shepherd' from an Old English perspective of *'scēphyrde'* (Marsden, 2004), shepherds were protectors and carers. Perhaps to move sustainable pedagogy into the 21st century we need to incorporate these two terms together and encourage children to become *wisdom shepherds* of their ecological world.

The positionality of wisdom shepherds contrasts with children being environmental *stewards*, which is seen as just a role of responsibility. A wisdom shepherd is positioned from an empathetic, caring and capable approach, aligning with both SDG 15 (Life on land) – which specifically asks for support to conserve, restore and take significant action for all aspects of the ecological systems – and SDG 14 (Life below water) (UNESCO, 2015).

Sustainable pedagogy (Scollan et al., 2024) can promote ecologically knowledgeable children as wisdom shepherds, and as activists for SDG 13 (Climate action) through place-based learning (Boyd, 2018c). However, Günther et al. (2024) conducted a research review into the necessary competencies needed for embedding sustainability teaching into practice. While all the UNESCO framework (2017b) competencies were mentioned, two additional ones were highlighted – one being the competency to deal with knowledge. Their findings (Günther et al., 2024, p. 8) stressed the need for children to have the capacity to 'evaluate and classify knowledge and/or information', specifically highlighting curiosity, the ability to question and openness to acquiring new knowledge. When you put these knowledge capabilities alongside the characteristics of effective learning (DfE, 2024), there are clear parallels to the UNESCO framework (2017b) competencies and a rights-based philosophy.

The final pillar of sustainability is economic, and is seen as the weakest in practice (Siraj-Blatchford et al., 2010) due to the lack of understanding, experience and dialogue as to what this actually encompasses.

The hands-on experiences, as advocated by the pioneers (Boyd, 2018a), reflects the economic pillar and links to SDG 8, Decent work and economic growth, SDG 9, Industry, innovation and infrastructure, and SDG 11, Sustainable cities and communities (UNESCO, 2015). Drawing on your community wisdom keepers (local volunteers, services, allotment keepers, etc.), children can be scaffolded in the use of tools, terminology and skills, embedding their intergenerational knowledge competencies organically.

The case study below demonstrates the interconnectedness of the three pillars and the importance of early childhood as a foundational base for both ethical and ecological fundamental values and capabilities. What is clear in this example is the whole-school approach to sustainability and the importance of powerful leadership that encouraged all staff (Gibson, 2015) and children to work together as one, strengthening their sustainable pedagogical ethos (Scollan et al., 2024).

CASE STUDY: IMMERSED IN A SUSTAINABLE ETHOS

Early childhood education for sustainability is a holistic interconnected pedagogical approach. At San Sior School in North Wales the children from three to 11 years are immersed in this sustainable ethos. The school proudly displays, both inside and outside, the 17 SDGs and they are used in everyday learning. When considering the three pillars the children engage creatively demonstrating all three. A key element of socio-cultural sustainability is the cultural pride every child feels for their Welsh heritage alongside their recognition of a rights-based approach; additionally, each class has its own business which the children run and make all economic decisions. For example, the Reception-aged children run a seed packet enterprise, designing and packaging products, and a vegan honey business. The children are aware and use the economic language of trade, recognising the terminology of profit and loss. The whole class decides how the profits are to be spent, and understands the need to redistribute money back into their business to be sustainable. Environmentally, the children understand and can sort different seeds and can identify them. They grow and cultivate the vegetables and plants and recognise the regenerative nature of their business. Their vegan honey uses dandelions, and they market it as a 'plant-based alternative', a positive ethos towards a cleaner world. As a result of running a business they engage locally within the community, selling their products alongside all the other

(Continued)

classes in the school fair, or outside the school grounds on the pavement drawing on the socio-cultural pillar of sustainability. This socio-cultural aspect draws the children into their community and gives them the confidence to interact with members of their locality. The Year 1 classes' business is focused on mental health, selling worry worms; they put their profits to good use by supporting the local MIND charity. By the time the Early Years children reach Year 6 they are strong advocates for the SDGs and all three pillars of sustainability (Boyd et al., 2024).

Figure 2.2 Designing and packaging

Figure 2.3 Pricing

Figure 2.4 Marketing vegan honey products

Figure 2.5 Year 1 worry worms

A key aspect of sustainable pedagogy (Scollan et al., 2024) is a valuable free resource that is available for all practitioners and students: *An Early Childhood Education for Sustainability Resource that Embeds the SDGs and STEM into Pedagogical Practice* (Boyd et al., 2021). This resource supports authentic engagement with all aspects of sustainability and helps children to learn about our responsibilities to others and the world in which we all live, becoming wisdom shepherds. The resource recognises that early childhood is situated in the ecological context of the family, locality, global world and bio-system. It draws on the philosophy of Reggio Emilia, which places children and the environment as protagonists in their learning through provocations, not learning outcomes or goals.

An example of a natural provocation is the book *It's a No-Money Day* (Milner, 2023) as an initial starting point to help young children begin to empathise with others less fortunate. This resonates with the earlier discussion on the economic pillar and the lived realities of the children in your care in terms of food poverty and food banks. Together, sustainable pedagogy and the resource reflect the urgency of the UNESCO 2015 document.

FIVE KEY TAKEAWAYS

1. Sustainable pedagogy is defined as a holistic, interconnected pedagogical approach that draws on all aspects of sustainability, experiential learning and the co-construction of knowledge and research.
2. Sustainable pedagogy needs embedding in curriculums so educators are aware of it.
3. Sustainable pedagogy should be mandatory in all training and qualifications from level 3 upwards for educators to be more confident.
4. Sustainable pedagogy highlights the importance of wisdom shepherds and their role in their ecological world.
5. Sustainable pedagogy should be recognised and actioned by all political parties.

CONCLUSION

This chapter highlights the disconnection between policy and practice, which is evident in practitioners' understanding around the three pillars of sustainability (WCED, 1987) and the SDGs (UNESCO, 2015). To move forward into the 21st century, there is a need for a new way of seeing children.

Children are active, competent wisdom shepherds who engage and could lead all aspects of sustainable pedagogy (Scollan et al., 2024), drawing on their cultural traditions and heritages, lived realities, knowledges and self-determination. The policy-makers need to recognise children are protagonists of their own future and support this in legislation and therefore practice.

REFERENCES

Arlemalm-Hagser, E. and Elliott, S. (2020). Analysis of historical and contemporary early childhood education theories in the Anthropocene. In S. Elliott, E. Arlemalm-Hagser and J. Davis (eds), *Researching Early Childhood Education for Sustainability: Challenging Assumptions and Orthodoxies* (Vol. 2). London: Routledge, pp. 3–12.

Borg, F. and Samuelsson, I. P. (2022). Preschool children's agency in education for sustainability: the case of Sweden. *European Early Childhood Education Research Journal*, 30(1), 147–63.

Boyd, D. (2018a). Early childhood education for sustainability and the historical legacies of two pioneering giants. *International Journal of Early Years*, 38(2), pp. 227–39.

Boyd, D. (2018b). The Legacy Café: a trial of intergenerational and sustainable learning in an early childhood centre in Liverpool. In W. Leal Filho (ed.), *Social Responsibility and Sustainability, World Sustainability Series*. New York: Springer, pp. 373–88.

Boyd, D. (2018c). Utilising place based learning through local contexts to develop agents of change in early childhood education for sustainability. *Education*, 3–13.

Boyd, D., King, J., Mann, S., Neame, J., Scollan, A. and McLeod, N. (2021). *An Early Childhood Education for Sustainability Resource that Embeds the SDGs and STEM into Pedagogical Practice*. Available at: www.ncfe.org.uk/media/xbcbjrfj/early-years-sustainability-resource.pdf. Accessed 29 May 2024.

Boyd, D. King, J., Mann, S. and Neame, J. (2022). *Sustainability Matters in Early Childhood*. Available at: www.ncfe.org.uk/media/p1socs4v/sustainability-matters-in-early-childhood-resource.pdf. Accessed 29 May 2024.

Bronfenbrenner, U. (1979). *The Ecology of Human Development: Experiments by Nature and Design*. Cambridge, MA: Harvard University Press.

Brundtland, G. (1987). Report of the World Commission on Environment and Development: Our Common Future. *United Nations General Assembly document* A/42/427.

Chapman, S. N. and O'Gorman, L. (2022). Transforming learning environments in early childhood contexts through the arts: responding to the United Nations SDGs. *International Journal of Early Childhood*, 54, 33–50.

Davis, J. and Elliott, S. (2024). What is early childhood education for sustainability and why does it matter? In J. Davis and S. Elliott (eds) (3rd edn), *Young Children and the*

Environment: Early Education for Sustainability. Port Melbourne: Cambridge University Press, pp. 7–26.

Department for Education (DfE) (2023). *Sustainability and Climate Change Strategy*. Available at: www.gov.uk/government/publications/sustainability-and-climate-change-strategy/sustainability-and-climate-change-a-strategy-for-the-education-and-childrens-services-systems. Accessed 29 May 2024.

DfE (2024). *Early Years Foundation Stage Statutory Framework for Group and School-Based Providers*. Available at: https://assets.publishing.service.gov.uk/media/65aa5e42ed27ca001327b2c7/EYFS_statutory_framework_for_group_and_school_based_providers.pdf. Accessed 29 May 2024.

Donaldson, M. (1978). *Children's Minds*. London: Harper Collins.

Early Childhood Studies Degrees Network (ECSDN) (2019). *Graduate Practitioner Competencies*. Available at: www.ecsdn.org/competencies/. Accessed 29 May 2024.

Farini, F. and Scollan, A. (2019). Introduction. In F. Farini and A. Scollan (eds), *Children's Self-Determination in the Context of Early Childhood Education and Services: Discourses, Policies and Practices*. International Perspectives on Early Childhood Education and Development, 25. Amsterdam: Springer, pp. 1–22.

Gibson, W. (2015). Leadership for creating cultures of sustainability. In Davis, J. (ed.) (2nd edn), *Young Children and the Environment: Early Education for Sustainability*. Port Melbourne: Cambridge University Press, pp. 55–74.

Günther, J., Muster, S., Kaiser, K. and Rieckmann, M. (2024). A multi-stakeholder perspective on the development of key competencies for sustainability in education for sustainable development at school. *Environmental Education Research*, 1–17.

Liebschner, J. (1992). *A Child's Work: Freedom and Guidance in Froebel's Educational Theory and Practice*. Cambridge: Lutterworth Press

Marsden, R. (2004). *The Cambridge Old English Reader*. Cambridge: Cambridge University Press.

Milner, K. (2023). *It's a No-Money Day* Edinburgh: Barrington Stoke.

Moss, P. (2006). Structures, understandings and discourses: possibilities for re-envisioning the early childhood worker. *Contemporary Issues in Early Childhood*, 7, 30–41.

Moss, P. (2017). Power and resistance in early childhood education: from dominant discourse to democratic experimentalism. *Journal of Pedagogy*, 8(1), 11–32.

Ritchie, J. (2012). Titiro Whakamuri, Hoki Whakamua: 1 Respectful integration of Mori perspectives within early childhood environmental education. *Canadian Journal of Environmental Education*, 17, 62–79.

Scollan, A. and McNeil, E. (2019). Discourse/2 Ireland: listening to children's voices in Irish social work through cultural and organisational filters. In F. Farini and A. Scollan (eds), *Children's Self-Determination in the Context of Early Childhood Education and Services: Discourses, Policies and Practices*. International Perspectives on Early Childhood Education and Development, 25. Amsterdam: Springer, pp. 151–68.

Scollan, A., Boyd, D. and Lee, K. (2024). Exploring UNITY underpinning early childhood sustainable pedagogy in the 21st century [manuscript submitted for publication].

Scottish Government (2020). *The Environment Strategy for Scotland: Vision and Outcomes*. Available at: www.gov.scot/publications/environment-strategy-scotland-vision-outcomes/. Accessed 29 May 2024.

Siraj-Blatchford, J., Smith, K. C. and Samuelsson, I. P. (2010). *Education for Sustainable Development in the Early Years*. London: World Organization for Early Childhood Education.

United Cities and Local Governments (2010). *Culture: Fourth Pillar of Sustainable Development*. Available at: https://agenda21culture.net/sites/default/files/files/documents/en/zz_culture4pillarsd_eng.pdf. Accessed 29 May 2024.

United Nations Convention on the Rights of the Child (UNCRC) (1989). Convention on the Rights of the Child. New York: United Nations.

UNCRC (2023). General Comment No 26. Available at: www.ohchr.org/en/documents/general-comments-and-recommendations/crccgc26-general-comment-no-26-2023-childrens-rights. Accessed 29 May 2024.

United Nations Educational, Scientific and Cultural Organization (UNESCO) (2015). *Sustainable Development Goals*. Available at: https://sdgs.un.org/publications/transforming-our-world-2030-agenda-sustainable-development-17981. Accessed 29 May 2024.

UNESCO (2016). *Education for People and Planet: Creating Sustainable Futures for All*. Global education monitoring report. Available at: www.unesco.org/gem-report/en/education-people-and-planet. Accessed 29 May 2024.

UNESCO (2017a). *Culture: At the Heart of Sustainable Development Goals*. Available at: https://courier.unesco.org/en/articles/culture-heart-sustainable-development-goals. Accessed 10 October 2024.

UNESCO (2017b). *Education for Sustainable Development Goals: Learning Objectives*. Paris: UNESCO.

UNESCO (2020). *Education for sustainable development: a roadmap*. Available at: https://unesdoc.unesco.org/ark:/48223/pf0000374802. Accessed 29 May 2024.

Welsh Government (2022). *Developing a Vision for Curriculum Design*. Available at: https://hwb.gov.wales/curriculum-for-wales/designing-your-curriculum/developing-a-vision-for-curriculum-design/#curriculum-design-and-the-four-purposes. Accessed 10 May 2023.

World Commission on Environment and Development (WCED) (1987). *Our Common Future: The World Commission on Environment and Development*. Oxford: Oxford University Press

3

TRANSFORMING THE ROLE OF THE SCHOOL NURSE TO MEET THE NEEDS OF YOUNG CHILDREN

Dr Pat Day and Delya Lane

KEY DEFINITIONS

Multi-agency collaboration: Multi-agency collaboration working is where practitioners from more than one agency work together jointly, sharing aims, information, tasks and responsibilities to intervene early to prevent problems arising which may impact on children's holistic needs.

Maternal health: Maternal health refers to the health of women during pregnancy, childbirth and the postnatal period.

Infant health: This is an area of practice concerned with the wellbeing and prevention of disease among children ages 0 to 36 months.

Cognitive behavioural therapy: Cognitive behaviour therapy (CBT) is a type of psychotherapy. It may help you to change unhelpful or unhealthy ways of thinking, feeling and behaving.

> **Emotional literacy:** Emotional literacy involves having self-awareness and recognition of your own feelings and knowing how to manage them, such as the ability to stay calm when you feel angry or to reassure yourself when in doubt. It includes empathy.

INTRODUCTION

This chapter advocates transformation of the role of the school nurse to meet the health needs of young children. This requires a refocus of children's services towards early intervention and prevention of ill health. The authors of this chapter are experienced school nurses who have worked in many different Early Years settings within the city of Sheffield. They have witnessed teachers, support staff, social workers, GPs and mental health practitioners working reactively to manage the crises experienced by struggling families. This often returns little success. Negative outcomes are frequent. These include disengaged parents, hostility from parents, children being taken into care, poor academic achievements and emotional wellbeing issues. We believe the time is right for significant resources to be allocated to the wellbeing of young children through upstream interventions. This chapter provides an evidence-based guide for these interventions.

EARLY CHILDHOOD INTO THE FUTURE

Marmot (2010, p. 22) identified that our biggest gains would be to support young children effectively.

> Giving every child the best start in life is crucial to reducing health inequalities across the life course. The foundations for virtually every aspect of human development – physical, intellectual, and emotional – are laid in early childhood. What happens during these early years (starting in the womb) has lifelong effects on many aspects of health and wellbeing – from obesity, heart disease and mental health, to educational achievement and economic status.

This requires effective multi-agency collaboration. In addition, it will need a significant increase in resources in health visiting, school nursing and other services. The *Healthy Child Programme* (PHE, 2018) is a national prevention and early intervention public health framework. It is commissioned by local authorities and its aim is to support every family in making healthy choices by bringing together health, education and other partners to deliver effective programmes on both a universal and targeted basis. The programme underpins delivery of health visiting and school nursing services and partnership working is a principal component.

Family hubs and the Start for Life programme are key to meeting the needs of children. Their aim is to meet the commitments set out in *The Best Start for Life: A Vision for the 1,001 Critical Days* (DHSC, 2021). The overall aims of the programme are to provide support to parents, reduce inequalities in health and education outcomes and building an evidence base of effective practice. The principles we have highlighted in this chapter fit with the overall aims of the family hubs and Start for Life and highlight that the work carried out in these settings can have lifelong benefits to the outcomes for children and young people.

Financial constraints have severely affected staffing provision within health and social care; however, fostering a culture of multi-agency working will help reduce the effects of this. Multi-agency working promotes the exchange of ideas between practitioners in addition to sharing expertise, knowledge and also resources. This practice does exist within family hubs, but, moving forwards, should be built on further. To enhance children's health and wellbeing we feel that services should be co-located within the hubs, as standard practice throughout the country, to meet the needs of the communities in which they serve. This should be inclusive and recognise the need for an expansion in the workforce to include workers from diverse backgrounds to improve understanding and facilitate culturally sensitive interventions for families accessing the service.

MENTAL HEALTH

The most pressing need for young children is good mental health. This determines their outcomes. Poor mental health affects a child's feelings, thoughts and communication (DoH, 1999). This can lead to a struggle to fulfil their potential and live an active life (Day, 2002, p. 22).

Mental health concerns among children were already an issue before the Covid pandemic, but Covid exacerbated the situation. Historical data shows that, prior to the pandemic, the number of hospital admissions across the UK for teenagers with eating disorders increased from 959 13–19-year-olds in 2010/11 to 1,815 in 2013/14. Although the numbers are small, the rate of increase (89 per cent) is mirrored by a larger number of cases that do not present at health services and are unreported (Whitworth, 2015). Apart from this specific information, current data about adolescent mental health is patchy and out of date. Two large-scale and robust surveys by the Office for National Statistics (ONS) in 1999 (Meltzer et al., 2000) and 2004 (Green et al., 2005) are the source of most information about this topic, but they have not been repeated since. Overall, around 13 per cent of boys and 10 per cent of girls were rated as having a mental health disorder. As school nurses, our experience suggests that these statistics represent just the beginning.

A recent research study found that children's anxiety increased significantly during the Covid pandemic, and this had an impact on school anxiety (Adegboye et al., 2021). This has affected the school-readiness of children as they enter nursery and their Foundation Stage 2

(Reception) and the readiness of schools to support these children and their families. Early intervention in mental health could make a real difference to adult outcomes. School nurses are well placed to support this work in early childhood settings if funding would allow and appropriate programmes developed. The most frequent adolescent disorders include anxiety and depression, eating disorders, conduct disorder, attention deficit and hyperactivity disorder (ADHD) and self-harm. Rarer psychotic disorders such as schizophrenia (Green et al., 2005) can also occur. Half of all lifetime cases of psychiatric disorders start by the age of 14 (Kessler et al., 2005). It is proposed that multi-agency working in early childhood could have a significant impact on reducing the numbers of young people affected.

PARENTING

Supporting maternal and infant mental health is a high-impact area for health visiting teams. Infant mental health is vital for the long-term development of emotional health and wellbeing throughout life. Preparation for parenthood is essential as it brings with it many challenges that can affect wellbeing. Preparation should begin with the health visiting team providing antenatal support to parents through an holistic assessment to provide them with information regarding the importance of attachment and attunement and identification of adverse childhood experiences (ACEs) (Kwint, 2022).

We believe that every parent should be offered the opportunity to attend a parenting skills programme to equip them with the most up-to-date information regarding childhood development. By offering this to all, it would reduce the stigma that is often associated with attendance and the feeling that you are a bad/inadequate parent if you are attending. Parenting strongly influences children's thinking and behaviour (Dadds et al., 2015, p. 1312). Overly critical or controlling parenting is linked to child and adolescent depression (McLeod et al., 2007, p. 997). Critical parents focus on children's defects; they can be controlling and lacking emotional attachment. Overprotective parenting risks anxiety disorders by placing restrictions on children due to fear (Rapee et al., 2009, p. 317). Calm, consistent parenting, emphasising problem-solving and behavioural experiments, mitigates these effects (Cartwright-Hatton et al., 2011, p. 250).

As school nurses we were involved in the delivery of a successful parenting programme called 'Coping with our kids'. The programme was designed to be universally available through schools and was promoted as being non-judgemental. It was based on the work of Webster-Stratton. The programme was successful and had a dramatic effect on children's behaviour. The most extensive changes reported in evaluation were seen in the decreased number of reported temper tantrums and interruptions, reduction in being defiant and improved bedtime routines. Results indicated calmer and more respectful relationships because of the five-week programme (Day, 2005). The potential exists for this practical and effective programme to be delivered in family hubs as part of a partnership approach to supporting parents. Staff working in universal services can be trained to deliver such programmes, with the advantage that, when delivered locally by staff familiar with parents, support can be ongoing.

NICE recommends parenting programmes as first-line interventions for conduct disorders in children aged three to 11 years (2013, p. 9). Reducing harsh, inconsistent parenting and promoting more positive parenting is attributed to the Incredible Years™ programme (Webster-Stratton and Reid, 2003, p. 138), using a partnership approach with parents to improve parent–child relationships. Parents learn behaviour management skills – for example, *rules, rewards and consequences* – becoming involved in role modelling and problem-solving. This programme shows sustainable effects on child conduct problems (Bywater et al., 2009). Child conduct disorders showed sustained improvement in randomised controlled trials of the intervention (McGilloway et al., 2012).

COGNITIVE BEHAVIOURAL THERAPY (CBT)

Children's emotional wellbeing can be strengthened with a programme which introduces both them and their parents to the principles of CBT and strategies for using CBT (Day, 2009). The care delivered by school nurses promotes mental health through psychoeducation within a safe environment. Promotion of resilience, problem-solving skills and healthy relationships is effective (Day, 2009).

All parents should be offered the opportunity to understand the principles of CBT. Children in primary schools should also have education about how thoughts affect feelings and behaviour. Work has been carried out in secondary schools to teach the principles of CBT to teenagers. Evaluation was positive and showed that these sessions could have the potential to be adapted for children in primary schools (Day, 2009). CBT has the best evidence base for any mental health intervention due to low relapse rates (Blenkiron, 2022). Research demonstrates CBT can be delivered as an upstream mental health promotion strategy (Barrera et al., 2007).

EMOTIONAL LITERACY

Emotional literacy is an essential part of a child's development. Many children lack the language to adequately express how they feel. This can affect their relationships with others. Children may experience problems with confidence, control and empathy. The Early Years Foundation Stage (EYFS) framework highlights the importance of supporting children to manage their emotions and develop a positive sense of self. It emphasises the need to provide words and meanings to names and express emotions (DfE, 2021). Staffing resources within Early Years settings do not always allow staff to provide the emotional support needed for children to develop these skills.

Children's emotional understanding has a direct impact on their behaviour and adjustment in later life (Denham and Burton, 1996). Good levels of emotional expression are associated with higher levels of empathy, sociable behaviours and popularity (Izard et al., 2001). A project in Sheffield looked at increasing the levels of emotional literacy in children (Day, 2002). Although the project was conducted over 20 years ago, we believe that challenges faced by children today and the low levels of emotional literacy experienced by children show that the project still has relevance. The work was delivered by teachers, learning mentors and school nurses, with support and advice provided by psychologists, drama specialists and behaviour support teachers. A ten-week programme was delivered, based on drama and 'circle time' (Mosley, 2005) to explore feelings and relationships and tackled the impact of issues such as bullying and violence in children's lives. Children were encouraged to discuss strategies and consider the sources of support that could be available to them to tackle these issues. The use of drama allowed children the opportunity to express themselves through an imagined scenario that reflects realistic situations that they may experience. Books were used to foster listening skills and emotional language. Evaluation of the work showed that the programme enabled children to significantly increase their understanding of feelings. Children described how the programme had enabled them to consider the impact of bullying and conflict and the need to care for each other. Of particular interest was the marked intention to seek help from others when needed. Class teachers reported increased levels of confidence for pupils and a reduction in disruptive behaviour (Day, 2002). The success of this programme indicates that the programme could be adapted to meet the needs of young children today. This could be used as a preventative universal programme to promote emotional wellbeing in young children before issues emerge. The current government priority is the need to deliver the academic requirements of the national curriculum, but we propose that a shift in focus should prioritise children's health and wellbeing. This would reap benefits in improving a child's ability to learn.

PROBLEM-SOLVING

Young men find it difficult to express their feelings and approach services for support. Therefore, this puts them at risk of harmful behaviours (Day et al., 1999). The ONS found that the male suicide rate was 16.1 per 100,0000 compared to a female suicide rate of 5.3 per 100,000 (ONS, 2022). A collaborative research project between school nursing and the child and adolescent mental health service was developed to strengthen young people's decision-making skills (Day et al., 1999). Following a scholarship to Australia to observe the work of clinical psychologist Lindy Peterson (1995), a programme of work, Stop, Think, Do, using traffic lights as an aide memoire, was developed. The work was delivered over four sessions and aimed to teach young people problem-solving skills.

These skills are very protective to an individual's mental health. A study into mental health provision for young offenders highlighted traffic light lessons as an effective intervention

(Tunnard et al., 2005, p. 65). Problem-solving skills training shows evidence of reducing anti-social behaviour and mental health problems (Tunnard et al., 2005, p. 62). The programme, Stop, Think, Act, Reflect, focuses on reducing offending behaviour, substance misuse and violence (Tunnard et al., 2005, p. 45). While there is evidence to support the effectiveness of the programme it does not reflect an upstream approach. We propose that the programme should be used as a preventative strategy and that the teaching of this could protect children from future risk-taking behaviours. Stop, Think, Do (Day et al., 1999) has been used to teach young people skills they lack, including communication, relationships and self-awareness (Tunnard et al., 2005, p. 65). The positive impact of this is demonstrated through pre- and post-psychometric testing, self-report evaluation forms, attendance records and improved literacy (Tunnard et al., 2005, p. 65). The programme uses a traffic light approach to encourage young people to consider decision-making processes and the impact their actions may have on both themselves and others. This can be delivered in a variety of ways, but uses interactive teaching methods such as circle time, drama and scenarios. Using a set of working traffic lights enhanced understanding of Stop, Think, Do. Encouraging children to think about decision-making and the consequences of actions could be developed from Early Years settings upwards. The principle of Stop, Think, Do continues to be delivered within our own clinical area as an effective model of practice.

FIVE KEY TAKEAWAYS

1. Early intervention is key.
2. Attachment is of the upmost importance and information needs to be provided for parents in a way that they can understand and become engaged in. Where issues exist rapid access to local parent and infant relationship services (PAIRS) are vital.
3. We need to focus on the mitigation of ACEs across all early childhood provision.
4. We need to provide supportive strategies to young children that will enable them to become resilient, confident and manage the challenges that they will face in life.
5. Government education policy needs to prioritise mental health and shift the focus away from purely educational targets.

CONCLUSION

The need to address the emotional wellbeing of young children so they can become healthy functioning adults is paramount. This can only be achieved with a major increase in funding which sees a rapid expansion in workforce numbers and a significant shift in policy and practice. Practice demands transformational leadership to reflect the position of school nurses as children's services leaders. They are vital advocates for children's health. Through the healthy child programme school nurses can promote health and wellbeing to enable children to achieve their full potential in school. Several areas in England have decommissioned school nursing services. We argue that this should be reversed, with the establishment of appropriately resourced school nursing services, possessing the key skills and knowledge to enhance multi-agency working across health, education and social care.

REFERENCES

Adegboye, D., Williams, F., Collishaw, S., Shelton, K., Langley, K., Hobson, C., Burley, D. and van Goozen, S. (2021). Understanding why the COVID-19 pandemic-related lockdown increases mental health difficulties in vulnerable young children. *JCPP Advances*, *1*(1), e12005.

Barrera, A., Torres, L. and Muñoz, R. (2007). Prevention of depression: the state of the science at the beginning of the 21st Century. *International Review of Psychiatry*, *19*(6), 655–70.

Blenkiron, P. (2022). *Cognitive Behavioural Therapy (CBT)*. Royal College of Psychiatrists. Available at: www.rcpsych.ac.uk/mental-health/treatments-and-wellbeing/cognitive-behavioural-therapy-(cbt). Accessed 10 October 2024.

Bywater, T., Hutchings, J., Daley, D., Whitaker, C., Yeo, S., James, K. and Edwards, R. (2009). Long term effectiveness of a parenting intervention for children at risk of developing conduct disorder. *British Journal of Psychiatry*, *195*(4), 318–24.

Cartwright-Hatton, S., McNally, D., Field, A., Rust, S., Laskey, B., Dixon, C., Gallagher, B., Harrington, R., Miller, C., Pemberton, K., Symes, W., White, C. and Woodham, A. (2011). A new parenting-based group intervention for young anxious children: results of a randomized controlled trial. *Journal of the American Academy of Child and Adolescent Psychiatry*, *50*(3), 242–51.e6.

Dadds, M., Moul, M., Hawes, D., Mendoza Diaz, A. and Brennan, J. (2015). Individual differences in childhood behaviour disorders associated with epigenetic modulation of the cortisol receptor gene. *Child Development*, *86*(5), 1311–20. Available at: https://srcd.onlinelibrary.wiley.com/doi/pdfdirect/10.1111/cdev.12391. Accessed 10 October 2024.

Day, P. (2002). Classroom drama acting for emotional literacy. *Young Minds*, *61*, 22–3.

Day, P. (2005). 'Coping with our kids': a pilot evaluation of a parenting programme delivered by school nurse. *Groupwork*, *15*(1), 42–60

Day, P. (2009). The use of CBT to strengthen emotional wellbeing. *British Journal of School Nursing*, *4*(3) 130–2.

Day, P., Murphy, A. and Cooke, J. (1999). Traffic light lessons: problem solving skills with adolescents. *Community Practitioner*, *72*(10), 322–4.

Denham, S. A. and Burton, R. (1996). A social-emotional intervention for at-risk 4-year-olds. *Journal of School Psychology, 34*(3), 225–45.

Department for Education (DfE) (2021). *Help for Early Years Providers*. Available at: https://help-for-early-years-providers.education.gov.uk/. Accessed 10 October 2024.

Department of Health (DoH) (1999). *Saving Lives: Our Healthier Nation*. London: HMSO. Available at: https://assets.publishing.service.gov.uk/media/5a7b8c8240f0b62826a044aa/4386.pdf. Accessed 10 October 2024.

Department of Health and Social Care (DHSC) (2021). *The Best Start for Life: A Vision for the 1,001 Critical Days*. Available at: www.gov.uk/government/publications/the-best-start-for-life-a-vision-for-the-1001-critical-days. Accessed 10 October 2024.

Green, H., Mcginnity, A., Meltzer, H., Ford, T. and Goodman, R. (2005). *Mental Health of Children and Young People in Great Britain, 2004*. London: ONS.

Izard, C., Fine, S., Schultz, D., Moslow, A., Ackerman, B. and Youngstrom, E. (2001). Emotional knowledge as a predictor of social behaviour and academic competence in children at risk. *Psychological Science, 12*(1), 18–23.

Kessler, R., Berglund, P., Demler, O., Jin, R., Merikangas, K. and Walters, E. (2005). Lifetime prevalence and age-of-onset distributions of DSM-IV disorders in the National Comorbidity Survey replication. *Archives of General Psychiatry, 62*, 593–602.

Kwint, J. (2022). NIHR Evidence: *Adverse Childhood Experiences: What Support Do Young People Need?* Available at: https://evidence.nihr.ac.uk/collection/adverse-childhood-experiences-what-support-do-young-people-need/. Accessed 10 October 2024.

Marmot, M. (2010). *Fair Society, Healthy Lives: The Marmot Review*. Available at: www.parliament.uk/globalassets/documents/fair-society-healthy-lives-full-report.pdf. Accessed 10 October 2024.

McGilloway, S., Mhaille, G., Bywater, T., Furlong, M., Leckey, Y., Kelly, P., Comiskey, C. and Donnelly, M. (2012). A parenting intervention for childhood behavioural problems: a randomized controlled trial in disadvantaged community-based settings. *Journal of Consulting and Clinical Psychology, 80*(1), 116–27.

McLeod, B., Weisz, J. and Wood, J. (2007). Examining the association between parenting and childhood depression: a meta-analysis. *Clinical Psychology Review, 27*(2), 986–1003.

Meltzer, H., Gatward, R., Goodman, R. and Ford, T. (2000). *The Mental Health of Children and Adolescents in Great Britain*. London: HMSO.

Mosley, J. (2005). *Circle Time for Young Children*. London: Routledge.

NICE (2013). Antisocial Behaviour and Conduct Disorders in Children and Young People: Recognition and Management. *Clinical guideline [CG158]*. Available at: www.nice.org.uk/guidance/cg158. Accessed 10 October 2024.

Office for National Statistics (ONS) (2022). *Suicide in England and Wales*. Available at: www.ons.gov.uk/peoplepopulationandcommunity/birthsdeathsandmarriages/deaths/datasets/suicidesintheunitedkingdomreferencetables. Accessed 10 October 2024.

Petersen, L. (1995). Stop think do: improving social and learning skills for children in clinics and schools. In H. van Bilsen, P. Kendall and J. Slavenburg (1995). *Behavioural Approaches for Children and Adolescents: Challenges for the Next Century*. New York: Plenum Press, pp. 103–11.

Public Health England (PHE) (2018). *Healthy Child Programme: Health Visitor and School Nurse Commissioning*. Available at: www.gov.uk/government/publications/healthy-child-programme-0-to-19-health-visitor-and-school-nurse-commissioning. Accessed 10 October 2024.

Rapee, R., Schniering, C. and Hudson, J. L. (2009). Anxiety disorders during childhood and adolescence: origins and treatment. *Annual Review of Clinical Psychology*, 5, 311–341.

Tunnard, J., Ryan, M. and Kurtz, Z. (2005). *Mapping Mental Health Interventions in the Juvenile Secure Estate: Report for the Department of Health*. London: DoH. Available at: www.ryantunnardbrown.com/wp-content/uploads/2012/11/Mapping-MH-Interventions-rtb-final-report-to-DH-October-2005.pdf. Accessed 10 October 2024.

Webster-Stratton, C. and Reid, M. (2003). Treating conduct problems and strengthening social and emotional competence in young children: the dinosaur treatment programme. *Journal of Emotional and Behavioural Disorders*, *11*(3), 130–43.

Whitworth, D. (2015). Eating disorder hospital admissions nearly double. *BBC Newsbeat*. Available at: http://bbc.in/1JoQNZ. Accessed 10 October 2024.

4
BABIES AND CHILDREN'S HEALTH AND WELLBEING

Dr Jackie Musgrave

> **KEY DEFINITIONS**
>
> **Health:** Health is a state of complete physical, mental and social wellbeing and not merely the absence of disease or infirmity (WHO, 1948).
>
> **Wellbeing:** A positive state experienced by individuals and societies. Similar to health, it is a resource for daily life and is determined by social, economic and environmental conditions (WHO, 2024c).
>
> **Mental health:** A state of mental wellbeing that enables people to cope with the stresses of life, realize their abilities, learn well and work well, and contribute to their community (WHO, 2024b).
>
> **Chronic health condition:** A disease or condition that usually lasts for three months or longer and may get worse over time (WHO, 2024a).

INTRODUCTION

This chapter outlines a manifesto for improving the health of babies and young children and foregrounds the role of early childhood professionals in achieving this goal. The content outlines my motivation for wanting to encourage all of us to be aware of what we can do individually, within society, as well as including key messages for government.

I am inspired by Margaret McMillan's (more about her later in the chapter) quote in which she urges nurseries 'to educate each child as if he were your own' (1924). I have adapted this quote and I urge every adult working with and caring for babies and young children to consider how you can make a difference to each child's health, as if he or she were your own child. In this chapter, I outline how giving babies and children access to high-quality early childhood education and care can help to support and promote their physical and mental health, as well as improving the wellbeing of parents and families.

Whenever we are considering contemporary issues, casting a glance back at history helps to understand why and how situations have emerged, so the next section gives a brief historical view of child health and summarises key events during the previous century.

HISTORICAL PERSPECTIVE OF CHILD HEALTH

At the start of the last century, infant mortality was high; one in six infants did not survive until their first birthday. Once a child reached the age of five, the chances of survival increased. Infectious, that is communicable, diseases were a common cause of death in infants and young children. Living in poverty, in crowded and unsanitary housing with inadequate nutrition, increased the risks to children's health.

During the 20th century, a raft of medical advances contributed to reducing child mortality levels – for example, immunisations that prevent life-threatening infectious diseases such as poliomyelitis and diphtheria. The discovery of antibiotics meant that many previously life-threatening infections could be treated. Better sanitation and improved housing with indoor toilets and the provision of fresh and safe water have contributed to fewer deaths and better health.

Babies and children who lived in poverty were most likely to die or have poorer health than those living in affluent families. In 1919, the McMillan sisters, Margaret and Rachel, set up nurseries in poor areas so that they could improve the health of children living in poverty. The provision of nutritious food, good hygiene and play opportunities illustrated the important role of nursery schools in improving health, especially for poor children. If the McMillan sisters were still alive, they may be very surprised to learn that over 100 years since they were working in their nurseries children's health is still of concern. Although child survival rates have improved, there are many factors that influence children's health and can create poor quality of life.

Infant mortality has improved dramatically in high-income countries (although it remains high in many low-income countries). Medical advances and interventions mean that many children who are born with or develop life-limiting or threatening health conditions can be kept alive. However, the quality of life for many children because of health conditions is not good. In a report by the Royal College of Paediatrics and Child Health (RCPCH) back in 2017, it was stated that:

> The health of infants, children and young people in the UK has improved dramatically over the last 30 years. Many will lead happy and healthy lives, but the future health and happiness of a significant number is in jeopardy. The bottom line is that the UK could do far more to improve child health and wellbeing.
>
> (2017, p. 4)

It is important to note that this report was published before the global pandemic which had a profoundly negative impact on children's health, especially for children living in poverty and deprivation. In a post-pandemic report by the Academy of Medical Sciences (2024), it states that:

> Health in the early years (which we define in this report as encompassing preconception, through pregnancy, to the first five years of childhood) forms the basis for mental and physical health and wellbeing through the rest of the life course with consequent benefits to population health, national productivity, innovation and the prosperity of the nation.
>
> (2024, p. 4)

Thus, the report clearly states the importance of laying the foundations before conception takes place. This chapter explores the contribution that early childhood practitioners can, and do, make to laying the foundations of good health. The following section looks at the factors that contribute to building firm foundations for health.

FACTORS THAT INFLUENCE CHILDREN'S HEALTH

Children's health is complex and there are many factors that contribute to their good, or poor, health. To illustrate the health factors that can impact on health, Figure 4.1 adapts Bronfenbrenner's ecological systems (1979) approach to separate factors that can be within the child, the family, community, country and across the world. Table 4.1 illustrates the factors in more detail.

Starting with the child, it is becoming increasingly clear that future health is strongly influenced by pre-conceptual care (PHE, 2018). Antenatal care of the unborn infant and mother are firmly established in high-income countries as a way of maximising the chance of a safe delivery of a healthy baby. Genetically inherited conditions such as cystic fibrosis or asthma can affect children's health in myriad ways (Musgrave, 2022).

Babies and children's health is most influenced by the family they grow up in. Socio-economic factors can determine the type of diet a child is provided with. Some parents have strong views about health; for example, because of religious or cultural beliefs, they may not want their child to be immunised against preventable, communicable diseases, such as measles (Kendall-Rayner, 2019).

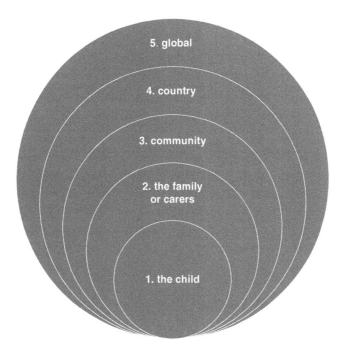

Figure 4.1 The factors within systems that influence children's health (adapted from Bronfenbrenner, 1979)

Table 4.1 Examples of factors within each of the layers

Factors in each layer	Examples of factors that influence health
The child	Pre-conceptual care Length of gestation (pregnancy) Quality of antenatal care Genetic conditions Trauma, physical and mental Age of child and level of development
The family or carers	Socio-economic status Family structure Religious beliefs Cultural beliefs
Community	Availability of child services for health and education Availability of safe outdoor play areas Pollution Availability of shops to buy reasonably priced food
Country	Availability of health services such as immunisations Political status and (in)stability Status of children
Global	Climate Politics Pandemics

As has already been mentioned, living in poverty remains, as it was in the days of the McMillan sisters, a negative influence on children's health and wellbeing (Wickham et al., 2016). However, it is important to remember that many children from more affluent families are also experiencing poor health.

Children who are in the care of the state and do not live with their biological parents are especially vulnerable to poor health outcomes (DfE, 2015).

The community that children and their families live in can heavily influence health. A welcoming environment that has outdoor spaces with well-maintained recreation and playground facilities means that children and families can safely play and engage with nature. A community where children's services are easily available, such as playgroups, nurseries, access to health clinics and education settings, means that parents can make use of facilities that contribute to good health. In contrast, inaccessible and poor housing in a hostile and dilapidated environment with no services are negative factors that influence children's health. In particular, lack of opportunity to be physically active means that children have less opportunity to meet the guidelines that are recommended for physical activity for children (WHO, 2020). In turn, this can lead to obesity and a range of health-related issues (Musgrave et al., 2024).

The country that a child is born in has a profound influence on their health. A nation's commitment to children's health can be measured by the services that are available to families. The political situation in a country impacts on children's health; war-torn countries can mean that there are higher levels of poverty, and children are more likely to suffer from starvation. The climate of a country also affects children's health; excessive temperatures can create famine and drought. Earthquakes and other natural disasters can destroy buildings and the infrastructure that supports children's health, thus leaving them vulnerable to poorer health.

Globally, there are many initiatives that are aimed at supporting children's health. Most notably, the United Nations Convention on the Rights of the Child (UNCRC) Article 24 states parties recognise:

> the right of the child to the enjoyment of the highest attainable standard of health and to facilities for the treatment of illness and rehabilitation of health.
>
> (UNCRC, 1989)

However, despite many countries ratifying the Rights of the Child, the ways that health is addressed remains inconsistent across the world.

The United Nations *Sustainable Development Goals* (SDGs) (UNESCO, 2015) Goal 3 aims to provide good health and wellbeing; however, in the 2023 report, it is evident there are still significant shortcomings in how individual countries can and do provide services and interventions that can improve children's health.

This section has summarised some of the factors that can influence all children's health within different systems. The following section focuses on some of the physical and mental health conditions that are jeopardising children's health in contemporary times.

CONTEMPORARY HEALTH ISSUES

As well as children's health being complex, the classification and causes of physical and mental health are complex. It can be helpful to think of health conditions as being *communicable* or *non-communicable*. Communicable diseases are illnesses or conditions that are passed between humans by 'germs' or parasites.

Communicable diseases:

- infections caused by 'germs' – for example, viruses, bacteria or fungi – that cause infections such as measles, poliomyelitis, diphtheria, whooping cough or rubella
- infestations such as parasites – for example, threadworms.

On the other hand, non-communicable health conditions are those that are not passed on by germs.

Non-communicable diseases:

- nutrition-related conditions such as obesity, poor oral health
- mental health conditions
- chronic health conditions: asthma, eczema, diabetes, sickle cell anaemia
- complex medical needs.

Many communicable diseases are preventable; as already mentioned, childhood immunisations are highly effective in reducing the spread of diseases such as whooping cough, measles and poliomyelitis. Despite the availability of immunisations that are provided free of charge, many children are not fully immunised, leaving them vulnerable to dying or being left with a legacy of disability because of developing the diseases. One of the most effective ways of preventing the spread of infectious diseases is a good handwashing technique using safe water.

Many non-communicable health conditions are preventable, but the factors that influence a child's health may mean that this is more difficult to achieve. Again, families living in poverty are likely to live in communities that are not conducive to good health. Children who are vulnerable to adversity are more likely to develop mental health difficulties and diagnosable mental health conditions. As many as 20 per cent of children are living with a chronic – that is, an ongoing – health condition that can have a negative impact on overall physical and mental health.

The context of children's health probably sounds bleak, but, as pointed out already, this is the reality of the situation. The health of many children is in jeopardy, as an RCPCH report states (2023). So, what can be done to improve this situation? As stated in the Academy of Medical Sciences Report (2024), good foundations for health need to be laid down in the preconception to age five period – this is where practitioners in early childhood education and care settings can, and do, make a significant contribution to supporting and improving children's health.

THE ROLE OF EARLY CHILDHOOD EDUCATION AND CARE SETTINGS

Many countries have a curriculum for the care and education of babies and pre-school children. And such curriculums often have aims and principles relating to health. In England, the Early Years Foundation Stage (EYFS) (DfE, 2024) includes more than 30 aims and principles that, if implemented with integrity, can support and promote babies' and children's health.

In the UK, more than 4 million children are living in poverty. This has a profound impact on their general health. And if they have a chronic or ongoing health condition, such as asthma, living in poverty can add an additional level of complexity to managing the symptoms of the condition.

To help to unpack some of the ways that practitioners contribute to improving children's health, please read the case study below and make a list of the ways that you think the practitioners are helping the family.

> **CASE STUDY: HELPING THE FAMILY**
>
> Jaxon and Skyla are two-year-old twins, their brother Emmerson is four.
>
> Marnie, the children's mum, lives in a small house on a recently renovated social housing estate. Marnie is a single parent following the death of her partner a year ago. She works three days a week at the local hospital. The children attend nursery while Marnie goes to work.
>
> The nursery has an excellent reputation, there is low turnover of staff, and low levels of staff sickness. The owners invest a great deal of time and money to ensure that the staff wellbeing is as good as it can be. The nursery has a small outdoor play area, but it is built next to a park that has well-maintained play equipment.
>
> Ameera is the twins' key person and Brett is Emmerson's key person.

Jaxon and Skyla are thriving and happy at nursery, they have regular routines, and enjoy a short afternoon nap which revives them for the rest of their stay at nursery. They enjoy the nutritious food that is cooked in the nursery, and they happily feed themselves. They are happy to drink water because the nursery doesn't serve squash. The twins enjoy playing on their own and with others; they especially enjoy playing in the sand and with other sensory play activities. They happily copy Ameera showing them how to clean their teeth, which is part of the practice within the nursery to ensure that children's oral health is attended to. Ameera has noticed that the twins are starting to show signs that they are ready to be toilet trained, so Ameera has devised an approach with Marnie to ensure that home and nursery are following the same approach. The twins are learning to wash their hands properly by following the other children and Ameera's hand-washing routine.

The twins' speech and communication are developing fast; they love listening to stories and mimicking words. Ameera listens carefully to the twins and supports their language development.

However, Emmerson has become withdrawn over the last six months. Emmerson has recently developed eczema, and it is causing him a lot of discomfort and it is interfering with his everyday activities. Brett has a very good understanding of how to manage the symptoms; he completed a health care plan with Marnie so that everyone knows when to apply cream to Emmerson's skin to relieve the itching and reduce the need for him to scratch his skin. Brett carries out regular observations of Emmerson to help him build a picture of what is going on with him.

The following section highlights some of the ways that the children's attendance at the setting is helping to support and promote health for all of the family.

REFLECTING ON THE CASE STUDY, HOW IS ATTENDANCE HELPING?

Marnie has a huge amount of responsibility in her life. As well as being a single mum to three pre-school-aged children, she is grieving for and still adjusting to life without her partner. If she couldn't access high-quality care for her children, she would miss out on the social aspects of her work which she enjoys hugely. Being able to go to work and earn money means that the family is better off financially. Without being able to go to work, her wellbeing and mental health could be negatively impacted.

The children's key people know the children well and they provide strong, warm and supportive relationships with them and with Marnie. In turn, they can plan for their needs exceedingly well. Brett knows how much Emmerson loves playing football, so he takes some of the children to the park as often as he can. This distracts Emmerson from scratching and Brett notices how much happier he is when he's outdoors and especially when he plays football. However, Brett is concerned that he is quieter than he used to be. By carrying out additional observations of Emmerson, he can keep an eye on him. Brett is wondering if Emmerson is grieving for his dad and is conscious that he may need some specialist counselling. However, Brett is also aware that it may be the eczema that is getting him down and causing him to be quieter. Marnie had mentioned that during a recent spell of hot weather, Emmerson's skin was angry-looking and itchy to the extent that he was awake during the night and his sleep was affected. So Brett is wondering if sleep deprivation is adding to him being quieter. Brett listens and observes Emmerson carefully, using inclusive nursery routines, such as circle time, to give him an opportunity to express his emotions.

The above case study is designed to illustrate how practitioners can support the physical and mental health of young children 'simply' by providing high-quality practice, including some of the ways that regular and predictable routines such as play, good hygiene, nutritious food, hydration and so on can improve children's health. And for children with other health conditions, such as Emmerson with eczema, the case study illustrates how excellent practice – for example, carrying out regular observations and working in partnership with parents – is important for managing children's ongoing health conditions. You may have identified other ways that early childhood education and care can improve children's health.

Much of what is outlined in the case study may be regarded as normal everyday practice, but it is important that practitioners see themselves as key professionals who make a significant contribution to promoting children's health. This is discussed in the next section.

HEALTH PROMOTION IN EARLY CHILDHOOD EDUCATION AND CARE SETTINGS

Health promotion is described by the WHO as:

> the process of enabling people to increase control over, and to improve, their health. It moves beyond a focus on individual behaviour towards a wide range of social and environmental interventions (2024a).

Clearly, children have limited options to control and improve their health; therefore, it is the responsibility of adults to promote children's health. And when families need additional support, and as children in your setting may be in your care for considerable periods of time, you are very well placed to promote children's health.

To help settings to address the health needs of children, I devised the early childhood Education Health Promotion Toolkit (Musgrave and Payler, 2023). This is a free downloadable resource. The toolkit supports settings to identify an aspect of health that needs to be improved. The five steps in the toolkit include guidance about implementing an intervention, such as one aimed at improving the nutritional value of the food provided to children. In the pilot research to trial the toolkit, one nursery in an area of high deprivation looked at ways of working sensitively with parents to increase their knowledge of healthy eating (Musgrave and Payler, 2021).

Key to the success of the healthy eating campaign was to devise an inclusive approach to working with parents and staff. To learn more about what went on at home, all parents were invited to complete an anonymous questionnaire. The responses helped them to identify some of the health issues they needed to address. Findings revealed that many parents didn't have the time or money to spend on food that they were concerned their children wouldn't eat. Some parents didn't have reliable cooking facilities. Some parents said that they had never taken their children to the dentist because of lack of services in the community, or lack of time to do so.

All these findings helped the setting to shape the campaign. To address the need for children to become familiar with going to the dentist and learning about oral health, a dental nurse was invited to come to the nursery, and the home corner became a dental surgery.

This section has briefly outlined some of the ways that you can make a valuable contribution to promoting children's health. The following section summarises the key points relating to how the early childhood community can make a positive contribution to children's health.

FIVE KEY TAKEAWAYS

1. The need for all children to have access to high-quality early childhood education and care. Increase the recognition that early childhood practitioners play an important role in supporting and promoting children's health. Early childhood curriculums, such as the Early Years Foundation Stage (DfE, 2024), when implemented in high-quality settings, are a way to enact the rights of the child to health.
2. As discussed in Chapter 8, the government must support the early childhood workforce to improve qualifications and ensure that qualifications

(Continued)

include health-related content, so they are prepared to address the complexities of children's health. High-quality CPD is important to update knowledge relating to health.
3. Support practitioners to develop inclusive approaches for children with health needs – for example, those with chronic health conditions – so that they have maximum participation and minimal exclusion in their early education experience.
4. Promote awareness that contemporary childhood is a root cause of childhood mental health difficulties. However, regular and reliable routines that are suited to each child's needs can help lay the foundations of good physical and mental health.
5. Change society's view of babies and children and put children's health needs in all policies. Local planners can improve children's health by providing services for children and families in communities – for example, town planning policies that put children's services and recreation as a priority.

CONCLUSION

The aim of this chapter is to say what I would want for children's health if I could wave a magic wand. The imperative for government is to reduce child poverty and ensure that every child has enough nourishing food for their needs. However, as reducing child poverty is a challenging and complex aim, it would be beneficial if government and policy-makers recognised the valuable role that early childhood practitioners can, and do, play in supporting and promoting health. Prioritising the provision of access to early childhood education and care for all babies and young children contributes to laying strong foundations for future good physical and mental health. The government is missing a trick by not doing so!

REFERENCES

Academy of Medical Sciences (2024). *Prioritising Early Childhood to Promote the Nation's Health, Wellbeing and Prosperity*. Available at: https://acmedsci.ac.uk/file-download/16927511. Accessed 5 April 2024.

Bronfenbrenner, U. (1979). *The Ecology of Human Development: Experiments by Nature and Design*. Cambridge, MA: Harvard University Press.

Department for Education (DfE) (2015). *Promoting the Health and Well-being of Looked-after Children* (updated 2022). Available at: www.gov.uk/government/publications/promoting-the-health-and-wellbeing-of-looked-after-children--2. Accessed 29 October 2024.

DfE (2024). *Early Years Foundation Stage (EYFS) Statutory Framework*. Available at: www.gov.uk/government/publications/early-years-foundation-stage-framework--2. Accessed 19 April 2024.

Kendall-Raynor, P. (2019). Measles outbreak: misinformation and poverty fuelling quadrupling of worldwide cases. *Nursing Children and Young People, 31*(3).

McMillan, M. (1924). Educate every child as if he were your own. *Handwritten manuscript*. Available at: https://discovery.nationalarchives.gov.uk/details/r/8af0db7f-c0e1-4d80-8cac-f8c9a243203b. Accessed 10 October 2024.

Musgrave, J. (2022). *Health and Wellbeing for Babies and Children: Contemporary Issues*. London: Routledge.

Musgrave, J. and Payler, J. (2021). Proposing a model for promoting children's health in early childhood education and care settings. *Children and Society, 35*(5), 766–83.

Musgrave, J. and Payler, J. (2023). *Early Childhood Health Promotion: A Toolkit for Early Childhood Education and Care Practitioners. A Resource to Support Your Practice in Improving the Health of Children in Pre-Schools Settings*. Available at: www.open.edu/openlearn/pluginfile.php/4015395/mod_resource/content/2/byc_1_early_childhood_health_promotion_toolkit_dec23.pdf. Accessed 10 October 2024.

Musgrave, J., Dorrian, J., Langdown, B. and Rodriguez-Leon, L. (2024). *Little Minds Matter: Promoting Physical Development and Activity in Early Childhood*. Abingdon: Routledge.

Public Health England (PHE) (2018). *Making the Case for Preconception Care: Planning and Preparation for Pregnancy to Improve Maternal and Child Health Outcomes*. Available at: https://assets.publishing.service.gov.uk/government/uploads/system/uploads/attachment_data/file/729018/Making_the_case_for_preconception_care.pdf. Accessed 10 October 2024.

Royal College of Paediatrics and Child Health (RCPCH) (2017). *State of Child Health*. Available at: www.rcpch.ac.uk/sites/default/files/2018-05/state_of_child_health_2017report_updated_29.05.18.pdf. Accessed 24 October 2024.

RCPCH (2023). *RCPCH Responds to Latest Obesity Figures for England, 2022/23*. Available at: www.rcpch.ac.uk/news-events/news/rcpch-responds-latest-childhood-obesity-figures-england-202223#:~:text=The%20prevalence%20of%20obesity%20in,higher%20than%20pre%2Dpandemic%20levels. Accessed 5 April 2024.

United Nations (2023). *The Sustainable Development Goals Report: Special Edition*. Available at: https://unstats.un.org/sdgs/report/2023/The-Sustainable-Development-Goals-Report-2023.pdf. Accessed 10 October 2024.

United Nations Convention on the Rights of the Child (UNCRC) (1989). Convention on the Rights of the Child. Available at: www.unicef.org.uk/wp-content/uploads/2016/08/unicef-convention-rights-child-uncrc.pdf. Accessed 10 October 2024.

United Nations Educational, Scientific and Cultural Organization (UNESCO) (2015). *Sustainable Development Goals*. Available at: https://sdgs.un.org/publications/transforming-our-world-2030-agenda-sustainable-development-17981. Accessed 10 October 2024.

Wickham, S., Anwar, E., Barr, B., Law, C. And Taylor-Robinson, D. (2016). Poverty and child health in the UK: using evidence for action. *Archives of Disease in Childhood*, 101, 759–66.

World Health Organization (WHO) (1948). Constitution. Available at: https://apps.who.int/gb/bd/PDF/bd47/EN/constitution-en.pdf?ua=1. Accessed 10 October 2024.

WHO (2020). *WHO Guidelines on Physical Activity and Sedentary Behaviour*. Available at: https://iris.who.int/bitstream/handle/10665/336656/9789240015128-eng.pdf. Accessed 8 April 2024.

WHO (2024a). *Health Promotion*. Available at: www.who.int/westernpacific/about/how-we-work/programmes/health-promotion#:~:text=Health%20promotion%20is%20the%20process,of%20social%20and%20environmental%20interventions. Accessed 10 October 2024.

WHO (2024b). *Mental Health*. Available at: www.who.int/health-topics/mental-health#tab=tab_1. Accessed 10 October 2024.

WHO (2024c). *Promoting Well-being*. Available at: www.who.int/activities/promoting-well-being. Accessed 10 October 2024.

FURTHER READING

NHS England (2023). *One in Five Children and Young People had a Probable Mental Disorder in 2023*. Available at: www.england.nhs.uk/2023/11/one-in-five-children-and-young-people-had-a-probable-mental-disorder-in-2023/#:~:text=One%20in%20five%20children%20and%20young%20people%20in%20England%20aged,probable%20mental%20disorder%20in%202023. Accessed 10 October 2024.

FREE RESOURCES

OpenLearn/Open University (n.d.). *Supporting Children's Mental Health and Wellbeing*. Available at: www.open.edu/openlearn/education-development/supporting-childrens-mental-health-and-wellbeing/content-section-overview?active-tab=description-tab. Accessed 10 October 2024.

OpenLearn/Open University (n.d.). *Supporting Physical Development in Early Childhood*. Available at: www.open.edu/openlearn/health-sports-psychology/supporting-physical-development-early-childhood/content-section-overview?active-tab=description-tab. Accessed 10 October 2024.

Open Learn Create/Open University (n.d.). *Antenatal Care*. A free course available at: www.open.edu/openlearncreate/course/view.php?id=10. Accessed 6 December 2024.

Open Learn Create/Open University (n.d.). Part of a collection of 17 courses. Health Education and Training. Available at: www.open.edu/openlearncreate/course/index.php?categoryid=23. Accessed 10 October 2024.

5
EARLY CHILDHOOD CURRICULUM

Professor Verity Campbell-Barr, Dr Katherine Evans and Sasha Tregenza

> **KEY DEFINITIONS**
>
> **Emergent curriculum:** A curriculum built on children's interests in support of their learning.
>
> **Contextual curriculum:** A curriculum that recognises the diversity of children's backgrounds.
>
> **Expressive curriculum:** A curriculum that builds on the autonomy of the child.
>
> **Hidden curriculum:** The unspoken or implicit rules of how children are expected to be and behave when learning.

INTRODUCTION

'Curriculum' is a commonly used term within educational contexts and is often associated with a course of study. However, in looking at curriculum for those aged birth to eight, it is evident that it is a term that can be variably interpreted. For example, a distinction can be made between curriculum in different educational contexts, such as the difference between a pre-school and primary school curriculum. Even within these different educational contexts there may be variability in how curriculum is interpreted when working with children of different ages – would a curriculum for a nine-month-old be the same as for a four-year-old? Here we consider a way of talking about curriculum that is not constrained by a child's age or a course of study. We present curriculum as emergent, expressive and contextual (Campbell-Barr et al., 2023) as a way of working with children irrespective of their age or educational context. We draw on literature primarily from Early Years education (EYE) by way of providing a stimulus to think of curriculum differently to the traditional definition of curriculum as a course of study (Mufti and Peace, 2012).

We begin with considering what is curriculum and who and what determines this, recognising the social-historical dimension of the epistemological framing of curriculum. We then consider the historical perspective in detail in order to ascertain what has shaped and influenced current perspectives on curriculum, but also recognising that these are often debated and contentious ideas. We then go on to consider curriculum as something based in children's rights and respectful of early childhood professionals' professional knowledge and agency.

WHAT IS CURRICULUM?

How curriculum is understood will inform how it is planned for and enacted. Embedded in the curriculum are understandings of knowledge and how to obtain that knowledge – providing messages as to what it is deemed worthwhile knowledge. Curriculum thus becomes the planned learning for acquiring the knowledge (Chawla-Duggan, 2019). The determining of the knowledge will be historically and socially formed (Popkewitz, 1997), whereby different knowledges are ascribed with different functions and meanings. As such, curriculums become socially constructed epistemological spaces. As Dillon (2009) sets out, curriculum comprises the legitimated bodies of knowledge and skill that are selected for early childhood professionals to transmit to children. For children aged from birth to eight, curriculum reflects the knowledge and skills that society wants them to learn.

Within the curriculum there are different social actors. While we may think of an early childhood professional and children when we consider who is involved in a curriculum, we also need to think carefully about who and what is influencing the curriculum. In many national contexts, there will be national curriculums, or what might be regarded as the official (state-bureaucratic and legislative) discourse (Bernstein, 2000). In such circumstances, the curriculum becomes a disciplining technology that sets out the knowledge that is to be learnt (Popkewitz, 1997). As such, the curriculum is *what* is to be taught and pedagogy is *how*. In this context, curriculum cannot be separated from notions of outcomes and competence, whereby there is an assessment of a child having acquired the prescribed knowledge and skills that formulate the 'what' is to be taught.

Historically, there have been different ideologies, theories and approaches that shape the curriculum. However, in early childhood contexts, there is little agreement on what is meant by curriculum (Hedges et al., 2011). In early childhood, curriculum is seen as a point of struggle, that has been influenced by theories of child development, but lacks significant theorising and development of its own (Wood and Hedges, 2016). The dominance of child development theories has influenced curriculum as being a series of stages that lead to prescribed outcomes for the child. If child outcomes inform the 'what' is to be taught, the risk is that this restricts the potential for alternative forms of knowledge and outcomes to be considered. This risk is particularly acute in contexts where the state has determined the outcomes to be achieved as this ascribes knowledge hierarchies that have consequences for both understanding the child and the early childhood professional.

Internationally, there is concern that the technology of the state has formulated a narrow definition of child outcomes (Moss et al., 2016) and, by association, curriculum. The English context is an interesting example, where the Early Years Foundation Stage for children from birth to five years of age (DfE, 2024) is a framework rather than a curriculum and it is early childhood professionals who determine the curriculum. The framework does stipulate both areas of learning and Early Learning Goals (ELGs), alongside the need for ongoing assessment that promotes teaching and learning to 'ensure children's "school readiness"' (p. 7), all of which will have a bearing on what is possible within the curriculum. Thus, while early childhood professionals are free to determine their curriculum, whereby there are no prescribed courses of study, the areas of learning and ELGs will shape what the curriculum looks like.

Conversely, Key Stage 1 of the national curriculum for children aged five to seven in England sets out compulsory curriculum subjects, with programmes of study (DfE, 2013). While Key Stage 1 (and later stages of the curriculum) can be seen as a technocratic curriculum that sets out what is to be taught, the concern is that the Foundation Stage, with its focus on school readiness, is equally resulting in expected ways of designing a curriculum (Roberts-Holmes, 2015). The concern with this technocratic approach is that it is counter to the philosophical traditions that are found within Early Years education.

EARLY YEARS PIONEERS

While the Early Years curriculum is predominantly informed by developmental theories (Wood, 2020) and has arguably become focused upon supporting school readiness and a performative culture (Roberts-Holmes, 2015), the longstanding and influential Early Years pioneers originally offered less technocratic approaches to curriculum and practice within early learning. Rousseau (1762) focused upon the naturalist view of learning, promoting an Early Years curriculum which fosters free thinking and well-balanced children, respecting the uniqueness of childhood. Rousseau (1762) encouraged the importance of listening to children and Malaguzzi (1996) has since emphasised the need to appreciate and respond to the hundred languages of children, to shape curriculum approaches and practices in line with children's interests and needs. Pestalozzi (1819) further considered the early learning curriculum to be driven by nature, fostering the importance of children exercising self-directed activity, through their hands (activity), head (making connections between knowledge) and heart (following interests and developing morals), appreciating the influence of the innate evolution of nature in guiding learning, without requiring unnecessary pressures or influences, to shape or prescribe curriculum content and early learning experiences.

The underpinning concepts relating to respecting nature, the uniqueness of children and self-directed learning experiences were additionally advocated by Froebel (1826), Montessori (1912), McMillan (1919) and Isaacs (1929), promoting an expressive curriculum which builds upon the autonomy and capabilities of children (Campbell-Barr et al., 2023). Starting with the child is a different interpretation to curriculum than starting with the outcomes to be achieved or the prescribed subjects to be covered or methods of how to support learning and educating the child. Instead, there is a greater focus upon pedagogical approaches which consider how children learn and the role of the early childhood professional and environment in supporting children's learning, as opposed to prescribing the content of what skills and knowledge should be taught. However, approaches to supporting children as autonomous learners varied between each pioneer's approach. Froebel (1826) promoted self-directed activity through play and exploration, offering children freedom with guidance from the early childhood professional. Similarly, the Montessori method (1912) included a curriculum which requires the early childhood professional to carefully plan and structure the environment, with natural open-ended resources. Montessori acknowledged the children's capabilities in directing their own learning, through self-directed play and exploration, referred to as *auto-education*. The Montessori method (1912) requires the early childhood professional to only intervene to direct and support learning when invited to do so by the child. Alternatively, McMillan (1919) and Isaacs (1929) focused upon the nurturing role of the early childhood professional, emphasising the importance of a curriculum which offers outdoor play to support children's health and wellbeing. Isaacs (1929) further promoted the self-directed activity of children, establishing a free-flow learning environment, which encouraged open-ended and unpredictable play.

The importance of children leading their own play and learning results in the inability to pre-plan the curriculum content, due to the children exercising their imagination, curiosity and active enquiry in the moment and on their own terms (Giardiello, 2014). While the importance of delivering a curriculum which fosters self-directed activity remains present within curriculum guidance documents for the Early Years Foundation Stage (Early Years Coalition, 2021; DfE, 2023), the current pressures placed upon early childhood professionals in supporting children to reach the ELGs (DfE, 2024) has arguably resulted in hesitation surrounding child-led practices within the Early Years, in favour of more structured approaches to learning (Roberts-Holmes, 2015).

While the Early Years pioneers promoted the connection between children, nature and the importance of self-directed activity, an aspect of their approaches considered the skills children needed for later life. Froebel (1826) considered childhood as a valid stage in life, but also acknowledged the preparation needed for adulthood. Froebel presented children with 'gifts' (open-ended resources to promote imagination and discovery) and 'occupations' (to develop life skills and invention), seeking to support self-directed play while building upon future life skills. Froebel (1826) and Montessori (1912) further promoted the importance of children's daily living skills in relation to supporting health and wellbeing (Giardiello, 2014), leading to Montessori's curriculum including opportunity to practise daily living skills, such as encouraging self-care and responsibility within the home-from-home learning environment. Similarly, McMillan (1919) established a contextual curriculum which nurtured the skills needed for lifelong learning, associating such skills with the importance of physical activity in promoting both happy and healthy future lives. Isaacs (1929) continued to build upon these concepts, establishing a home-from-home learning environment with a curriculum which encouraged children to take responsibility for the environment, through helping to plan and prepare mealtimes and care for nature. A curriculum without outcomes is not devoid of recognition for child development, instead a curriculum centred on the child takes a broad and holistic view of child development, learning and the knowledges needed in life.

CONTEMPORARY PERSPECTIVES

The lack of consideration for curriculum theory in early childhood means that mainstream discussions of education policy tend to adopt the language and concepts of curriculum in other age phases, such as the national curriculum in England (DfE, 2013). The more traditional notions of curriculum as what is to be taught sits counter to a more child-centred interpretation of curriculum seen in the philosophy of the early childhood pioneers. As such, curriculum narrative frequently fails to recognise the unique nature of early childhood as a phase of education and runs the risk of promoting a 'schoolified' (Moss, 2013; OECD, 2017) version of early learning. Drawing on empirical research with early childhood experts and educators, Campbell-Barr et al. (2023) argue that Early Years curriculums need to be viewed as distinctive from other phases of education. They advocate the need for a clear definition of curriculum in the Early Years, one that recognises the emergent and iterative nature of early learning. In their study exploring 'Insights into a High Quality Early Years

Curriculum' (Campbell-Barr et al., 2023), they propose a model of curriculum that is expressive, contextual and emergent. Such a model responds to children's needs, interests and developmental stages (An emergent curriculum), recognises diversity in children's backgrounds and the ecological context in which the child exists (A contextual curriculum), and builds on children's autonomy, shaping curriculum through their active participation (An expressive curriculum). This notion of curriculum aligns with other contemporary ideas in this area, including the concept of funds of knowledge (Hedges et al., 2011), working theories (Wood and Hedges, 2016) and the location of children's interests as a site of intra-action (Chesworth, 2019).

An emergent curriculum (Campbell-Barr et al., 2023) draws on knowledge of child development, while building on children's interests in support of learning. It is therefore not completely free, emanating not just from the children but arising dynamically in response to a range of factors, including the physical and social environment, early childhood professionals' interests and social and cultural values (Hedges, 2022). This valuing of emergence is in contrast to more traditional views of curriculum that are built on clear outcomes that act to determine what is of value in terms of knowledge, skills and experience. An emergent curriculum is also a dynamic curriculum. According to Chesworth (2019), accepting curriculum and pedagogy as dynamic necessitates an openness to learning as uncertain and unpredictable, as occurring within 'the complexity of classroom intra-actions' (p. 14).

A contextual curriculum, according to Campbell-Barr et al. (2023) builds on children's cultural capital, recognising the different socio-cultural backgrounds that children have, in support of learning experiences in which they can express their interests and capabilities. This appreciation of children's interests is akin to Hedges et al.'s (2011) notion of 'funds of knowledge', which argues for a move away from the consideration of interests as a choice of play activity (in an environment curated by adults) towards an appreciation of children's 'funds of knowledge' as being rooted in their lives as part of families, cultures and communities.

An expressive curriculum (Campbell-Barr et al., 2023) recognises and builds on the autonomy of the child and creates space for children's active and authentic participation. Considering curriculum in this expressive form helps to raise questions about if and how it might be understood from children's perspectives as part of a specific ecological context, as opposed to a model built on the organisation of a specific set of knowledge and skills. Wood and Hedges' (2016) articulation of children's 'working theories' supports this notion of an expressive curriculum, identifying knowledge construction as tentative, creative and unpredictable, being rooted in community and cultural experiences (p397). They consider that, 'Working theories offer a way to incorporate social pedagogic and academic goals within the context of valuing children's play alongside the conversations, inquiries and debates that occur within participatory learning experiences' (Wood and Hedges, 2016, p.398).

These theorisations of curriculum are embedded in an Early Years context built on the legacy of pioneers who advocated for education that values children's uniqueness, autonomy, independence and wellbeing, while maintaining a focus on knowledge and skills needed for later life. They offer an alternative to normative models of curriculum that view learning as linear, predictable and progressive. They offer another way of talking about curriculum, with terms such as 'working theories', 'funds of knowledge', 'expression' and 'emergence' challenging the vocabulary of goals, outcomes and standardised assessment.

However, we also have to reflect on how all forms of curriculum set expectations as to how children are to be and behave within the learning context (Popkewitz, 1997), as well as setting expectations of the professional actions of the early childhood professional. While the traditional curriculum model, with discreet subject areas and clear outcomes, may invoke a pedagogy that one associates with school and more formal methods of teaching and learning whereby the early childhood professional is at the front of the class and the children sit at desks, a curriculum that is child-centred also presupposes a particular pedagogical approach. Intra-action and working with children's funds of knowledge in emergent, contextual and expressive ways requires early childhood professionals and children to behave in particular ways.

CASE STUDY: A CURRICULUM IN OUR HEADS

An example of the expectations of an emergent, contextual and expressive curriculum can be seen in the following extract from the *Insights into a High Quality Early Years Curriculum* project (Campbell-Barr et al., 2023). Speaking about the emergent nature of learning in an Early Years setting, the curriculum lead of a day nursery setting in the South West of England commented,

> for some random reason a group of girls the other day got all the tissue paper out and started making dresses ... and it's just see where that goes and then you got the cutting of the sticky tape ... you've got all the holding of the scissors ... but that ... for that to happen and that learning opportunity to be maximised for want of a better term ... you need every practitioner to be able to spot that learning opportunity.

The expectation therefore is that the early childhood professional will be able to carry specific knowledge of learning, development and pedagogy with them in their day-to-day practice, making in-the-moment connections with children's activities in order to maximise learning opportunities.

EARLY CHILDHOOD INTO THE FUTURE: WE NEED TO TALK ABOUT CURRICULUM

For early childhood curriculums of the future, there is much to be gained from looking at the rich theories of early childhood past. There is much in the work of the early childhood pioneers that has provided a way to talk about curriculum and we need to embrace that and take it into the future. To call early childhood unique as compared to other stages of education is insufficient in getting the wider education community to understand this uniqueness. Talking about how an early childhood curriculum is emergent, expressive and contextual is to distinguish it from other stages of education and to establish a model that says we do things differently here. However, what is perhaps missing from this model is a clear articulation of how such a curriculum does provide the knowledge and skills that will support later learning.

Future steps need to be made to not only establish early childhood curriculum as unique, but to ensure that this uniqueness is not about it being in opposition to other stages of curriculum; rather it is an approach to curriculum that is centred on the child at a stage when children's development is so formative. To talk of a curriculum as being child-centred is not to negate that a curriculum is still related to children's development (Chung and Walsh, 2000) and associated with socio-cultural perspectives around knowledge and skills and how a child learns these.

Talking about early childhood curriculum is also important to avoid it becoming a hidden curriculum. All curriculums have unspoken or implicit rules and values about how a child is expected to be and behave that are not written down or articulated (Bernstein, 1971). Those children who understand or have an insight into those rules and values are more likely to succeed; in essence, they know the rules of the game. There is an inherent risk that a curriculum that emerges (possibly even moment by moment) and is based on the context, whereby there are thousands of different contexts, may not support a child's self-expression if the child is not aware of what the rules are. Therefore, talking about early childhood curriculum is not just for the purposes of the education community, but those who are participating in it as well.

Equally, we wish to stress that working with a curriculum that is emergent, contextual and expressive requires a skilful and knowledgeable early childhood professional. Being able to engage with children's interests and support them in expressing their capabilities in support of their development requires early childhood professionals who draw on a rich knowledge-base (Campbell-Barr, 2019); this should not be underestimated.

FIVE KEY TAKEAWAYS

1. For policy to acknowledge that early childhood is distinct to other stages of education, in support of a model of early childhood curriculums that is befitting of its uniqueness (and does not rely on misfitting ideas developed for school contexts).
2. For curriculums to be shaped by the socio-cultural and historical context and recognise the cultural capital of children and families.

3. To develop curriculums that encompass all of early childhood, thus extending to eight years of age, but are no less focused on supporting children's learning and development.
4. To have curriculum guidance that has the flexibility to recognise the holistic nature of the knowledge and skills that are valued within society and, in turn, set out what is deemed important for children to learn.
5. To recognise that an emergent, expressive and contextual curriculum requires knowledgeable and skilful early childhood professionals, in support of the highest-quality provision.

CONCLUSION

In writing this chapter, we recognise that just as curriculum is shaped by its socio-cultural and historical context, we too have been shaped by ours. Curriculum feels contested in the English context, but in other national contexts (even within the UK), this is not the case. Nonetheless, we still feel it is important to talk about the uniqueness of an early childhood curriculum. Expressing the unique ways of working in early childhood is to resist curriculum being defined by other stages of education or being imposed by technocratic models that are not befitting the rich history of early childhood education. There are particular ways of talking about early childhood curriculum that support its emergent, expressive and contextual character.

REFERENCES

Bernstein, B. (1971). *Class, Codes and Control*, Vol. 1. London: Routledge.

Bernstein, B. (2000). *Pedagogy, Symbolic Control, and Identity*. Rev. edn. Oxford: Rowman & Littlefield.

Campbell-Barr, V. (2019). Professional knowledges for early childhood education and care. *Journal of Childhood Studies*, 44(1), 134–46.

Campbell-Barr, V., Evans, K., Georgeson, J. and Tragenza, S. (2023). *Insights into a High Quality Early Years Curriculum*. Montessori Global Education/University of Plymouth. Available at: https://montessori-globaleducation.org/wp-content/uploads/2023/05/A-high-quality-early-years-curriculum.pdf. Accessed 10 May 2024.

Chawla-Dggan, R. (2019). The sociology of knowledge: the intended and enacted curriculum. In C. A. Simon and S. Ward (eds), *A Students' Guide to Education Studies*. London: Routledge, pp. 143–54.

Chesworth, E. A. (2019). Theorising young children's interests: making connections and in-the-moment happenings. *Learning, Culture and Social Interactions*, 23.

Chung, S. and Walsh, D. J. (2000). Unpacking child-centredness: a history of meanings. *Journal of Curriculum Studies*, 32(2), 215–34. https://doi.org/10.1080/002202700182727

Department for Education (DfE) (2013). *The National Curriculum in England, Key stages 1 and 2 Framework Document*. Available at: https://assets.publishing.service.gov.uk/media/5a81a9abe5274a2e8ab55319/PRIMARY_national_curriculum.pdf. Accessed 10 May 2024.

DfE (2023). *Development Matters: Non-Statutory Curriculum Guidance for the Early Years Foundation Stage*. Available at: https://assets.publishing.service.gov.uk/media/64e6002a20ae890014f26cbc/DfE_Development_Matters_Report_Sep2023.pdf. Accessed 9 October 2024.

DfE (2024). *Early Years Foundation Stage Statutory Framework*. Available at: www.gov.uk/government/publications/early-years-foundation-stage-framework--2. Accessed 11 October 2024.

Dillon, J. T. (2009). The questions of curriculum. *Journal of Curriculum Studies*, 41(3), 343–59.

Early Years Coalition (2021). *Birth to 5 Matters: Non-Statutory Guidance for the Early Years Foundation Stage*. Available at: https://birthto5matters.org.uk/wp-content/uploads/2021/04/Birthto5Matters-download.pdf. Accessed 9 October 2024.

Froebel, F. (1826). *The Education of Man*. New York: Lovell and Co.

Giardiello, P. (2014). *Pioneers in Early Childhood Education*. London: Routledge.

Hedges, H. (2022). *Children's Interests, Inquiries and Identities: Curriculum, Pedagogy, Learning and Outcomes in the Early Years*. Abingdon: Routledge.

Hedges, H., Cullen, J. and Jordan, B. (2011). Early years curriculum: funds of knowledge as a conceptual framework for children's interests. *Journal of Curriculum Studies*, 43(2), 185–205.

Isaacs, S. (1929). *The Nursery Years: The Mind of a Child from Birth to Six*. London: Routledge.

Malaguzzi, L. (1996). *The Hundred Languages of Children: The Reggio Emilia Approach to Early Childhood Education*. New Jersey: Ablex.

McMillan, M. (1919). *The Nursery School*. London: J. M. Dent & Sons.

Montessori, M. (1912). *The Montessori Method*. New York: Frederick Stokes.

Moss, P. (2013). The relationship between early childhood and compulsory education: a properly political question. In Moss, P. (ed.). *Early Childhood and Compulsory Education: Reconceptualising the Relationship*. Abingdon: Routledge, pp. 2–50.

Moss, P., Dahlberg, G., Grieshaber, S., Mantovani, S., May, H., Pence, A., Rayna, S., Swadener, B. B. and Vandenbroeck, M. (2016). The Organization for Economic Co-operation and Development's International Early Learning Study: opening for debate and contestation. *Contemporary Issues in Early Childhood*, 17(3), 343–51.

Mufti, E. and Peace, M. (2012). *Teaching and Learning and the Curriculum: A Critical Introduction*. London. Continuum-3PL.

Organization for Economic Cooperation and Development (OECD) (2017). *Starting String 2017: Key OECD Indicators on Early Childhood Education and Care*. Available at: www.oecd.org/education/starting-strong-2017-9789264276116-en.htm. Accessed 10 May 2024.

Pestalozzi, H. (1819). *Letter XXIX. April 4, 1819*. Available at: https://en.heinrich-pestalozzi.de/letters-on-early-education/overview/letter-xxix-april-4-1819-1. Accessed 8 May 2024.

Popkewitz, T. S. (1997). The production of reason and power: curriculum history and intellectual traditions. *Journal of Curriculum Studies*, 29(2), 131–64.

Roberts-Holmes, G. (2015). The 'datafication' of Early Years pedagogy: if the teaching is good, the data should be good and if there's bad teaching, there is bad data. *Journal of Education Policy*, 30(3), 302–15.

Rousseau, J. J. (1762). *Emile: On Education*. Auckland: Floating Press.

Wood, E. (2020). Learning, development, and the early childhood curriculum: a critical discourse analysis of the Early Years Foundation Stage. *Journal of Early Childhood Research*, 18(3), 321–36.

Wood, E. and Hedges, H. (2016). Curriculum in early childhood education: critical questions about content, coherence and control. *Curriculum Journal*, 27(3), 387–405.

6
PARTNERSHIP OR COPRODUCTION WITH PARENTS?

Philippa Thompson

> **KEY DEFINITIONS**
>
> **Parent:** Any person who has parental responsibility or cares for a young child during their early childhood (conception to eight years).
>
> **Professional:** Adult who is qualified to work with young children (conception to eight years) across health, education and social care.
>
> **Community:** A group of people sharing the same early childhood provision.
>
> **Participation:** The concept of children's participation recognises that children are 'active in the process of shaping their own lives, learning, and future. They have their own view on their best interests, a growing capacity to make decisions, the right to speak and the right to be heard' (Woodhead, 2010, p. xviii).
>
> **Agency:** 'The ability to act and make decisions that influence events and affect one's world' (Early Years Coalition, 2021, p. 118).

Coproduction: 'A model of partnership working where public services are planned, designed, commissioned and delivered in an equal and reciprocal relationship between practitioners, people using services and their close communities' (Fleming and Borkett, 2023, p. 16).

Neoliberalism: Neoliberalism is a political and economic ideology advocating for free markets, deregulation, privatisation, reduced government spending and individual responsibility.

INTRODUCTION

This chapter explores and challenges current approaches to 'partnership' in early childhood with a focus on all services that connect across health, education and social care in particular. As the title suggests, the idea of coproduction is considered as a way of engaging in a reciprocal way and listening to those who have lived experiences of the services they receive. Those that have parental responsibility or who are involved in the care of young children, and also the care of a pregnant mother, are an essential part of ensuring the best care is received and a quality learning and development environment is supported with shared knowledge and no bias towards a particular style of parenting.

The chapter will focus on a manifesto idea of community which disrupts the often-proposed idea of engagement with parents where they are positioned from a deficit perspective and as one homogeneous group. Urban et al. (2020, p. 3) identified three pillars that have proposed a provocation for this chapter and could be applied potentially to all chapters – and certainly a manifesto for change. It is important to share these in the introduction and consider them as the golden thread that runs throughout:

- recognition of early childhood as a common good
- the right to locally and culturally appropriate and responsive early childhood development, education and care for all children
- the central role and responsibility of governments in establishing, resourcing and sustaining such 'competent systems' (Urban et al., 2011, 2012) for children, families and communities.

(Urban et al., 2020, p. 3)

With these three pillars in mind, the chapter continues with further explanation of what shifting the narrative might look like, how the policy has shaped narrative thus far and how we may sustain society through this approach in early childhood. As the book suggests, this is a manifesto for early childhood so the concluding sections will consider what this will look like when working in communities and the five key takeaways. It is important to state that this chapter appreciates that there will always be financial implications for any changes in policy approach. However, critical thinking about accepted approaches does not incur financial constraints and small changes initially can have dramatic impact on the lives of those involved.

SHIFTING THE NARRATIVE

Both education and health policy and practice in the UK can tend to position parents homogeneously (Thompson and Simmons, 2023). While potentially well intentioned, this can often continue the narrative of parents as outsiders who can be included, but only in the way the professional may deem appropriate. This perhaps leads us to return to the traditional proverb, 'it takes a village to raise a child' and the role we all play to engage within a community and return to our social values.

> ### REFLECTION 6.1
>
> What do you consider should be at the forefront for provision for all children? Educational outcomes as a sole focus, or developing contributors to a functioning society where everyone can be included?

Wagner (2006, p. 292) reflected on her experiences of visiting Scandinavia and her own American early childhood perspective. She describes the foundations of early childhood in Nordic society as being 'democracy, egalitarianism, freedom, emancipation, cooperation, and solidarity'. In thinking about early childhood policy in the UK, are these words at the forefront of how we consider those earliest years, or do we mostly hear the terms 'quality', 'affordable childcare', 'best start in/for life', 'school readiness', 'ready to learn'? What does this suggest about us as a society? Urban et al. (2020) explore the possibility of moving away from the neoliberalist focus of outcomes, highly focused on the individual and the concept of school readiness. Instead, they consider perspectives that allow for social cohesion and community, where the lens moves away from the individual and measured success.

In the UK the outgoing government (at the time of writing) could claim that social mobility and inclusion has been at the forefront in public health and education. The proposal in the Best Start for Life strategy (DHSC, 2021) proposed the idea of *family hubs* in a return to the well-documented previous successes of Sure Start: 'seamless support for families' (p. 8) and a 'modern skilled workforce to meet the changing needs of families' (p. 8). However, if we return to the narrative behind this, parents are still in danger of being positioned as needing to be helped and a one-size-fits-all approach with little coproduction evident.

Penn and Kjørholt (2019, p. 211) approach the narrative from a different perspective by suggesting not only an approach that involves the communities that it will serve, but also that this work should be intergenerational and recognise the 'cultural, economic and political complexities of working with young children and their families and communities'. This introduces the idea of community rather than the narrative of parents with a heavy emphasis on what parents can do to support the education agenda. The idea of intergenerational working is an area that has gathered speed more recently, with programmes being developed between care homes and nurseries. These could be viewed as replicating the positive impact of socio-cultural learning in families and communities from the moment a pregnancy is announced. The idea that communities, rather than just parents, are involved in raising a child is one that lends itself to the idea of coproduction.

The chapter asks that early childhood considers the concept of community as part of the narrative surrounding parents and shifts the narrative away from that constructed by policymakers. Considering the role of early childhood professionals as part of a social cohesion agenda could potentially also be a way of achieving recognition for the role. Aligning this with truly working to understand the needs of communities and families within, it can shift us away from a deficit model. Raising a child is one of the most complex challenges that involves the child, parents, families, communities and society. There are many different ways that this practice is viewed; therefore applying ubiquitous approaches to child development (Penn and Kjørholt, 2019) and learning can potentially be damaging to the practice and concept of parent partnerships. Taking into account socio-cultural contexts means that successful partnerships can be built (Kettleborough, 2023), with the key starting point ensuring that the needs of communities are identified (Urban et al., 2020).

POLICY AND PRACTICE: THE POSITIONING OF PARENTS IN EARLY CHILDHOOD

It has long been documented that involving parents in their child's education can have educational benefits for both the child and their family (PISA, 2001). However, there is less consideration of parental and child rights in both policy and practice; this section seeks to explore the importance of language and perceptions. The chapter considers the wider benefits of coproduction than simply educational outcomes and proposes it is not these alone that will enhance children's life chances. Language in both research and practice can determine how practice is perceived and how it develops, so it is therefore important to critique the impact of this on the positioning of parents in a child's earliest years.

A starting point could be from the lens of a professional working with young children. Cottle and Alexander (2014) suggest that parental engagement can often be positioned as either active or inactive. This simplified understanding of coproduction suggests that parents *must* engage with the setting in order for their child to succeed. It also proposes that the onus is on the parents to engage with what the setting offers whether or not it is what they need. Once parents become positioned in this way it can lead to further social isolation and labelling of families as hard to reach (Osgood et al., 2013; Sims-Schouten, 2016).

To reflect on our own practice, it is important to consider how policy may have consciously or unconsciously influenced our bias. Thompson (2023, p. 91) proposes there are six key positions at the forefront of policy and research literature that require acknowledgement:

- parents as generators of school/setting improvement
- parents as the first educator with the power to improve outcomes for children
- parents as workforce
- parents as achievers of social and economic success
- parents as empowered with choice: a consumerist voice
- parents as marginalised by parenting styles and accessibility.

This in itself demonstrates the complexities of the issue. For those across the discipline of early childhood and in policy-making it suggests we require an analysis of our own position before we can begin to develop ways of working together. For example, if a headteacher perceives parents as *generators of school improvement* then the language used would probably focus on parental engagement or involvement putting the onus on parents to engage in whatever the school determines are the required educational outcomes. If professionals perceive parents as *the first educators with a power to improve outcomes for children*, then the focus might be on the transition of knowledge when a child first begins in a setting, but after that there may be a perception of little requirement for the transfer of knowledge as the professionals have taken over. When considering the six positions above, are there any that suggest community input and coproduction to support the wellbeing of the child and family?

Hakyemez-Paul et al. (2020) explore the issue further by considering the differences between what research suggests and educational establishments actually do. They strongly present the argument that there is a failure in collaboration that needs exploration and positions the setting as leading on this and understanding what successful parental involvement could look like. Equally they explore the range of language used across research and policy such as 'parental involvement', 'parental engagement', 'parental partnership' and, more recently, 'coproduction'. Therefore, it is proposed that the language is linked to the six positions suggested which then create different meanings.

So, how could policy and practice change to improve relationships with parents and communities? Manifesto outlines during the 2024 UK general election for all political parties were disappointing, with continued emphasis on educational outcomes and the 'driving up' of standards. However, there is hope that there is an emphasis on the wellbeing of the child which potentially cannot be achieved without support from parents and communities and is a turn in a differing direction. This chapter proposes that there is a need to remove the deficit model of 'poor parenting', particularly in areas with high levels of child poverty. This continues to drive the white middle-class narrative of parenting with an emphasis on parenting courses. This can often alienate rather than encourage families to be partners in the care and education of their child.

REFLECTION 6.2

Consider your own response to the four terms below. How would you define the theme and what do you see as the difference between them?

- parental involvement
- parental engagement
- parental partnership
- coproduction.

SOCIAL AND CULTURAL SUSTAINABILITY THROUGH COPRODUCTION?

Fleming and Burkett (2023) propose the idea of coproduction as a way forward to working across disciplines to support children, families and communities from conception to eight years old. They explore two key microsystems (Bronfenbrenner, 1994) – home and early childhood settings – and how they can work together to co-construct a positive learning environment for both children and families. They also explore the idea of an inclusive environment with an emphasis on professionals having the ability to communicate, without judgement, with diverse groups, developing trusting relationships. This idea of coproduction requires training that supports professionals to challenge their own unconscious bias towards parents and community values and needs to be done sensitively. Without this, it is proposed that coproduction will never take place as the power imbalance will continue and mutual respect will be difficult to obtain.

Bessell and Kjørholt (2023) raise the concept of social and cultural sustainability as an integral part of parental relationships and coproduction. Their discussion around the idea that knowledge acquisition is not the sole domain of the school or setting is an interesting one. Many of us can take a look back at our childhoods and think of things we have learnt from wider family members or our wider communities that would not have been part of our formal education, but rather our daily interactions or shared experiences. This returns us to the suggestion in neoliberalist politics that education is driven by outcomes and only by achieving these outcomes can an individual be successful.

Hawkes (2001) suggests that the success of a society can be measured in other ways and that the 'primary function of education is the transmission of values' (p. 28). The idea that as a society (and community) we can determine our own future by engaging with our society's culture and values, rather than advanced capitalism, aligns well with coproduction. If professionals could work towards understanding the local area and aspirations of their families rather than assuming that all of them are working towards material wealth and high grades in exams, we may see very different, successful and sustainable community outcomes. Reconsidering the idea that the only place for knowledge acquisition at a young age is formal schooling is a challenge, but could create positive and lasting change. As Bessell and Kjørholt (2023, p. 35) state,

> Informal or outside-of-school learning is especially important in communities where traditional skills are valued and transferred outside formal education systems, often as a result of children and young people engaging in activities alongside parents, grandparents, or other adults.

WHAT DOES PRACTICE LOOK LIKE?

Many early childhood professionals will attest to the fact that their role is enhanced by their relationships with parents and the wider family. It can enable the curriculum to evolve as meaningful and develop deep understandings. There are currently many examples of positive practice in UK early childhood settings which is well documented by research. Early childhood professionals are often willing to learn and develop despite the fact that their role is under constant pressure in terms of ratios, policy and lack of resources. The *Graduate Practitioner Competencies* (ECSDN, 2020), which form part of the QAA subject *Benchmark Statement for Early Childhood Studies* (2022), recognise the key role that professionals play and encourage all of their graduates to demonstrate evidence that they understand the role through both academic understanding and practice experience.

Competency 7 of the *Graduate Practitioner Competencies* is entitled Partnership with Parents and Caregivers and is set out below:

7.1. Evidence understanding of the importance of partnership with parents and/or caregivers in their role as infants and young children's first educators.

7.2 Demonstrate in practice the co-construction of learning in respectful partnership with parents and/or caregivers.

7.3 Apply knowledge to practice, about the diversity of family life and society.

7.4 Demonstrate skills in communicating and working in partnership with families.

(QAA, 2022, p. 18)

This competency sets out the need for graduates to show evidence that they have developed their skills in working with parents as well as children, in recognition that this has equal importance. However, even these competencies are using language that has been examined as part of the chapter. This demonstrates the constant need for review and updating our practice as we learn and research more and listen to those we work alongside. This could also be reflected in policy.

MANIFESTO FOR CHANGE

On reflection, while there is agreement that working with parents, families and communities can be beneficial for all in early childhood, there is still a way to go in agreeing how this should be done, who should be included and what the outcomes should be. This chapter also proposes that perspectives need to be addressed, not only through policy but also through training and education for professionals. Furthermore, this uncovers further complexities as the sector is not straightforward in the qualifications offered and who offers them. This is even before we consider the quality and ethos of the range of training providers.

If policy and training are focused on neoliberal ideals of outcomes and individualism, then it becomes difficult at graduate level to critique theory without being perceived as critical. Early childhood professionals work with cultural and linguistic diversity on a daily basis (Norheim and Moser, 2020) requiring a depth of knowledge and enquiry that is seen at graduate level. However, rarely are they prepared in teacher education or Level 2 and 3 qualifications to develop strong, meaningful partnerships that can be coproductive. Learning about curriculum as part of training does not go far enough to explore the language of parental partnership discussed previously in this chapter.

REFLECTION 6.3

- Are early childhood professionals and those that educate them really exploring the potential needs of those who have moved from another home culture with differing expectations?
- Are they prepared to understand that socio-economic status may have an influence on parental and community priorities on the needs of the family and the child?
- Do training providers enable future professionals to challenge their own unconscious bias and understand how their behaviour and action may marginalise families, whole communities and their children?

FIVE KEY TAKEAWAYS

1. Coproduction requires co-constructive approaches to parent and community engagement where the balance of power is shared, and everyone benefits.
2. Provision offered in early childhood should be based on a deep understanding of the local needs of young children, families and the community.
3. Early childhood professionals require support and training at graduate level to work in a transdisciplinary, coproductive way in communities.
4. Policy-makers need to consider key pillars of sustainability in order to understand the benefits of a successful society that lifts children out of poverty without the requirement for neoliberalist approaches.
5. The role of the early childhood professional should be considered as part of a social cohesion agenda.

CONCLUSION

The chapter has raised many ideas that challenge the current approach to working with parents and families. It also introduces the importance of situating early childhood within the wider community. While considering these ideas it is important to challenge our own assumptions and beliefs. As a young teacher in early childhood, I can remember feeling very nervous at the thought of working with parents. All my confidence laid with working with young children, but my teacher training had not prepared me for the child being part of the family and community. While this was nearly 40 years ago, I still hear young Early Years teachers saying they feel the same. Those working in early childhood settings can feel similarly, which can lead to personal protective barriers and deficit models developing. By shifting the narrative and understanding how policy is developed, there is a chance to take down barriers and start to listen. Being an early childhood professional is a role with many challenges and a requirement for knowledgeable and sustainable strategies. Many do this on minimum wage and without opportunities for further training. Maybe, just maybe, with a new government we have a chance to lobby for change and to take our communities with us.

REFERENCES

Bessell, S. and Kjørholt, A. T. (2023). Coastal communities past, present, and future? The value of social and cultural sustainability. In A. Kjørholt, S. Bessell, D. Devine, F. Gaini and S. Spyrou (eds), *Valuing the Past, Sustaining the Future? Exploring Coastal Societies, Childhood (s) and Local Knowledge in Times of Global Transition*. New York: Springer International, pp. 23–42.

Bronfenbrenner, U. (1994). Ecological models of human development. *International Encyclopaedia of Education*, 3(2), 37–43.

Cottle, M. and Alexander, E. (2014). Parent partnership and 'quality' Early Years services: practitioners' perspectives. *European Early Childhood Education Research Journal*, 22(5), 637–59.

Department for Health and Social Care (DHSC) (2021). *The Best Start for Life: A Vision for the 1,001 Critical Days*. Available at: https://assets.publishing.service.gov.uk/media/605c5e61d3bf7f2f0d94183a/The_best_start_for_life_a_vision_for_the_1_001_critical_days.pdf. Accessed 11 October 2024.

Early Childhood Studies Degree Network (ECSDN) (2020). *Early Childhood Graduate Practitioner Competencies*. Available at: www.ecsdn.org/wp-content/uploads/2021/09/ECSDN-Booket-Rev-July-2020.pdf. Accessed 11 October 2024.

Early Years Coalition (2021). *Birth to 5 Matters: Non-Statutory Guidance for the Early Years Foundation Stage*. Available at: https://birthto5matters.org.uk/wp-content/uploads/2021/04/Birthto5Matters-download.pdf. Accessed 9 October 2024.

Fleming, K. and Borkett, P. (2023). The potential of co-production. In P. Thompson and H. Simmons (eds), *Partnership with Parents in Early Childhood Today*. London: Learning Matters, pp. 16–29.

Hakyemez-Paul, S., Pihlaja, P. and Silvennoinen, H. (2020). Parental involvement in Finnish day care: what do early childhood educators say? *European Early Childhood Education Research Journal*, 26(2), 258–73.

Hawkes, J. (2001). *The Fourth Pillar of Sustainability: Culture's Essential Role in Public Planning*. Champaign, IL: Common Ground.

Kettleborough, W. (2023). Practice perspective: parents as experts. In P. Thompson and H. Simmons (eds), *Partnership with Parents in Early Childhood Today*. London: Learning Matters, pp. 145–57.

Norheim, H. and Moser, T. (2020). Barriers and facilitators for partnerships between parents with immigrant backgrounds and professionals in ECEC: a review based on empirical research. *European Early Childhood Education Research Journal*, 28(6), 789–805.

Osgood, J., Albon, D., Allen, K. and Hollingworth, S. (2013). 'Hard to reach' or nomadic resistance? Families 'choosing' not to participate in early childhood services. *Global Studies of Childhood*, 3(3), 208–20.

Penn, H. and Kjørholt, A. T. (2019). Early childhood: a panacea for Intervention? Theories, approaches and practices in development work. In H. Penn and A. T. Kjørholt (eds), *Early Childhood and Development Work: Theories, Policies, and Practices*. London: Palgrave Macmillan, pp. 209–23.

Programme for International Student Assessment (PISA) (2001). *PISA Knowledge and Skills for Life: First Results from PISA 2000*. Paris: OECD.

QAA (2022). *Subject Benchmark Statements: Early Childhood Studies*. Available at: www.qaa.ac.uk/the-quality-code/subject-benchmark-statements/early-childhood-studies. Accessed 11 October 2024.

Sims-Schouten, W. (2016). Positioning in relationships between parents and Early Years practitioners. *Early Child Development and Care*, 186(9), 1392–405.

Thompson P. (2023). Partnership with parents and caregivers: competency seven. In A. Bradbury, J. Musgrave and H. Perkins (eds), *A Practical Guide to Early Childhood Studies Graduate Practitioner Competencies*. London: Learning Matters, pp. 87–96.

Thompson, P. and Simmons, H. (eds) (2023). *Partnership with Parents in Early Childhood Today*. London: Learning Matters.

Urban, M., Cardini, A., Costin, C., Floréz-Romero, R., Guevara, J., Okengo, L. and Priyono, D. (2020). *Policy Brief: Upscaling Community-Based Early Childhood Programmes to Counter Inequality and Foster Social Cohesion During Global Uncertainty*. Saudi Arabia: 2020 Think, Task Force.

Wagner, J. T. (2006). An outsider's perspective: childhoods and early education in the Nordic countries. In W. J. Einarsdottir and J. T. Wagner (eds), *Nordic Childhoods and Early Education*. Charlotte, NC: Information Age, pp. 289–306.

Woodhead, M. (2010). In B. Percy-Smith and N. Thomas (eds), A Handbook of Children and Young People's Participation: Perspectives from Theory and Practice. Abingdon: Routledge.

7
GLOBAL DYNAMICS OF EARLY CHILDHOOD: WELCOMING PRACTICES TO SUPPORT BELONGING IN EARLY CHILDHOOD EDUCATION AND CARE (ECEC)

Dr Donna Gaywood, Professor Tony Bertram and Professor Chris Pascal

> **KEY DEFINITIONS**
>
> **Forced displacement:** This is an umbrella term used to refer to people who have been forced to leave their homes for a variety of reasons which may include war, persecution, human rights abuses, natural or man-made disasters. This term covers people who are seeking asylum and those who are refugees.
>
> *(Continued)*

> **Belonging:** Describes a sense of knowing to whom we belong, to the places that are familiar and where we can be fully accepted as ourselves.
>
> **Transitions:** Refers to any movement, large or small, that a child might make within ECEC, from one place to another.
>
> **Welcoming practices:** This term is used to describe everyday activities or pedagogical approaches which act as a means to make children who have experienced displacement welcome.

INTRODUCTION

In 2022, the United Nation High Commission for Refugees (UNHCR) published figures which suggested that 108.4 million people worldwide experienced *forced displacement* (UNHCR, 2022) and about 43.3 million of those were children. By the end of 2024, UNHCR estimates that this figure could have risen to 130.4 million. Given the current geopolitical landscape, this figure is only likely to rise in the next ten years. The Institute for Economics and Peace, a London-based think tank, estimates that over the next 30 years around 1.2 billion people could be negatively affected by climate change and experience displacement as a result (Apap and Harju, 2023).

Although the UK Conservative government (2016–24) pursued regressive policies regarding people seeking asylum with its Rwanda Bill (HM Government, 2024) and the ongoing mantra of 'stop the boats' (HM Government, 2023b), children impacted by forced migration are already attending early childhood education and care (ECEC) settings in England. According to the Office of National Statistics (ONS) Census in 2023, 11,000 children were resettled in Britain as part of the Vulnerable Persons Resettlement Scheme and the Vulnerable Children Resettlement Scheme between 2014 and 2021 (ONS, 2023), while in 2022 and 2023 the total number was approximately 9,000 children, indicating an 81 per cent rise between the year ending June 2022 and June 2023 (HM Government, 2023a). Given these figures, early educators across the country will have to further develop practice to support children who have been impacted by forced displacement in the next ten years.

This chapter draws on the PhD study: 'The post migration lived experiences of Syrian refugee children in early childhood education and care in England: four children's stories' (Gaywood, 2023) and will specifically be considering elements of the *pedagogy of welcome* (Gaywood, 2023, p. 295). It also considers research conducted by the EECERA Special Interest Group: Children from refugee and migrant backgrounds in 2022 and the Inclusive Education Toolkit that was developed and evaluated (a link to this resource can be found at the end of the chapter). The aim of this chapter will be to support early educators to think about the impact of forced displacement on children and reflect on their own practice as a powerful tool to enable the children to develop a new sense of belonging.

Matters of migration, asylum and refuge seeking are political, emotional and complex (Gaywood et al., 2020; Gaywood, 2023; Gaywood et al., 2023) so this chapter intends to also try to capture the nuances that early educators may encounter when working with children impacted by these issues. Although it is important to recognise that forced displacement brings a unique set of life challenges, which should not be ignored or underestimated, this chapter purposefully situates children as global citizens (Pascal and Bertram, 2009) and powerful creators of their own 'scripts of refuge' (Kyriakides et al., 2018, p. 59), thus rejecting the notion of traumatised children needing 'saving' by host country adults. Moll et al. (1992) first coined the term 'funds of knowledge' referring to the wealth of knowledge and experience that children from migrant backgrounds brought with them into an education setting. Although this is now a commonly held belief about all children within early education, it is worth noting the findings of Ortega and Oxford (2023), who suggested that refugee children potentially draw from more extensive funds of knowledge because of their 'wide-ranging experiences in multiple places and their encounters with many kinds of people events and challenges' (Ortega and Oxford, 2023, p. 4).

Through her research with young refugee children, Gaywood (2023) concludes,

> As very young 'persons of self-rescue' (Kyriakides et al., 2018, p. 65) they clearly demonstrated their capacity to build connections, establish themselves in the face of both open and hidden hostility, rise about [sic] negative conceptualisations and positioning, navigate significant personal challenges, and thrive in spite of it all.
>
> (Gaywood, 2023, p. 274)

However, it is equally important for early educators to understand that forced displacement can and does have a significant impact on very young children. While some may believe that because of their young age children within the Early Years will retain little memory of their early experiences, the impact will most likely resonate throughout their lives. Not only will family stories become embedded in their identities, but also navigating the sense of not quite belonging and trying to develop a dual identity will continue to be a challenge. The loss of home, of loved ones and all that is familiar will surround the children, even if they themselves have no experiential memory. Fear of racially motivated attack might be a reality, but equally may haunt their everyday interactions. Refugee children are often sensitive to the emotional atmospheres they inhabit, both in their families and within the community they have been resettled in. Von Knorring and Hultcrantz (2019) report the phenomena of resignation syndrome, which was noticed in asylum-seeking children in Sweden, where children fall into an involuntary catatonic state. The final trigger appears to be negative news about their family's asylum claim. It seems that the anxiety of waiting and the tension had a severe impact on young children. For the adults, being forced to leave their country of origin in distressing circumstances can also undermine ongoing trust, particularly with those who hold power. This can impact the parental engagement and relationship building within ECEC. Early educators need to be mindful of these often-invisible pressures and experiences, ensuring ongoing sensitivity is employed when making relationships with the children and their parents. It is likely the parents may need more time and a higher amount of contact with the practitioners to feel safe enough to engage in a meaningful way.

UNDERSTANDING TRANSITIONS

Transitions for many very young children can be destabilising and challenging. *Birth to 5 Matters* (Early Years Coalition, 2021) notes the importance of support around times of transitions, suggesting that transitions can be both linear and horizontal to include movement to other settings and smaller movements over one day. Examples of transitions may include ending a play activity and moving to a mealtime, moving from a baby room (birth to two) into a toddler room (two years old) or moving into Reception class. It is not uncommon for children to find these times of transition and others quite difficult. Children who have been impacted by forced migration will most likely need a greater sensitivity from early educators, to help them navigate transitions successfully. Gaywood (2023) found that refugee children and their families often had conflicting feelings about their ECEC settings and preferred to keep their home lives and their time at ECEC separate. This created a significant divide between the two places, with the children rarely speaking about their homes in their Early Years setting. Figure 7.1 demonstrates these feelings.

Figure 7.1 Ahmed, drawing activity, 7 March 2018 (Gaywood, 2023, p. 225)

These conflicted feelings about their ECEC as being a place they like to go to, on one hand, and at the same time, on the other, a place of distress potentially makes the transition from their home into the ECEC setting even more challenging.

In conversation with Tamar Garb, Eva Hoffman discusses her own experiences of moving from Poland as a political refugee in the 1950s. She describes another type of transition which she needed to navigate, an internal transition of self. She says, 'One kind of identity of self, is left behind, and a new self has not yet been created' (Garb, 2020, p. 42). For very young children to develop a sense of who they are, when the two worlds they inhabit (home and their ECEC setting) are separated by language, cultural practices and differing expectations, is a complex process. For refugee or migrant children to feel safe, accepted and included they need to develop a sense of belonging.

THE IMPORTANCE OF BELONGING

The notion of belonging is recognised as important within *Belonging, Being and Becoming: The Early Years Learning Framework for Australia* (Australian Government, 2009) which places a high emphasis on young children feeling that they belong, suggesting that it is 'integral to human existence' (2009, p. 7). However, there is no mention of belonging in the Early Years Foundation Stage (EYFS) in England (DfE, 2021). Instead, it suggests that 'children should be supported to … develop a positive sense of self' (DfE, 2021, p. 9). While a strong sense of self is obviously important for all young children to develop, for refugee children, feelings of belonging are significant and more complex because of their experiences. Seker and Aslan (2015) acknowledge that refugee students encounter, 'problems like alienation, discrimination, or otherization in their relationships at school and in class' (Seker and Aslan, 2015, pp. 88/9).

Tajfel and Turner's (1979) *social identity theory* is helpful to consider belonging. Following his own experience of the Holocaust (1939–45), Tajfel began to wonder how it was possible for a nation (Germany) to be coerced into accepting the negative narrative of the Third Reich which resulted in millions of people being murdered. Alongside Turner, he studied intergroup conflict, social categorisation and social comparisons. They noticed that to form their social identities people tended to locate themselves in a distinct grouping which Tajfel and Turner (1979) described as *in-groups* and *out-groups*. They found that members of groups satisfied their sense of belonging to their group (in-group) by exaggerating shared positive characteristics, while at the same time negatively framing and overstating the differences of those who were outside of their group (the out-group). This increased their self-esteem and improved their sense of belonging to their in-group. They suggested that this process of developing a sense of belonging in this way leads to: 'stereotyping, prejudice, and discrimination towards out-group members in addition to producing a homogeneity effect, which casts all out-group members as a homogenous [sic] group' (Gaywood, 2023, p. 124).

Due to the current legislation and political climate in England, there already exists a negative narrative around people who have experienced forced migration. By applying Bronfenbrenner's ecological systems theory (Gaywood et al., 2023) it is clear the impact these wider concerns in children's meso-, exo-, macro- and chronosystems tend to have on refugee children within ECEC. Therefore, it is not surprising to note that very young refugee children experience the same levels of isolation as their older peers described by Seker and Aslan (2015), being subtly socially positioned within an out-group.

Gaywood (2023) noted that this out-group status meant that refugee children found it more difficult to make friends with the host country children. They seemed drawn naturally to other children who were also located in out-groups – for example, other children for whom English was a second language or who faced challenges with their social, emotional, or mental health needs.

All children need to forge meaningful relationships with their peers; however, because of the increased sense of isolation experienced by refugee children, it is even more important. Early childhood professionals can play an important role in facilitating this, particularly for children impacted by forced migration. Through peer relationships they can begin to understand to whom they belong and become familiar with the space they inhabit and know that they are fully accepted as themselves. Transitions and belonging are closely linked for refugee children. The internal transition previously mentioned by Eva Hoffman, in which children must navigate two identities and then find a new sense of a dual identity, is commonplace for children impacted by forced migration but is often invisible to early educators. To support children's growing sense of belonging educators need to be mindful of this emotional identity formation and actively work to support children, through sensitive welcoming practices.

WELCOMING PRACTICES

Alison Clark's (2023) work on the unhurried child and developing slow pedagogies is useful to draw on when thinking about creating welcoming practices. She advocates allowing children time and space to develop in a less hurried educational setting. This approach is good for children who have experienced forced migration as it reduces performative stress and provides time for their sometimes-daily orientation as they learn to manage both physical and emotional transitions.

Welcoming practices will be unique to each setting and each group of children, but one of the most important aspects is to ensure there is adequate space, time and support for children to develop friendships. It is often harder for refugee children to form bonds with other children in their ECEC settings, so early educators need to consider the ways they are overtly offering support in this area. Practically, this might be through promoting adult-supported small group games, locating an educator within the home corner to actively include children in role play or developing small group circle times, where the membership of the group is fixed, to support feelings of belonging. Children can consider how to be a good friend or staff can create a *kindness tree* (EECERA SIG, 2022) where children are rewarded for acts of kindness to one another. All of these will create an atmosphere where refugee children can feel safe enough to begin to form bonds.

A second welcoming practice is for early educators to give refugee children opportunity to understand their own stories. This is not necessarily about their migration stories, but rather the everyday stories of their lives.

> Strekalova-Hughes and Wang (2019) highlight the importance of family story telling noting that for refugee children it is a 'culturally sustaining practice' (Strekalova-Hughes and Wang, 2019, p. 11) which is significant for the children's identity formation, cultural and linguistic transference.
>
> (Gaywood, 2023, p. 96)

Children begin to develop their sense of self when they can actively represent their own experiences. This could take many forms; for example, children can be encouraged to take photographs of their homes, toys or people that are special to them or the things they enjoy most at their early childhood setting. Being supported to draw their homes, a map of their journey to their nursery, their families or their friends also offers children further opportunities to represent their lives. In addition, through working with parents, collecting and including home songs, greetings and other language-sharing can become standardised welcoming practice. These types of activities have a variety of functions. Not only do they allow children representation, but they also support children in developing an identity which encompasses the fullness of their experiences. For this reason, these types of activities are positive welcoming practices which help refugee children to know who they are, enhance feelings of belonging and enable them to draw on their rich funds of knowledge.

Developing welcoming practices is a philosophical approach as well as a practical one. For early educators, intercultural sensitivity (Strekalova-Hughes, 2017) is an important aspect of welcoming practice and should be addressed through staff meetings, so a whole-team approach can be undertaken. Intercultural sensitivity allows educators to interrogate their everyday taken-for-granted practices to be able to ascertain whether they are culturally specific. For example, children in England are expected to eat using cutlery and are encouraged to use 'please' and 'thank you' as part of their everyday interactions. This is a very British expectation, but could remain largely hidden as a British cultural norm unless early educators actively chose to develop intercultural sensitivity. Intercultural sensitivity acknowledges the value and status of *all* cultural ways, without promoting one over another. It suggests that there are many ways of living, each with richness and strength, and offers educators the opportunity to examine their own cultural norms in order to identify any which may be acting as barriers for children and inadvertently galvanising their isolation. Through this process a deeper level of understanding is developed that allows educators to be far more alert to cultural miscues which are often inevitable. Both refugee children and their families are sensitive to the unspoken and unseen aspects within communications. Early educators who can develop intercultural sensitivity are more aware of these miscues which, if left unchecked, can translate as a coldness or lack of welcome. Attending to this aspect of welcoming practices is vital.

> **FIVE KEY TAKEAWAYS**
> 1. Children who have been impacted by forced migration will often be able to draw on larger funds of knowledge.
> 2. Transitions can include physical, emotional and psychological aspects, which can mean they require extra support and time.
> 3. Developing a sense of self and belonging is complex as refugee children experience a high degree of isolation and are living with multiple identities.
> 4. Welcoming practices are vital to include refugee children and can help them develop feelings of belonging, make friendships and understand their own lived experiences.
> 5. Promoting intercultural sensitivity as a whole-team approach can address the often-unseen barriers for refugee children and their families to feel welcome.

CONCLUSION

Given the current geopolitical and global climate change crisis, it is likely that in the next ten years, the global North will need to welcome many more people who have experienced forced migration. Early educators are well placed to support very young children who find themselves displaced. Currently, public narratives about refugees in the UK tend to be either negative or position children as merely traumatised victims who need sympathy and rescue by well-qualified professional adults. However, our work has shown that very young refugee children's lives are more complex. Many of their experiences are invisible and, when they remain so, it can deepen the isolation often felt, with refugee children situated in out-groups. When educators understand the complexities of transitions, how children develop a sense of self and are able to support them to make friends, this can improve their feelings of belonging. Welcoming practices are both practical and philosophical. We advocate in this chapter and in our other works (Gaywood et al., 2020; Gaywood et al., 2023) that taking time to develop unique contextualised welcoming practices is important. Equally vital is for early educators to spend time developing intercultural sensitivity so they can interrogate their own culturally specific practices which may be preventing refugee children and their families from feeling welcome. Recognising the deep and rich funds of knowledge that refugee children bring and acknowledging the equal status of all cultural practices rather than prioritising taken-for-granted norms can also promote feelings of welcome. When children and their families who have experienced forced migration are welcomed and enabled to form relationships, our work has shown that they can develop a sense of belonging in their early education setting, which enables and promotes community cohesion.

REFERENCES

Apap, J. and Harju, S. J. (2023). The concept of 'climate refugee': Towards a possible definition. *European Parliamentary Research Service*. European Union. Available at: www.europarl.europa.eu/RegData/etudes/BRIE/2021/698753/EPRS_BRI(2021)698753_EN.pdf. Accessed 11 October 2024.

Australian Government, Department of Education and Workplace Relations (2009). *Belonging, Being and Becoming: The Early Years Learning Framework for Australia*. Canberra: Council for Australian Governments.

Clark, A. (2023). *Slow Knowledge and the Unhurried Child: Time for Slow Pedagogies in Early Childhood Education*. London: Routledge.

Department for Education (DfE) (2021). *Statutory Framework for the Early Years Stage: Setting the Standards for Learning, Development and Care for Children from Birth to Five*. Available at: https://dera.ioe.ac.uk/id/eprint/37697/1/EYFS_framework_-_March_2021.pdf. Accessed 11 October 2024.

Early Years Coalition (2021). *Birth to 5 Matters: Non-Statutory Guidance for the Early Years Foundation Stage*. Available at: https://birthto5matters.org.uk/wp-content/uploads/2021/04/Birthto5Matters-download.pdf. Accessed 11 October 2024.

EECERA Special Interest Group: Children from refugee and migrant backgrounds (2022). Inclusive Education for Refugee and Migrant Children: A Toolkit for Early Childhood Education and Care Settings. Available at: https://refugee-early-years.org/. Accessed 11 October 2024.

Garb, T. (2020). Stories of migration and belonging: Eva Hoffman and Honny Steinberg in conversation with Tamar Garb. In Fidduan-Qasmiyeh, E. (ed.), *Refuge in a Moving World: Tracing Refugee and Migrant Journeys Across Disciplines*. London: UCL Press.

Gaywood, D. (2023). The post migration lived experiences of Syrian refugee children in early childhood education and care in England: four children's stories. *Doctoral dissertation, Birmingham City University*. Available at: www.open-access.bcu.ac.uk/14739/1/Donna%20Gaywood%20PhD%20Thesis%20published_Final%20version_Submitted%20Sept%202022_Final%20Award%20Jul%202023.pdf. Accessed 11 October 2024.

Gaywood, D., Bertram, T. and Pascal, C. (2020). Involving refugee children in research: emerging ethical and positioning issues. *European Early Childhood Education Research Journal*, 28(1), 149–62. Available at: https://doi.org/10.1080/1350293X.2020.1707369. Accessed 11 October 2024.

Gaywood, D. Bertram, T. and Pascal, C. (2023). Supporting refugee families. In P. Thompson and H. Simmons (eds), *Partnership with Parents in Early Childhood Today*. London: Learning Matters, pp. 114–29.

HM Government (2023a). Home Office Immigration System statistics. *Asylum and Resettlement summary tables*. Available at: www.gov.uk/government/statistical-data-sets/asylum-and-resettlement-datasets. Accessed 11 October 2024.

HM Government (2023b). PM statement on the Stop the Boats Bill, 7 March. Available at: www.gov.uk/government/speeches/pm-statement-on-the-stop-the-boats-bill-7-march-2023. Accessed 11 October 2024.

HM Government (2024). Safety of Rwanda (Asylum and Immigration) Bill: factsheet. Available at: www.gov.uk/government/publications/the-safety-of-rwanda-asylum-and-immigration-bill-factsheets/safety-of-rwanda-asylum-and-immigration-bill-factsheet-accessible. Accessed 11 October 2024.

Kyriakides, C., Bajjali, L., McLuhan, A. and Anderson, K. (2018). Beyond refuge: contested Orientalism and persons of self-rescue. *Canadian Ethnic Studies*, 50(2), 59–78.

Moll, L. C., Amanti, C., Neff, D. and Gonzalez, N. (1992). Funds of knowledge for teaching: using a qualitative approach to connect homes and classrooms. *Theory into Practice*, 31(2), 132–41.

Office for National Statistics (ONS) (2023). *Experiences of Displaced Young People Living in England: January to March 2023*. Available at: www.ons.gov.uk/peoplepopulationandcommunity/populationandmigration/internationalmigration/articles/experiencesofdisplacedyoungpeoplelivinginengland/januarytomarch2023. Accessed 13 October 2024.

Ortega, Y. and Oxford, R. (2023). Immigrants' and refugees' 'funds of knowledge(s)' on the path to intercultural competence. *Journal of Multilingual and Multicultural Development*, 1–12.

Pascal, C. and Bertram, T. (2009). Listening to young citizens: the struggle to make real a participatory paradigm in research with young children. *European Early Childhood Education Research Journal*, 17(2), 249–62.

Seker, B. D. and Aslan, Z. (2015). Refugee children in the educational process: a social psychological assessment. *Journal of Theoretical Educational Science*, 8(1), 86–105.

Strekalova-Hughes, E. S. (2017). Comparative analysis of intercultural sensitivity among teachers working with refugees. *Journal of Research in Childhood Education*, 31(4), 561–70.

Strekalova-Hughes, E. and Wang, X. C. (2019). Perspectives of children from refugee backgrounds on their family storytelling as a culturally sustaining practice. *Journal of Research in Childhood Education*, 33(1), 6–21.

Tajfel, H. and Turner, J. C. (1979). An integrative theory of intergroup conflict. In W. G. Austin and S. Worchel (eds), *The Social Psychology of Intergroup Relations*. Monterey, CA: Brooks/Cole, pp. 33–47.

UNHCR (2022). *Figures at a Glance*. Available at: www.unhcr.org/uk/about-unhcr/who-we-are/figures-glance. Accessed 13 October 2024.

von Knorring, A. and Hultcrantz, E. (2019). Asylum-seeking children with resignation syndrome: catatonia or traumatic withdrawal syndrome? *European Child and Adolescent Psychiatry*, 29(8), 1103–9.

USEFUL RESOURCE

EECERA Special Interest Group: Children from refugee and migrant backgrounds (2022). *Inclusive Education for Refugee and Migrant Children: A Toolkit for Early Childhood Education and Care Settings*. Available at: https://refugee-early-years.org/. Accessed 11 October 2024.

8

EARLY CHILDHOOD WORKFORCE DEVELOPMENT

Dr Aaron Bradbury

> **KEY DEFINITIONS**
>
> **Early childhood workforce:** Workers in the early childhood workforce are involved in educating or caring for young children in the first eight years of a child's life.
>
> **Workforce strategy:** A workforce strategy seeks to guide governments and the sector in delivering a sustainable, highly qualified and professional workforce.
>
> **Early Childhood Studies Graduate Practitioner Competencies (GPCs):** The GPCs aim to support with the confusion in the sector about how Early Childhood Studies (ECS) degrees are aligned to practice requirements in the four nations of the UK.

INTRODUCTION

This chapter only offers a snapshot of a discussion for the future for our early childhood workforce. It does not suggest that it holds all of the answers, but it tries to convey that, for the vision needed for the sector to become sustainable for children and families, change is inevitable – and now is the time to start that change.

In recent years, it has become increasingly evident that skilled and well-qualified early childhood and education practitioners contribute significantly to the quality of early childhood education and care. They make a significant difference to the development of children from low-income and at-risk families (Sylva, 2014). Over the past decade, qualifications in the early childhood sector have been continually scrutinised and evaluated, but little has changed in scope and recognition for our early childhood professionals. These early childhood (Early Years) qualifications are regulated by the Department for Education (DfE). According to Nutbrown (2012), some of the current qualifications lack rigour and depth, and the quality of these qualifications is inconsistent. It is concerning to find that there is a considerable climate of mistrust in the current early childhood education system. We are now in 2025 and, even though there has been some tinkering around the edges with qualifications, we have yet to see some well thought out key changes to benefit the early childhood profession.

SETTING THE CONTEXT

There are two broad categories of early childhood and education settings:

- the maintained sector (nursery schools and nursery classes within schools)
- private, voluntary and independent sectors (such as day nurseries and childminders) (Nuffield Foundation, 2021).

It is therefore possible for children to be educated and cared for in very small groups, such as in the home of a childminder, or in larger groups in a day nursery or maintained nursery school. Moreover, the way in which settings are funded and the expertise of the staff differ from each setting. As a result of all these factors, children may have a different experience in different types of settings. There is a large and diverse workforce in the early childhood sector. Early education is a *split system*, meaning that practitioners can work as sole childminders or in nursery settings and schools. There are many professional roles and titles in the early childhood sector: childminder, nanny, Early Years practitioner, pre-school teacher. This contributes to the complexity of language within the early childhood workforce.

The professional identity of an early childhood (Early Years) professional is a key component of how we move forwards with a workforce development goal. In the last 15 years, early childhood education and care in England have received unprecedented attention and sustained change; some of this has been intended to eliminate the pervasive divide between the maintained state sector and the non-maintained private, voluntary and independent sectors regarding the diversity of settings and services they provide. Moreover, there is a profound, historical institutional divide between Early Years education in maintained nursery and primary schools and the provision of care for babies and toddlers, such as by childminders and those who are cared for in day care settings. Historically, there has been tension between members of the workforce who are regarded as maternal and caring, as opposed to those who are degree-educated and highly qualified. Employees in the private, voluntary and independent sectors are generally paid less, have fewer holidays and work fewer hours than those in the education sector (Lightfoot and Frost, 2015). Teaching staff in maintained nursery schools, maintained nursery classes and Reception classes are considered part of the early childhood workforce, even though they work according to the pay and conditions of school teachers. The examination of the early education workforce is therefore a complex process.

EARLY CHILDHOOD GRADUATES ARE THE FUTURE

The GPCs aim to support with the confusion in the sector about how ECS degrees are aligned to practice requirements in the four nations of the UK. The competencies also address the inherent challenges of different types of early childhood degrees and study pathways, enabling the wider workforce to be clear about individual early career graduates' expected level of knowledge, skills and actual experience in practice. The GPCs also acknowledge that there are different pathways that lead a learner to undertake a degree and enhance their practice which support graduate employability skills. They ensure that higher education academic routes are responsive to the changing needs and training routes in Early Years practice, education and the wider children's services workforce and afford students with placement opportunities to critically apply theory to practice in a range of early childhood settings and/or schools, social care and health settings. This will enable students to develop graduate skills in the application of the interdisciplinary early childhood knowledge base to reflective practice and also provide new opportunities for graduates who want to strengthen their practice in early childhood and/or progress to post-graduate academic programmes or professional training, including Early Years teacher (0–5), teacher (3–11), social work and health professions (ECSDN, 2020).

To gain the competencies, students have to complete a portfolio, evidencing their ability to critically reflect and apply knowledge to practice, all at a Level 6 standard, in the following areas:

- advocating for young children's rights and participation
- promoting holistic child development
- working directly with young children, families and colleagues to promote health, wellbeing, safety and nurturing care
- observing, listening and planning for young children to support their wellbeing, early learning, progression and transitions

- safeguarding and child protection
- inclusive practice
- partnership with parents and caregivers
- collaborating with others
- ongoing professional development.

When researchers examine the quality of early childhood settings, they examine both *process quality* (children's experiences in the setting) and *structural quality* (staff ratios and qualifications). There is a close connection between these two aspects of quality. In the case of staff with higher qualifications, this results in better outcomes for the children (OECD, 2020). The Organization for Economic Co-operation and Development (OECD) has published several reports identifying what needs to be done to attract a high-quality workforce in the early childhood sector. Among them are:

- promoting the status of jobs in early childhood
- enhancing the qualifications of early childhood educators
- increasing the level of pay. (OECD, 2020)

In order to deliver a high-quality early childhood experience, a highly qualified and skilled workforce is required. Recent reports indicate, however, that the early childhood workforce continues to face challenges in terms of recruitment, retention, wage stagnation and changing employee qualification requirements (*Guardian*, 2022; LEYF Nurseries, 2022; Early Years Alliance, 2021). The chapter explores three key areas of the early childhood workforce and the ongoing development which may be needed to enhance the offering of qualifications, professional recognition and workforce development for early childhood practitioners. These are:

- early childhood (Early Years) qualifications
- what we have learnt from the early childhood workforce
- refocusing and working towards a strategy.

EARLY CHILDHOOD (EARLY YEARS) QUALIFICATIONS

Qualifications in the early childhood sector have continually been under scrutiny and assessment over the last 10 years. The regulator, the DfE, sets out the standards of these qualifications. Nutbrown (2012) completed a review of qualifications and stated:

> Some current qualifications lack rigour and depth, and quality is not consistent. I was concerned to find a considerable climate of mistrust in current early years qualifications, and anxiety, which I share on reading of evidence that standards have in some respects declined in recent years.
>
> (Nutbrown, 2012, p. 50)

The Nutbrown Review (2012), commissioned by the Coalition government, recommended that educators should be equipped with the necessary depth and breadth of knowledge and experience to overcome the challenges they face in their work. A new role replacing the Early Years professional status was the Early Years educator (EYE) Level 3 role and the Early Years teacher (graduate) role. As a result of these new roles and qualifications, there has been some unrest within the early childhood education and care community, particularly since the Early Years teacher role does not confer the status of qualified teacher (QT). According to the Association for the Professional Development of Early Years Educators (TACTYC, 2013), this new qualification will result in graduates earning less, having different terms and conditions of employment and having fewer career opportunities than their primary school counterparts. As of 2024, we now know that this has come to fruition and the recruitment and retention of Early Years teachers has declined considerably. TACTYC's view back in 2013 is very much the view still today.

As early childhood has evolved over the past century, different political administrations have engaged with and intervened in its provision to varying degrees. A qualification in English and mathematics was not required at the point of entry for trainees in 2012. Nutbrown (2012), however, identified that practitioners' literacy and numeracy skills are crucial to improving the quality of early childhood education and care. This initiative aimed to enhance the academic abilities of trainees entering the early childhood workforce. According to Nutbrown, entry requirements for the profession should include Level 2 English and mathematics (GCSE grade C or higher, current gradings, grade 4 or 5). Applicants to Level 3 EYE courses must meet this new policy, which was implemented by the Coalition government in 2014. In spite of this, many trainees no longer saw this profession as an opportunity, resulting in a decline in applications for this course.

The Conservative government under Theresa May underwent an impact assessment which introduced deregulatory measures that came into effect in 2017. The reasoning behind this was that they did not deem the skills needed to do the job at Level 2 and 3 warranted a grade C GCSE level or above. This resulted in the deregulation of the GCSE requirements which was carried out to alleviate the recruitment crisis of staff and trainees, especially at this time. It was clear that the higher entry requirements ended up acting as a deterrent for many applicants, which resulted in a recruitment challenge for training providers, so the deregulation was welcomed by others. This meant that they allowed Level 2 functional skills to be accepted alongside other suitable Level 2 qualifications, including GCSEs, which also meant that they could continue to be counted in ratios within the settings. The Childcare Act 2006 made reforms to inspection and Early Years regulation with the new Ofsted Childcare (Compulsory and Voluntary) Register, which was introduced in the same year. In 2008, the Early Years Foundation Stage (DCSF, 2008) was introduced. From this, qualifications which allowed a licence to practise in the sector became a regulated qualification due to the staff to child ratio.

Let us take a look at the current opportunities for early childhood qualifications and what this looks like in practice.

Example qualifications at Level 3:

- EYE
- Level 3 apprenticeship in EYE
- T-levels
- Scottish Vocational Qualification Early Years Care and Education
- Level 3 Children's Care, Play, Learning and Development (Wales and Northern Ireland).

Example qualifications at Level 4:

- Year 1 of an undergraduate degree or foundation degree
- Higher National Certificate.

Example qualifications at Level 5:

- Completion of a foundation degree, for example: Early Childhood, Early Years, Children, Young People and Families
- Higher Technical Qualification
- Apprenticeship Standard at Level 5 (Early Years leader)
- Higher National Diploma.

Example qualifications at Level 6:

- BA (Hons) Early Childhood Studies with Early Childhood Graduate Practitioner Competencies
- BA (Hons) Early Childhood Studies with EYE Assessed Practice
- BA (Hons) Early Childhood Studies
- BA (hons) Early Years.

From Level 6–7:

- Early Year initial teacher education (EYTS).

Professionals in early childhood have become increasingly interested in acquiring the skills and knowledge they need to graduate. As government policies on early childhood professionals constantly change, the GPCs were introduced in 2018. In this complex sector, a myopic assumption about the knowledge and skills needed for working in it has been made due to a lack of understanding of the breadth of the early childhood workforce, which encompasses health, education and care in all its manifestations. A homogeneous 'one size fits all' workforce led to government initiatives focusing on education at the expense of holistic child-centred policy and practice which differs across the four nations of the United Kingdom. In response to the shifting policy landscape, the Early Childhood Studies Degree Network (ECSDN) developed the GPCs to provide early childhood studies students with 'the skilful application of knowledge to practice and practice to knowledge' (ECSDN, 2020, p. 1). As a graduate practitioner, no matter what area of early childhood you work in or plan to work in, you will be able to critically apply theory to practice in your work with babies, young children and families (Bradbury et al., 2023). Research exploring practitioner, academic tutor and student experiences and perspectives of ECGPC by Richardson et al. (2022) found that:

> I learnt that it would be helpful to carry Post-It's with me to be able to instantly note anything that could go towards my evidence. I also wrote down all the competencies onto a set of revision cards that I kept handy so I could track across my evidence whenever I had some free time.
>
> Catilin Armstrong (early childhood graduate practitioner), University of Sunderland

> The competencies help to give the student a focus … When collecting evidence, the student can link the competencies specifically and give examples to show they have achieved them.
>
> (Voice of a mentor, in Richardson et al., 2022, p. 14)

WHAT WE HAVE LEARNT FROM THE EARLY CHILDHOOD WORKFORCE

The current model we have in England is that there is limited scope in the qualifications and workforce strategy for the sector. The lack of vision towards moving past the 'childcare narrative' still exists in the 21st century. Parents need early education and care for their children, but this should not be at the detriment of the recognition of early childhood professionals who are caught within the crossfire of policy and practice. It would be naive of us to see the childcare narrative as anything other than parents being able to go to work and support the economy. Thus, we need to be radical and think creatively. There is a continuing need for graduates in the workforce, and this is one of the topics we hear about all the time. The early childhood workforce continues to be dominated by women and is deeply rooted in the concept of motherhood (Bonetti, 2019). The Labour government (1997–2010) made universal provision for children, young people and families to reduce poverty and increase employment opportunities for working mothers. However, government policies have emphasised funding childcare costs to meet the employment needs of parents since 2010 (Payler and Davis, 2017). Despite this, successive governments have failed to make sufficient investments in childcare. Hevey (2014) explains that every new administration brings changes in policies and different views on qualification levels and funding, resulting in the persistence of problems related to low status, pay and qualifications among the workforce.

Furthermore, in contrast to some other European countries, ECEC is still viewed as a separate system rather than as part of a comprehensive system (Oberheuemer and Schreyer, 2018). Parents and carers need to consider a variety of factors, including those associated with services that allow them to work (Fenech et al., 2022). Consequently, a graduate-led system has not been possible because of this division and the mixed economy of pre-school education and childcare. Lumsden and Musgrave (2023) state that graduates like those in early childhood studies began their degrees back in 1992, a time when there were different perspectives on qualification levels, policy changes and ideologies. They state that:

> Early Childhood degrees were first started in 1992, at a time when there were ideological, political and social debates advocating that the distinction between 'education' and 'care' systems in England was not appropriate in the early years (Calder, 1999; Calder, 2018; Miller and Hevey, 2012).
>
> (Lumsden and Musgrave, 2023, p. 1088)

Further to this, the Nuffield Foundation (2021) states:

> The presence of a graduate in private, voluntary and independent early years settings – which include nurseries, pre-schools and childminders, demonstrates a small but positive association with young children's educational attainment.

We have continually spoken about why we need graduates, but we are still moving at a terribly slow pace when it comes to real investment and a workforce strategy which values the input of those graduates within the early childhood sector. To be able to achieve this it is important that early childhood degree courses are designed to prepare graduates to deliver high-quality early childhood outcomes. Several initiatives were undertaken to create a graduate-led workforce in ECEC. As a result of the widening participation education initiative, people who were traditionally less likely to attend higher education were now able to gain access to higher education (O'Hara and Bingham, 2004). It was possible to cover the first two years of a degree by studying a foundation degree for experienced practitioners who were already working in the field. A top-up route was created to enable undergraduate students to complete their studies to a bachelor's degree. EYPS (Early Years professional status) was another important opportunity for early childhood educators to become graduate practitioners. The *Every Child Matters* agenda (DfES, 2004) was a key policy focus during the period of aforementioned Labour government.

According to Professor Nutbrown's report (2012), career structures are important in the profession. As she argued, there was a need to mediate the division between qualified teacher status (QTS) and EYPS. According to Nutbrown, to achieve this goal, an Early Years teacher would need to be created who could work with children from birth to age seven. As a result, the government proposed that EYPS be replaced by Early Years teacher status (EYTS) to work with children from birth to five, which would be provided through Early years initial teacher training (EYITT). Although EYTS and QTS share the same entry requirements, those with EYTS cannot be called teachers in maintained schools nor be entitled to similar wages and benefits. This move has further divided those who work with children from birth to five from their colleagues in the teaching profession.

REFOCUSING AND WORKING TOWARDS A STRATEGY

It has been argued by researchers that high-quality early childhood settings can positively impact children's outcomes (Sylva et al., 2004), which has wider economic benefits in both the short and long term. To be able to look at what is needed for the workforce, it is essential to understand the environments of all early childhood settings and how different they are. It is important to note that no settings are identical, and many have different early childhood approaches when it comes to pedagogy and practice. However, workplaces have begun to be recognised as sites of learning. Research is providing insight into how theories and concepts are incorporated into work practices, resulting in early childhood professionals gaining knowledge within the workplace (Bradbury, 2023).

On reflection on the above, there are ways in which the sector could support the recruitment and retention issues being faced now. One area of this is to look closely at the training which is provided and how much of this is actually good-quality training. Bradbury (2023) considers how we can reconceptualise the third teacher in an early childhood education setting. He argues that we need to value those professionals who have been in the profession and have built up experience and knowledge, so that they can support the training of new professionals. Conversely, by learning lessons from the data of his research, he believes that there could be several improvements to the training landscape which could support the early childhood workforce further. This could include the following:

- increased funding for training and professional development
- a mentorship programme which supports qualified colleagues within the early childhood and education setting to support all trainees in the sector; a national mentoring programme by the government would support recruitment and retention for the sector
- a clear and updated workforce strategy which maps out a clear pathway for training which includes progression

- greater professionalism for the workforce, including higher pay and progression
- improving the perception of what Early Years education and care is and the value of investing in all early childhood professionals
- diversifying training. We have seen a work-based model of apprenticeships but allowing more flexible approaches to college-based and university courses must be at the forefront of the changes needed.

(Bradbury, 2023)

One of the investments we can see is that of apprenticeships or work-based learning and how we can utilise this area of training and learning to gain qualifications. We have yet to see the impact of how apprenticeships can benefit the sector when looking at higher-level apprenticeships and how this can then lead to a graduate role as we are behind many other areas of industry in this field. Bradbury (2023) argues that early childhood settings that recruit apprentices should invest in capacity to build the support needed to deliver quality and the expectations of the apprenticeship. However, continual professional development (CPD) must be placed at the centre of development for early childhood professionals and an acknowledgement of the importance of the theory to practice is very much needed. Ensuring that those settings supporting development of early childhood professionals have a manager or supervisor undergoing a mandatory training requirement, such as that of an assessor/trainer qualification which is work-based, is important. These roles are common in other professions such as work-based assessors in social work and nursing, so having these embedded into the early childhood sector is an idea to enhance our training offer (Bradbury, 2023); also investing in work-based programmes which have placement opportunities must be a plan moving forwards for qualifications from Level 3–6. Bradbury (2023) recommends that early childhood qualifications should be work-based as it is an important part of building and sustaining a high-quality employment relationship. Conversely, early childhood providers need to see themselves as part of the workforce strategy that builds on child-centred outcomes that result in competent and resilient early childhood professionals.

FIVE KEY TAKEAWAYS

1. A deeper understanding among policy-makers and professionals of the complexities of the early childhood sector is required. You cannot work on workforce development without bringing in factors such as pay and conditions, recruitment and retention, child development and economic growth.

(Continued)

2. Early childhood workforce strategic development needs a well thought out process map which is supported by a demonstration of progress from Level 3 qualifications and moves towards graduate roles across the sector, not necessarily just for teachers.
3. Early Childhood Graduate Practitioner Competencies to be mandatory for all early childhood graduates and given the same credibility as a Level 3 Early Years educator and Early Years teacher.
4. Improving the perception of what Early Years education and early childhood is and the value of investing in early childhood professionals. There needs to be a national college for early childhood professionals which works with national bodies on behalf of early childhood professionals.
5. A fully funded workforce development fund which gives early childhood professionals a range of training and qualifications that are accessible for all colleagues whether they work in the maintained or private sectors.

CONCLUSION

In order for young children to receive high-quality learning, development, family support and wellbeing experiences, the early childhood workforce is crucial. Rather than providing in-depth discussion of each area, this chapter is intended to be a starting point, highlighting opportunities that could be engaged in:

- early childhood (Early Years) qualifications
- what we have learnt from the early childhood workforce
- refocusing and working towards a strategy.

The purpose of this chapter is to provide and encourage further dialogue on what the workforce needs in terms of development. Policies that support the development of the early childhood workforce must address the requirements for qualifications, education in general and CPD. An increased focus should be placed on the working conditions of colleagues in early childhood and the value and respect they provide to an undervalued, under-resourced and under-represented sector. The concept of changing this to one that underpins, values, respects and recognises the vital work early childhood professionals do for families and children must be developed.

REFERENCES

Bonetti, S. (2019). *The Early Years Workforce in England: A Comparative Analysis Using the Labour Force Survey*. London: Education Policy Institute. Available at: https://epi.org.uk/publications-and-research/the-early-years-workforce-in-england/. Accessed 1 June 2024.

Bradbury, A. (2023). Reconceptualising the third teacher: A study of trainee experiences of work-based learning on Level 3 Early Years programmes. *Prof Doc Thesis*. Available at: https://doi.org/10.48773/q218z. Accessed 14 October 2024.

Bradbury, A., Musgrave, J. and Perkins, H. (2023). *A Practical Guide to Early Childhood Studies Graduate Practitioner Competencies*. London: Learning Matters.

Childcare Act (2006) *C.1*. Available at: www.legislation.gov.uk/ukpga/2006/21. Accessed 1 January 2024.

Department for Education and Skills (DfES) (2004). *Every Child Matters: Change for Children*. London: HMSO.

Department for Children, Schools and Families (DCSF) (2008). *Statutory Framework for the Early Years Foundation Stage: Setting the Standards for Learning, Development and Care for Children from Birth to Five*. Available at: https://dera.ioe.ac.uk/id/eprint/6413/7/statutory-framework_Redacted.pdf. Accessed 2 June 2024.

Early Years Alliance (2021). *Early Years Staffing Shortages Reaches Crisis Point*. Available at: www.eyalliance.org.uk/news/2021/12/early-years-staffing-shortages-reaches-crisis-point. Accessed 1 January 2022.

Early Childhood Studies Degree Network (ECSDN) (2020). *Early Childhood Graduate Practitioner Competencies*. Available at: www.ecsdn.org/wp-content/uploads/2021/09/ECSDN-Booket-Rev-July-2020.pdf. Accessed 1 June 2024.

Fenech, M., Wong, S., Boyd, W., Gibson, M., Watt, H. and Richardson, P. (2022). Attracting, retaining and sustaining early childhood teachers: an ecological conceptualisation of workforce issues and future research directions. *Australian Educational Researcher*, 49(1), 1–19.

Guardian (2022). *UK faces childcare crisis as staff shortages force nurseries to close*. Available at: www.theguardian.com/education/2022/apr/30/uk-faces-childcare-crisis-as-staff-shortages-force-nurseries-to-close. Accessed 1 January 2023.

Hevey, D. (2014). Professional work in early childhood. In T. Waller and G. Davis (eds), *An Introduction to Early Childhood*. London: Sage, pp. 265–85.

LEYF Nurseries (2022). *Tackling the Early Years Recruitment Crisis Head On*. Available at: www.leyf.org.uk/news/ey-recruitment-crisis/#:~:text=35%25%20of%20respondents%20are%20actively,and%20poor%20pay%20(57%25). Accessed 1 May 2024.

Lightfoot, S. and Frost, D. (2015). The professional identity of Early Years educators in England: implications for a transformative approach to continuing professional development. *Professional Development in Education*, 41(2), 401–18.

Lumsden, E. and Musgrave, J. (2023). 'Early childhood studies is more than a degree; it is an experience': undergraduate students' motivations, professional aspirations and attributes. *International Journal of Early Years Education*, 31(4), 1086–104.

Nuffield Foundation (2021). *The Deaton Review, Inequality*. Available at: https://ifs.org.uk/inequality/. Accessed 1 June 2024.

Nutbrown, C. (2012). *Foundations for Quality: The Independent Review of Early Education and Childcare Qualifications (Nutbrown Review)*. Available at: www.gov.uk/government/uploads/system/uploads/attachment_data/file/175463/Nutbrown-Review.pdf. Accessed 5 June 2024.

Oberheuemer, P. and Schreyer, I. (2018). *Workforce Profiles in Systems of Early Childhood Education and Care in Europe*. Available at: www.seepro.eu/English/Home.htm. Accessed 10 May 2024.

OECD (2020). *Building a High Quality Early Childhood Education and Care Workforce. Further Results from the Starting Strong Survey 2018*. Available at: www.oecd.org/education/talis/building-a-high-quality-early-childhood-education-and-care-workforce-b90bba3d-en.htm. Accessed 1 June 2024.

O'Hara, M. and Bingham, R. (2004). Widening participation on early childhood studies and Early Years education degrees. *Journal of Further and Higher Education*, 28(2), 207–17.

Payler, J. and Davis, G. (2017). Professionalism: Early Years as a career. In *BERA-TACTYC Early Childhood Research Review 2003–2017*, Edited by British Educational Research Association Early Childhood Special Interest Group and TACTYC: Association for Professional Development in Early Years. 9–29. Available at: www.bera.ac.uk/project/bera-tactyc-early-childhood-research-review-2003-2017. Accessed 1 July 2024.

Richardson, T., Wall, S. and Brogaard Clausen, S. (2022). *A Report on Findings from the Early Childhood Graduate Practitioner Competencies (ECGPC) Research Project: Exploring Practitioner, Academic Tutors and Student Experiences and Perspectives of ECGPC: Building Professional Identities*. Early Childhood Studies Degrees Network. Available at: https://mcusercontent.com/351ba87f63305d1461f8e3320/files/e3082df9-bc6f-4df9-d148-2e8138c5ddfb/ECSDN_Report_JB_6.pdf. Accessed 29 June 2024.

Sylva, K. (2014). The role of families and pre-school in educational disadvantage. *Oxford Review of Education*, 40(6), 680–95.

Sylva, K., Melhuish, E., Sammons, P., Siraj-Blatchford, I. and Taggart, B. (2004). *The Effective Provision of Pre-School Education (EPPE) Project: Final Report: A Longitudinal Study Funded by the DfES 1997–2004*. Available at: https://discovery.ucl.ac.uk/id/eprint/10005309/. Accessed 14 October 2024.

TACTYC: Association for the Professional Development of Early Years Educators (2013). *TACTYC Response to More Great Childcare*. Available at: www.tactyc.org.uk/pdfs/2013-response-1.pdf. Accessed 1 June 2024.

9
CHILDREN'S RIGHTS AND PARTICIPATION

Dr Nathan Archer and Dr Jo Albin-Clark

> **KEY DEFINITIONS**
>
> **Rights:** We are all born with rights that protect our dignity as humans: 'Human rights are universal, inalienable, indivisible and accountable. In other words, they apply equally to everyone, including babies and very young children' (Murray et al., 2019, p. xxiii).
>
> **Participation:** The concept of children's participation recognises that children are 'active in the process of shaping their own lives, learning, and future. They have their own view on their best interests, a growing capacity to make decisions, the right to speak and the right to be heard' (Woodhead, 2010, p. xviii).
>
> **Voice:** UNCRC Article 12: All children have a right to have their voices heard and taken into account. Children's voices are 'beyond words including behaviour, actions, silences, movement, body language, glances, and artistic expression' (Wall et al., 2019, p. 268).
>
> **Agency:** 'The ability to act and make decisions that influence events and affect one's world' (Early Years Coalition, 2021, p. 118).

INTRODUCTION

A manifesto is widely understood to be a publication which states a position and advances a set of ideas, opinions, or views. Here we take that idea to illustrate the research and our own positions (Albin-Clark and Archer, 2023) on the importance of children's rights, voice and participation in early childhood education and care (ECEC).

Historically childhood was seen as an early biological/physiological stage of life, marked by widely accepted stages of growth and development. Pre-sociological perspectives considered childhood as a time where innocence needed protection and where children needed discipline as they were an adult in the making. These perspectives were based on a number of assumptions, namely that children are passive recipients of knowledge and guidance, that it is the adult's work to *shape* children, and that human development is a linear and normative trajectory. More recently, post-sociological perspectives on childhood reflect ideas that children are human beings in their own right and that their development is shaped by the dynamic contexts in which they live and are cared for.

We work from the assumptions that:

- children are rights bearers
- children are active agents with growing capacity for self-determination
- children are capable and creative
- children influence adults in addition to being influenced by them
- children's competencies develop in relation to peers, adults and wider social networks. Within this relationality, other species, the environment, places, spaces and materialities of the more-than-human world have a role to play.

Moss, in Cameron and Moss (2020), asks: 'What is our image of the child, the early childhood centre, the worker in the centre? What are the fundamental values of ECEC, and what ethics should it work with?' (p. 7) We suggest that answers to these questions are shaped by and, in turn, shape perspectives on young children's rights and understandings of their voices and agency. This topic raises broader questions of the role of citizenship and democracy in early childhood education and care, as well as ideas of community and entitlements. As Wall et al. (2019) suggest, 'If we are to foster democratic skills and understanding in children and young people, we need to develop practices that support this from the earliest age' (p. 265).

In this chapter we explore the concepts of (and relationships between) young children's rights, voices, participation and agency in early childhood education and care.

CHILDREN HAVE RIGHTS

All children are born with rights, regardless of where they live and into which family they are born. Children are defined as anyone under 18; they acquire rights just by being born.

These rights are outlined in the United Nations Convention on the Rights of the Child (UNCRC) (OHCHR, 1989). The UNCRC is the most ratified international policy about childhood and does important work in positioning children as rights holders and social agents able to have influence on their life, rather than passive recipients of adult direction (Murray et al., 2019). The UNCRC has 54 articles that are interrelated and encompass social, political, civic, cultural and economic entitlements (OHCHR, 1989). Four articles in particular act as gateways to other rights and are framed as *general principles* that relate to non-discrimination, acting with children's best interests, survival and development and the right to be listened to (Murray et al., 2019).

When a young child is positioned as a citizen with rights it can alter an adult's view of them. It means a young child is seen as someone capable, competent and entitled to have their views and ideas taken seriously. For educators, the way we build relationships, organise environments for play and actively encourage children to make choices and decisions for themselves is central to daily life. Thus, ECEC is a critical period for rights to be realised and involves seeing children as beings rather than becomings (Cameron and Moss, 2020). Subsequently the sector can do important work in positioning young children and their early education as a vital period of life, and not solely a preparatory stage for their next phase of education.

An interest for ECEC is children's access to play. Children's entitlement to play is outlined in Article 31 of the UNCRC (OHCHR, 1989). Thus, children are entitled to and have the right to play. In early childhood, this is no surprise because play is recognised as intrinsic to early learning and development and often a principal factor in any early childhood curricula such as the Early Years Foundation Stage (EYFS) in England (Early Years Coalition, 2021). The non-statutory curricula guidance for EYFS that has been written by the sector does articulate the importance of rights and the agency of children, but rights agendas can be absent from many educational policies and curricula guidance. Moreover, play can be marginalised in everyday practice as educators feel the pull of outcomes-led and formalised approaches that foreground passive forms of learning. Unfortunately for children, their opportunities for play can become squeezed out and seen as of less value than adult-led activities.

But it is important to recognise that play is a fundamental gateway for children in accessing their wider rights. In play, children use their whole bodies to actively navigate their enquiries about how the world works; it can be viewed as holistically connecting physical, social, emotional and communicative developmental domains (Early Years Coalition, 2021). Because children are problem-solving, understanding what is fair and not fair, making their own decisions and learning to take control through play, we can see how this supports their overall development and general health and wellbeing.

Play is fundamental to child rights agendas, but educators can sometimes find themselves having to justify why play happens. Our recent research (Albin-Clark and Archer, 2023) has considered how educators find ways to resist and subvert formalisation learning discourses to foreground playful pedagogies. What we found was educators build their resistance practices to find ways for children to exercise their right to play. For example, one educator was a teacher of three- and four-year-old children in a nursery class in a primary school who found herself under scrutiny from her literacy coordinator asking for evidence of handwriting. What the teacher did was use her documentation of children hanging and swinging from a piece of fabric hung from a tree in outdoor play as a way of demonstrating the benefits of physical and imaginative play for later formalised writing skills. This shows that often educational professionals working in later primary stages (and perhaps families too) may not appreciate the vital work that ECEC does and particularly how play is so vital to early development and learning.

What we propose (Albin-Clark and Archer, 2023) is that educators need to tell and share stories of children's play and articulate how play and child rights agendas interrelate. Telling stories of play to other professionals, their families and children themselves is a joyful sharing of the power of play. In practice, this would entail making environments and time where play can happen and educators who enable it and act as play partners for children. Photographing and making observations of play are accessible ways of foregrounding children's right to play and more importantly can share those hopeful stories and enable other people to appreciate the connections between early learning and children's rights.

CHILDREN ARE EXPERTS IN THEIR OWN LIVES

In order for children to be fully involved in decision-making and to be heard in early education and care, all actors need to recognise children's right to participation and the right to be heard.

VOICE

Article 12 of the UNCRC (OHCHR, 1989) states that 'every child has the right to express their views, feelings and wishes in matters affecting them'. However, understandings of what constitutes children's voice differ. An understanding we value is offered by Murray (2019, p. 1):

> A definition of children's voices that ... puts the onus on not only hearing – but attending to – children's feelings, beliefs, thoughts, wishes, preferences and attitudes is indicated, perhaps along the lines of '... views of children that are actively received and acknowledged as valuable contributions to decision-making affecting the children's lives'.

It is important to note that voice constitutes more than verbal expression. Article 13 of the UNCRC states that children have the right to express themselves in any way they choose, not just the spoken word. Wall et al. (2019, p. 268) suggest that any definition of voice will be, by necessity, broader and more inclusive of a greater range of communication strategies beyond words, including behaviour, actions, silences, movement, body language, glances and artistic expression. One method which employs such an ethos to research is the *mosaic* approach.

The Mosaic approach (Clark and Moss 2011) is a multimethod method in which children's own photographs, tours and maps can be combined with talking and observing to gain deeper understanding of children's perspectives in relation to matters that directly affect them.

In exploring a definition of voice, Wall et al. (2019, p. 269) encourage educators to ask:

- what does voice look like/sound like in my setting?
- how do I identify voice in practice?
- how do I tune into different types of voice(s)?
- how do I listen to silence?
- if voice is important, what is it more important than?
- how does voice change over time?

Listening to children's voices is an active process of receiving (hearing and observing), interpreting and responding to communication. It is an ongoing way of tuning in to all young children as individuals in their everyday lives. Really listening to children has benefits for the child, the educator and the setting and builds a culture of respect, trust, openness, collaboration and patience.

However, contemporary contexts can create challenges to this listening in practice. Hayes (2024) draws attention to the pressures of accountability for educators and how policy demands can create tensions between a commitment to listening to children and opportunities in reality to enact this. Against the backdrop of these tensions educators will ideally create calm, supportive environments which enable time and space to access children's voices.

PARTICIPATION

Participation of children and young people is one of the General Principles of the Convention on the Rights of the Child (OHCHR, 1989). When we think about what true participation looks like, we think about how young children are fully involved in discussions and decision-making processes which affect them. Children's full participation in their early education and care can create significant transformations towards a culture of respect for children's rights. Such an approach demonstrates a commitment to principles of democracy and citizenship. Indeed, as Cameron and Moss (2020, p. 226) suggest: 'early childhood services, including schools, nurseries or children's centres are portals into the community'.

Meaningful participation requires educators to challenge historical power dynamics between adults and young children, and to embed participation into daily life and routines rather than as a separate 'tick box' exercise.

In practice, educators can:

- consider a democratic approach of decision-making – for example, children could explore voting on relevant issues
- encourage children to think about fairness and equity within the setting, local community and wider world
- support children's voice within the community and connect with community planning and consultation in all matters that affect children.

Early childhood professionals can draw on research and guidance to facilitate and enable children's full participation in the life of the early childhood setting. However, children seldom have opportunities for participation in policy-making processes. Their voices are often absent. The development of *Birth to 5 Matters* (Early Years Coalition, 2021) is an example of policy-making with children. Developers of the guidance undertook research through a survey gathering children's voices about what was important in their Early Years setting, and conducted a literature review of existing research on children's voices.

The importance of children's voice and participation is acknowledged in *Birth to 5 Matters* non-statutory guidance. It is noted:

> From the earliest age children should be involved in choices about their own learning. The UN Convention on the Rights of the Child Article 12 states the right of the child to express their views and have their views taken seriously.
>
> (Early Years Coalition, 2021 p. 39)

CHILDREN HAVE AGENCY

One definition of agency is 'the ability to act and make decisions that influence events and affect one's world' (Early Years Coalition, 2021, p. 118). Agency goes to the heart of teaching and learning – it reflects debates about power, control, choice and wellbeing.

This notion of agency leads us to look at how children learn and implies a particular way of looking at the relationship between teaching and learning. It turns on its head the idea that a prescribed curriculum comes first, or that the teacher always decides what needs to be learnt, tells the child and the child then soaks up this knowledge by remembering what has been said. Recognising children's agency offers a different perspective.

In ECEC, children's *funds of knowledge* and tuning in to their interests offer rich inspiration and motivation for further learning (Chesworth and Hedges, 2024). The funds of knowledge approach acknowledges and respects children's home and community experiences and cultural practices and explores how educators might use these funds of knowledge to help individual children to create personalised ways of knowing. This approach not only recognises what children bring to their early childhood setting but acknowledges their agency in shaping their own learning. Such an approach acknowledges 'that children have agency in their involvement with people, objects, the environment, ideas and events children build working theories about the world around them' (Early Years Coalition, 2021, p. 18).

The physical and emotional environments of early childhood settings offer many opportunities to enable children's agency to be expressed. A physical environment which is designed and resourced to facilitate freedom of movement and a choice of resources and activities will likely support the development of independence and autonomy. Studies suggest that wellbeing and motivation are enhanced in very young children when they feel a sense of control. Children's *locus of control* has also been related to academic achievement, so where an environment nurtures choice and motivation (and agency) research suggests that through an internal locus of control (rather than external) children thrive and excel.

An emotional environment which affords and enables expressions of agency is one of respect and trust. Such an environment involves adults engaged in responsive interactions: listening and talking respectfully with children, and having conversations where children's ideas and thoughts are genuinely sought and valued. Some examples of responsive interactions which acknowledge and nurture agency are:

- promoting autonomy, independence and self-help skills through the opportunity to participate in routine tasks like setting up environments, preparing snacks and selecting resources
- acknowledging and responding to children's contributions by ensuring their ideas and interests are reflected in the life of the setting
- affording children opportunities to establish their own routines, behaviour, guidelines and consequences
- providing flexible and unhurried routines which allow children to make choices about decisions which affect them
- promoting independent choice, movement, exploration and appropriate risk-taking
- offering children the opportunity to participate in long periods of uninterrupted play.

In policy terms, young children's agency has rarely been recognised. Curricular documents seldom acknowledge children's agentic drive, but rather stipulate knowledge, skills, competencies and attitudes to be acquired in their Early Years. The idea of children's agency does not currently feature explicitly in the Early Years Foundation Stage statutory guidance. However, the idea of agency can be read in the Characteristics of Effective Learning (Early Years Coalition, 2021, p. 22):

- playing and exploring
- active learning
- creative and critical thinking.

The idea of agency does, however, take a central role in *Birth to 5 Matters* (Early Years Coalition, 2021, p. 22, emphasis original) being recognised as key to children's learning and development:

> When there is support for children's sense of *agency* – knowing they have control of their own decisions, goals and actions rather than simply being passive in their experiences – children are likely to be effective in their learning. Experiences which endorse children's agency and autonomy reinforce and develop their learning powers.

If children are genuinely to be valued as unique human beings, there is a continuing need to develop conditions, both in practice and policy, in which children's agency can be expressed and can flourish.

EARLY CHILDHOOD INTO THE FUTURE

The future for ECEC is already here. One vital aspect we cannot ignore is what kind of world children are inheriting and will grow old into beyond our own life spans. Article 24 of the UNCRC is related to children's rights to health standards and recognises that environmental pollution poses both danger and risk (OHCHR, 1989). The sorry fact is that young children are made vulnerable by a world in environmental crisis where increasing climate temperatures, pollution and a depleted natural world pose a real and growing threat to their health and development (Cameron and Moss, 2020). How children access their rights is in a precarious relationship with the relentless effects of environmental harms (Murray et al., 2019).

Anyone who shares time with young children understands how closely related health, education and development are. So, as educators, we have an important role in nurturing practices that notice and appreciate the places and spaces we occupy with children and our collective role and responsibility in caring for the environment.

Some interesting research about children's relationship to the world comes from posthuman theories. Malone et al. (2020) use posthuman theories to imagine children in an extricable relationship with all the elements of the world (as well as humans) that they term 'childhoodnature'. Such theorising recognises 'the blurring of the boundaries between children and nature, to acknowledge that children are nature, that we human/animals are always part of the ecosystem in which we are entangled' (p. 103).

While posthuman theories can feel complex to understand, in fact they offer an interesting image of thought where play is positioned as a relationality in between the humans and the spaces, materials and more-than-human elements of the world. In the example earlier of the young children hanging and swinging, the outdoor space, the tree the fabric hung from are all in relation. In this way, we can see how play is a generative way to appreciate childhoodnature. When you begin to see children as already part of nature, rather than nature as a separate idealised place beyond the scope of most ECEC outdoor play spaces it makes you realise that children's time spent outside is vital. Not only does outdoor play give children an opportunity to develop their physical capabilities and overall health, they are experiencing the weather and noticing the small plants and creatures that cohabit those shared spaces. This is significant, as paying attention to their relationalities and responsibilities to the place and multiple species they share their world with may well be something positive. In this way, children can frame their relationships to the environment and other species as an interdependence that is in close connection with their own wellbeing.

It is certainly the case that the UNCRC is an important treaty, but it should be noted that how children access their rights depends on adults understanding them as rights holders (Murray et al., 2019). Indeed, children that you know and from around the world face much inequality and injustice and their access to rights can be severely limited. In posthuman views of childhood, it is helpful to see how intertwined seemingly disparate elements are; in this way children's rights, the natural world, curriculum documents and adult agendas are not separate, but rather:

> the child as always part of an entangled, hybrid assemblage, being-with and a part of all living things. That is, the child as an entity is not separated from fluid categories of humans, animals, earthlings, energy, atoms and so forth.
>
> (Malone et al., 2020, p. 147)

Educators are important advocates for young children, and sharing stories of children's play is one way that promotes their rights but can also draw attention to how spaces, time and materialities that fold in the environment we are part of all have a role to play (Albin-Clark and Archer, 2023).

FIVE KEY TAKEAWAYS

1. Children should be viewed as capable and competent citizens with rights, where play has a non-negotiable role in enabling children to access their rights. Educators need to advocate for children's right to play, and find ways to make room, space and give permission for children to play that resists the pressure to rush to formalised modes of learning.
2. Early educator and teacher professional standards should have an explicit requirement to engage with child voice.
3. Children's rights and their agency need to be foregrounded in and actively shape early educational curricula and guidance.

(Continued)

4. Children need outdoor play experiences where they can develop relationality and responsibility with the environment and the multiple species they share their world with.
5. Educators, policy-makers and researchers need to be advocates and activists for children's rights agendas and actively resist inappropriate formalisation agendas.

CONCLUSION

These manifesto statements matter. They matter because they are underpinned by an image of the child that is widely held in ECEC about the importance of children's rights, voice and agency. The manifesto statements are also a call for attitudinal change to reflect the value that wider society should place on children and childhood.

In children's earliest years, spaces for formal education and care can and should be sites of democracy where citizenship and participation can flourish. Within these spaces, early educators have a crucial role as advocates and activists with and for young children, ensuring that their rights, voice and agency are recognised and celebrated. Children can also come to know about their rights through their ECEC experiences. Additionally, ECEC has an important role in nurturing children's alliance and comfort with the more-than-human world around them for now and for the future.

Looking ahead to the next ten years, there are opportunities to further consider and reconsider these statements and the principles which underpin them. We hope they will be better understood and embedded in practice and policy-making with and for young children. Prosser and Contreras (2024) advocate for national leaders to have the courage to shape a child-centred nation and for all citizens to have the courage to speak up and be child-centred champions. We hope that early childhood educators continue to support this advocacy work.

REFERENCES

Albin-Clark, J. and Archer, N. (2023). *Playing social justice: how do early childhood teachers enact the right to play through resistance and subversion? PRISM Journal*, 5(2), 1–22. Available at: https://openjournals.ljmu.ac.uk/prism/article/view/714. Accessed 15 October 2024.

Cameron, C. and Moss, P. (2020). *Transforming Early Childhood in England*. 1st edn. London: UCL Press. Available at: https://library.oapen.org/handle/20.500.12657/51784. Accessed 15 October 2024.

Chesworth, E. and Hedges, H. (2024). Children's interests and early childhood curriculum: a critical analysis of the relationship between research, policy, and practice. *The New Zealand Annual Review of Education, 29*, 5–22.

Clark, A. and Moss, P. (2011). *Listening To Young Children: The Mosaic Approach* (2nd ed.). London: National Children's Bureau.

Early Years Coalition (2021). *Birth to 5 Matters: Non-Statutory Guidance for the Early Years Foundation Stage.* Available at: https://birthto5matters.org.uk/wp-content/uploads/2021/04/Birthto5Matters-download.pdf. Accessed 15 October 2024.

Hayes, N. (2024). 'It's not fair': hearing the voices of young children. *Education 3–13*, 1–13.

Malone, K., Tesar, M. and Arndt, S. (2020). Posthuman pedagogies in childhoodnature. In K. Malone, M. Tesar and S. Arndt (eds), *Theorising Posthuman Childhood Studies*. New York: Springer, pp. 103–42.

Murray, J. (2019). Hearing young children's voices. *International Journal of Early Years Education, 27*(1), 1–5.

Murray, J., Smith, K. and Swadener, B. (2019). *The Routledge International Handbook of Young Children's Rights*. Abingdon: Routledge. Available at: www.taylorfrancis.com/books/9781000682168. Accessed 15 October 2024.

Nutbrown, C. (2019). Respectful educators, capable learners: then and now. In J. Murray, K. Smith and B. Swadener (eds), *The Routledge International Handbook of Young Children's Rights*. Abingdon: Routledge, pp. 331–41. Available at: www.taylorfrancis.com/books/9781000682168. Accessed 15 October 2024.

Office for the High Commissioner for Human Rights (OHCHR) (1989). *United Nations Convention on the Rights of the Child (UNCRC)*. 20 November. Available at: www.ohchr.org/en. Accessed 15 October 2024.

Prosser, J. and Contreras, M. J. (2024). *Young at Heart*. Royal Society of Arts. Available at: www.thersa.org/rsa-journal/2024/issue-1/features/young-at-heart. Accessed 15 October 2024.

Wall, K., Cassidy, C., Robinson, C., Hall, E., Beaton, M., Kanyal, M. and Mitra, D. (2019). Look who's talking: factors for considering the facilitation of very young children's voices. *Journal of Early Childhood Research, 17*(4), 263–78.

Woodhead, M. (2010). Foreword. In B. Percy-Smith and N. Thomas (eds), *A Handbook of Children and Young People's Participation: Perspectives from Theory and Practice*. Abingdon: Routledge, pp. xiv–xxii.

10
HARNESSING THE POTENTIAL OF DIGITAL DEVICES IN EARLY CHILDHOOD

Dr Lorna Arnott and Professor Rosie Flewitt

> **KEY DEFINITIONS**
>
> **Digital technology:** 'Digital technology is a broad term for the multitude of media and devices that are used for communication, entertainment and gaming' (Teichert et al., 2021, p. 107).
>
> **Post-digital:** 'The post-digital pertains to a moment in human history whereby practices and digital technologies are intertwined with the daily actions and interactions of people' (Edwards, 2023, p. 777).
>
> **Educators:** The term 'educators' is used here to refer to all people responsible for supporting children's learning and care in formal, non-formal and informal settings, including those who support children at home and in the wider community.

INTRODUCTION

The progression in digital artefacts from radio, television, computers, touch screen technologies, internet-connected toys and increasingly to artificial intelligence (AI), has been persistently queried in early childhood education and care (e.g. Howard, 2002; Su et al., 2023). Widely felt anxieties about the potentially harmful effects of digital and online technologies on childhood are fuelled by persistent moral panics in the media about the safety and security of young children's digital lives, and their physical and mental health. Although these concerns are well founded in an era when the digital industry is often not held accountable for safeguarding personal data, there is a wealth of research that points to the limitations of deficit perspectives on the role and usefulness of technologies in children's lives (Delfin and Wang, 2023; Oakley et al., 2020; Scott and Marsh, 2018). Yet educators continue to be bombarded with deficit discourses about children's technology use, with advice focusing on restricting children's digital access and protecting children from the dangers of the digital world (American Academy of Paediatrics, 2016), often referred to under the umbrella term of 'screen time'.

While respecting and sharing widespread concerns about technology, in this chapter we offer alternatives to predominantly negative narratives about childhood and technology and suggest the need to support educators and children to evaluate the creative and critical potential of digital technologies for young children's learning, development and enjoyment. To achieve this, we need resources that are informed by reliable research, that are openly accessible for all, and that can help to build educators' confidence with technology and its purposeful use. In this way, we can move gradually towards all young children being enabled to flourish as they grow up in a digital world, where they can learn to make thoughtful and carefully crafted decisions about their own digital lives under the mentorship of informed and confident educators in a post-digital world.

WHAT IS POST-DIGITAL?

The term 'post-digital' is used to describe the era in which we now live, where digital data monitoring systems, surveillance and sensing around our bodies have become so ubiquitous and entwined in everyday life that it is difficult to distinguish between digital and non-digital aspects of life. And it starts early! Increasingly, the technologisation of life begins pre-birth. In utero, a foetus is already subjected to ultrasound technologies and a host of other digital experiences such as 'belly buds' hearing devices to play music to the unborn child. The neonate also experiences technologies outside the womb minutes from birth, as the joyful moment is immortalised through photographs and as midwives use digital technologies to check babies' weight and monitor their heartbeat.

The presence of digital devices in everyday life is a global phenomenon. While many households in the global North may on average have more and a wider range of technological devices than those in the global South, mobile connectivity has become a feature of everyday life across the world. The networked society in which we live (Flewitt and Clark, 2020) is now so deeply entwined in the fabric of our lives that technologies have become inseparable from human action (power supply and satellite communication permitting). This in turn shapes early childhood experiences, where post-digital play and learning are emerging as important concepts for consideration (Edwards, 2023).

CRITICALLY REFLECTIVE TECHNOLOGY USE IN EARLY CHILDHOOD

Scaffolding children's learning with technologies is complex. Educators and children currently experience a paradox between what is 'recommended' (American Academy of Paediatrics, 2016) versus the reality of how technology is so enmeshed in everyday life. We know that our youngest citizens are engaging with a multitude of digital devices (Arnott et al.,2020; Marsh et al., 2021) against a backdrop of negative narratives associated with screen time and its potentially negative outcomes for healthy child development (Takahashi et al., 2023). Consequently, many educators often have deep-seated reservations about whether it is appropriate for young children to use digital devices, and may restrict children's device access, irrespective of research evidence showing the potential benefits of integrating digital media into child-centred pedagogy (Vidal-Hall et al., 2020).

These two facets of contemporary life sit in uneasy company with each other. On the one hand, technologies have become so integral to life in the post-digital world it is difficult to discern when technology is not present. On the other hand, concerns about the potential harm of technology for children have led to a tendency among educators to try to restrict children's access to them. The ubiquitous nature of technologies highlights the need to shift the focus away from children's protection *against* technology towards a more optimistic approach, where children and their educators are offered guidance and support about how to navigate and learn safely and securely *with, about* and *through* digital media. If educators continue to focus on restricting children's technology use, this may in turn result in educators limiting their own learning about the opportunities that technologies offer for early learning, including opportunities to develop their own practices to harness technologies more purposefully, creatively and critically for children's learning.

To counter the deficit perspective that still tends to dominate public debate about childhood and technology, we propose a more nuanced vision for how technologies can be integrated meaningfully in children's learning in ways that enhance their creativity, criticality, skills and wider development, and how educators can support children as apprentices in their digital literacy journey.

CHANGING CHILDHOODS AND NEW POSSIBILITIES

Early childhood is a crucially important life stage. Not only does the quality of early childhood experiences lay the foundation for later success and achievement (Cooper et al., 2014), but, if we view children as beings (as well as becomings) (Uprichard, 2008), it is also a finite period that is invaluable in its own right.

The unquestionable significance of childhood as a crucially important phase of human development may well lay behind vehement deficit arguments that technology risks reducing the quality of early childhood experiences. However, romanticising the virtues of childhood in former non-digital eras fuels the illusion that the quality of childhood is diminishing (Plowman et al., 2010). Deficit views of technology in contemporary life include arguments about the overuse of screen-based technologies as 'babysitters' that result in lower-quality interactions for children with their educators, which in turn may lead to fewer opportunities to learn to talk (Lev and Elias, 2020).

The narrative that technologies are harming the quality of contemporary childhood experiences is often either fuelled by fear, hearsay or assertion, or evidence is presented in a linear causal manner, skewed towards the negative. Research demonstrating that technologies play a positive role in supporting children's cognitive, social and emotional development is often overlooked. For example, research has found strong evidence that interpersonal and intergenerational relations can be fostered via video calls, which also enhance cultural learning and social relationships (Demirsu, 2022). There are therefore many different factors to consider when comparing past childhoods with contemporary child rearing – life has changed.

Contemporary childhood benefits from new possibilities offered by technological advances. For example, video calls and online conferencing platforms have materialised as educational platforms to learn new skills, and interactive digital books provide rich environments for literacy learning. Although not all families were able to offer their children opportunities for remote learning during periods of pandemic lockdown, research has documented how some children were brought together online to share music lessons synchronously via Skype, Facetime and Zoom (Koops and Webber, 2020). Children were also observed learning gymnastics and contortion skills by viewing YouTube clips of these activities (Potter and Cowan, 2020). Further research has identified how cognitive development can be scaffolded via the use of open digital applications, which, when carefully planned with educators, can support reading, writing and spoken-language development (Oakley et al., 2020). These new experiences provided enjoyable and sociable, playful learning opportunities.

> **REFLECTION 10.1**
>
> Consider your own childhood and think about the ways in which technologies may have improved a challenging aspect of your own learning and development.

CREATIVE AND CRITICAL LEARNING WITH TECHNOLOGIES THROUGH PLAY

In early childhood, play is the main vehicle through which children learn and make sense of their world (Vygotsky, 2016). While there is evidence to suggest that technology use can be sedentary (Lev and Elias, 2020), Huber et al. (2018) illustrate the interactive potential of new technologies that differ from the passive viewing associated with television, offering the potential for play. For example, interactive digital resources offer scaffolding for children's experiences because of the immediacy of their in-built feedback, which can be further tailored to individual children if a confident educator joins in playfully with a child's digital activity.

The interactivity of many technologies means that children often fluidly transition and actively make connections between digital and non-digital play (Scott and Marsh, 2018), blending traditional play forms with technology. For example, children playing tablet games about dinosaurs often then engage with tactile toy dinosaurs in the non-digital environment (Neumann et al., 2020). These children engage in traditional–digital *converged play* (Edwards et al., 2020) that positions technologies as complementary resources in play.

Play*ful* learning applications for children have also been available for many years, leading to enjoyment with some structured elements, while offering some opportunities for intrinsically motivated play that is not outcome-driven or linear (Howard, 2002). These applications have had their limitations, but advances in the sophistication and complexity of digital processing have created opportunities for open-ended experiences with technologies and the possibility for digital play (Kervin, 2016).

Technology has advanced at such a rate that digital play may not involve a screen at all. Instead, children engage with soft toys that are internet-connected or have augmented digital elements (Arnott et al., 2020). Children creatively integrate digital household devices when they play in the home corner (Bird, 2020), by pretending to make phone/video calls (Scriven et al., 2018) or role playing being YouTubers (Potter and Cowan, 2020). Delfin and Wang (2023) found that symbolic play with 'pretend' technologies can positively influence cognitive development, including the progression of abstract thought. Here, technologies do not have to be working or 'real' to be valuable for children's play – children's imaginations contribute all the functionality needed to fuel their flights of fanciful playfulness.

Debates continue about whether digital experiences, whether actual or pretend, constitute play because they take place in a virtual world, and this challenges long-established definitions of play. Despite fears to the contrary, research has found that technologies are not replacing the fundamental, highly valued characteristics of childhood and play. Rather, they are extending the potential to enrich children's playful learning and to foster play and creativity if they are adopted thoughtfully and creatively through playful encounters (Marsh et al., 2021). Children are still enjoying eclectically rich activities alongside the digital world (Plowman and McPake, 2013; Rosanda et al., 2022). Critical reflection on the quality of experiences and learning being offered to, and with, children is central to ensuring that technologies support children's learning and development through playful activities.

REFLECTION 10.2

How do children in your practice integrate technologies, real or pretend, into their play?

CHILDREN'S APPRENTICESHIP INTO DIGITAL LITERACY

Depending on how they are used, many everyday technological devices offer the potential to support children's learning, but only if children develop a relationship with technologies that is self-aware and critically reflective. Optimal use of technology is often reached when a child is jointly engaged in a purposeful digital activity with another person, usually an educator. Joint attention to an activity creates an ideal communicative environment for the exchange of views about the activity and to speculate about how to achieve the desired outcome, in exchanges that are rich in spoken language and unfold in warm, loving relationships.

Children are apprentices in a digital literacy journey and educators play a key role in nurturing their learning rather than stifling their potential through fear or their own lack of digital confidence. Plowman et al. (2008) used the term 'guided interaction' to describe how educators can scaffold children's digital learning through proximal and distal interaction. 'Distal' refers to how adults enable children's digital device use by providing the resources, spaces and meaningful opportunities for their use. 'Proximal' refers to the face-to-face interactions between adults and children that have a direct influence on learning, characterised by joint shared attention that mirrors non-technological learning. These include the concepts of *guided participation* and *apprenticeship* (Rogoff, 2008), which describe how children become actively involved in learning within the cultural practices and values of their community, as well as the concept of *intent participation* where children may learn from observing others closely and listening in to what they are saying (Rogoff et al., 2003).

These concepts help us to understand that the characteristics for children's learning with technologies closely mirrors learning without technology – especially if the learning involves joint attention, rich interactions with others, is participatory, fun and culturally meaningful.

Post-digital perspectives and the recognition that technologies are culturally bestowed resources help us to understand why it is important for children to navigate their learning through active participation, while observing and *listening in* to educators' ways of being and doing with digital devices. Learning digital literacy in this 'empowered' manner (Craft, 2012) has to be central to children's education. In this scenario, our youngest children become digital apprentices learning alongside their educators about how to navigate the complexities of their intertwining digital and non-digital experiences.

The role that educators play in scaffolding this learning process should not be underestimated, because as Scott and Marsh (2018) articulate, we must 'enable children to become critical and engaged digital citizens who, in time, will be able to navigate the complex online terrain of "false" news and disinformation that appears to characterize the contemporary media landscape' (p. 17). Contemporary guidance focuses on the need to plan children's technology use around the quality of their experiences rather than quantity of screen time (Livingstone and Blum-Ross, 2020). Thus, co-use of media between educators and children is encouraged (Picherot et al., 2018).

Educators are already supported by resources to inform how they scaffold children's digital play, but they additionally need to develop internal critically reflective narratives to allow in-the-moment decision-making. Plowman's (2020) Digital Play resource provides helpful examples about what high-quality digital play entails. However, static resources and guidance are time-bound in their useability given the rapidly evolving landscape of digital play materials and technological devices, creating a barrier for educators' ability to make decisions as technologies evolve. Thus, it is essential to encourage educators to feel confident to move away from equating children's digital activity with risk (Craft, 2012), and to support educators to learn along with children to reflect on their own digital choices and help children to develop the critical reflective skills they will need to map out their own digital footprint in an informed and knowledgeable way.

REFLECTION 10.3

What is your role as a mentor if you want children in your care to learn as digital apprentices?

EARLY CHILDHOOD INTO THE POST-DIGITAL FUTURE

Childhood today already comprises an entanglement of digital and non-digital worlds, and children make meaning of this complexity through rich play episodes that bring together their diverse knowledge of contemporary material culture. Play is children's most powerful meaning-making activity. Play resources and materials, typically toys, are considered to offer an insight into the child's world and their interpretation of societal values (Cowan et al., 2024). The inclusion of technology in children's play, whether real or invoked through imagination, will almost inevitably become increasingly central to young children's play – where no-longer-functional mobile phones already form part of children's play resources, or where children make imaginary phone calls using a plastic brick held to their ear in place of the real item. Whether or not functioning digital devices are provided for children to explore, they will somehow or other feature in their play because children see and watch these devices being used in their homes and communities. It is therefore fundamentally important that educators start developing appropriate support mechanisms and pedagogy to propel children's confident, knowledgeable and independent decision-making when using digital devices in a culturally meaningful and reflective manner.

FIVE KEY TAKEAWAYS

1. A narrow understanding of digital technologies as screen time is unhelpful to support children's learning.
2. When optimally framed by educators, children's learning with technologies is often eclectic and rich.
3. The world is post-digital and it is very difficult to disentangle the many ways that digital technology is woven through the fabric of our everyday lives in the third millennium.
4. There is a need to conceptualise technologies as meaningful artefacts in play, embroiled in children's everyday worlds, ready to be harnessed for their rich potential.
5. Evidence-based resources and training are needed to support educators in young children's creative, critical, purposeful and reflective technology use.

CONCLUSION

This chapter adopts an optimistic and nuanced stance towards the potential of digital technologies in early childhood, from pre-birth to eight years. We have articulated how responsive scaffolding can enrich young children's everyday encounters with technological artefacts in ways that offer great potential for children's holistic learning experiences. The role of educators in this process is fundamental in supporting children to manoeuvre the complex – and at times, risky or dangerous – digital world. Yet, fear should not overshadow opportunities. Instead, adults can become confident to walk alongside young children as apprentices in a digital society. With appropriate support, young children can be encouraged to reflect on and make informed decisions about the role of technologies in their play, life and learning. Recognising the post-digital world that children are born into, our manifesto is for early childhood educators to be confident mentors for children's digital endeavours, in safe and secure ways that enrich their education, health and happiness.

REFERENCES

American Academy of Paediatrics, A. (2016). *Media and Young Minds*. Available at: http://publications.aap.org/pediatrics/article-pdf/138/5/e20162591/1061988/peds_20162591.pdf. Accessed 15 October 2024.

Arnott, L., Kewalramani, S., Gray, C. and Dardanou, M. (2020). Role-play and technologies in early childhood. In Z. Kingdon (ed.), *A Vygotskian Analysis of Children's Play Behaviours*. London: Routledge, pp. 76–92.

Bird, J. (2020). 'You need a phone and camera in your bag before you go out!': Children's play with imaginative technologies. *British Journal of Educational Technology*, 51(1), 166–76.

Cooper, B. R., Moore, J. E., Powers, C. J., Cleveland, M. and Greenberg, M. T. (2014). Patterns of early reading and social skills associated with academic success in elementary school. *Early Education and Development*, 25(8), 1248–64.

Cowan, K., van Leeuwen, T. and Selander, S. (2024). Pandemic playthings: a multimodal perspective on toys and toy play in the time of COVID-19. *Global Studies of Childhood*, 14(1), 62–80.

Craft, A. (2012). Childhood in a digital age: creative challenges for educational futures. *London Review of Education*, 10(2), 173–90.

Delfin, A. B. and Wang, W. (2023). The influence of pretend 'technologies' on children's cognitive development in symbolic play. *International Journal of Play*, 12(3), 387–402.

Demirsu, I. (2022). Watching them grow: intergenerational video-calling among transnational families in the age of smartphones. *Global Networks*, 22(1), 119–33.

Edwards, S. (2023). Concepts for early childhood education and care in the postdigital. *Postdigital Science and Education*, 5(3), 777–98.

Edwards, S., Mantilla, A., Grieshaber, S., Nuttall, J. and Wood, E. (2020). Converged play characteristics for early childhood education: multi-modal, global-local, and traditional-digital. *Oxford Review of Education*, 46(5), 637–60.

Flewitt, R. and Clark, A. (2020). Porous boundaries: reconceptualising the home literacy environment as a digitally networked space for 0–3 year olds. *Journal of Early Childhood Literacy*, 20(3), 447–71.

Howard, J. (2002). Eliciting young children's perceptions of play, work and learning using the activity apperception story procedure. *Early Child Development and Care*, 172(5), 489–502.

Huber, B., Highfield, K. and Kaufman, J. (2018). Detailing the digital experience: parent reports of children's media use in the home learning environment. *British Journal of Educational Technology*, 49(5), 821–33.

Kervin, L. (2016). Powerful and playful literacy learning with digital technologies. *Australian Journal of Language and Literacy*, 39(1), 64–73.

Koops, L. H. and Webber, S. C. (2020). 'Something is better than nothing': early childhood caregiver–child music classes taught remotely in the time of COVID-19. *International Journal of Music in Early Childhood*, 15(2), 135–56.

Lev, Y. B. and Elias, N. (2020). Digital parenting: media uses in parenting routines during the first two years of life. *Studies in Media and Communication*, 8(2), 41–8.

Livingstone, S. and Blum-Ross, A. (2020) *Parenting for a Digital Future: How Hopes and Fears about Technology Shape Children's Lives*. London: Oxford University Press.

Marsh, J., Lahmar, J., Plowman, L., Yamada-Rice, D., Bishop, J. and Scott, F. (2021). Under threes' play with tablets. *Journal of Early Childhood Research*, 19(3), 283–97.

Neumann, M. M., Merchant, G. and Burnett, C. (2020). Young children and tablets: the views of parents and teachers. *Early Child Development and Care*, 190(11), 1750–61.

Oakley, G., Wildy, H. and Berman, Y. E. (2020). Multimodal digital text creation using tablets and open-ended creative apps to improve the literacy learning of children in early childhood classrooms. *Journal of Early Childhood Literacy*, 20(4), 655–79.

Picherot, G., Cheymol, J., Assathiany, R., Barthet-Derrien, M. S., Bidet-Emeriau, M., Blocquaux, S., Carbajal, R., Caron, F. M., Gerard, O., Hinterman, M., Houde, O., Jollivet, C., Le Heuzey, M. F., Mielle, A., Ogrizek, M., Rocher, B., Samson, B., Ronziere, V. and Foucaud, P. (2018). Children and screens: Groupe de Pediatrie Generale (Societe francaise de pediatrie) guidelines for pediatricians and families. *Archives De Pediatrie*, 25(2), 170–4.

Plowman, L. (2020). *Digital Play*. Available at: www.de.ed.ac.uk/sites/default/files/2020-07/Digital%20Play%20-%20Plowman%202020.pdf. Accessed 15 October 2024.

Plowman, L. and McPake, J. (2013). Seven myths about young children and technology. *Childhood Education*, 89(1), 27–33.

Plowman, L., McPake, J. and Stephen, C. (2008). Just picking it up? Young children learning with technology at home. *Cambridge Journal of Education*, 38(3), 303–19.

Plowman, L., Stephen, C. and McPake, J. (2010). *Growing Up With Technology: Young Children Learning in a Digital World*. London: Taylor & Francis.

Potter, J. and Cowan, K. (2020). Playground as meaning-making space: multimodal making and re-making of meaning in the (virtual) playground. *Global Studies of Childhood*, 10(3), 248–63.

Rogoff, B. (2008). Observing sociocultural activity on three planes: participatory appropriation, guided participation, and apprenticeship. *Pedagogy and Practice: Culture and Identities*, 58–74.

Rogoff, B., Paradise, R., Arauz, R. M., Correa-Chávez, M. and Angelillo, C. (2003). Firsthand learning through intent participation. *Annual Review of Psychology*, 54, 175–203.

Rosanda, V., Kavčič, T. and Istenič, A. (2022). Digital devices in early childhood play: digital technology in the first two years of slovene toddlers' lives. *Education and Self Development*, 17, 83–99.

Scott, F. and Marsh, J. (2018). Digital literacies in early childhood. In *Oxford Research Encyclopedia of Education*. Available at: https://oxfordre.com/education. Accessed 15 October 2024.

Scriven, B., Edwards-Groves, C. and Davidson, C. (2018). A young child's use of multiple technologies in the social organisation of a pretend telephone conversation. In S. Danby, M. Fleer, C. Davidson and M. Hatzigianni (eds), *Digital Childhoods: Technologies and Children's Everyday Lives*. New York: Springer, pp. 267–84.

Su, J., Ng, D. T. K. and Chu, S. K. W. (2023). Artificial intelligence (AI) literacy in early childhood education: the challenges and opportunities. *Computers and Education: Artificial Intelligence*, 4, 100124.

Takahashi, I., Obara, T., Ishikuro, M., Murakami, K., Ueno, F., Noda, A., Onuma, T., Shinoda, G., Nishimura, T., Tsuchiya, K. J. and Kuriyama, S. (2023). Screen time at age 1 year and communication and problem-solving developmental delay at 2 and 4 years. *JAMA Pediatrics*, 177(10), 1039–46.

Teichert, L., Anderson, A., Anderson, J., Hare, J. and Mctavish, M. (2021). Access and use of digital technologies in early childhood: a review of mixed messages in popular media. *Language and Literacy*, 23(3), 106–28.

Uprichard, E. (2008). Children as 'being and becomings': children, childhood and temporality. *Children and Society*, 22(4), 303–13.

Vidal-Hall, C., Flewitt, R. and Wyse, D. (2020). Early childhood practitioner beliefs about digital media: integrating technology into a child-centred classroom environment. *European Early Childhood Education Research Journal*, 28(2), 167–81.

Vygotsky, L. S. (2016). Play and its role in the mental development of the child. *International Research in Early Childhood Education*, 7(2), 3–25.

11
EARLY CHILDHOOD PLAY AND PEDAGOGY

Ruth Swailes

KEY DEFINITIONS

Agency: An individual's ability or freedom to act in accordance with their own wishes regardless of social context.

Executive function: A set of mental skills we use as adults every day to manage our daily lives. There are three key aspects to executive function:

- **working memory:** we draw on our working memory to make sense of the world around us, by relating what we are experiencing to previous experiences
- **impulse control:** being able to control impulses which might prevent success or cause distress for ourselves or others
- **cognitive flexibility:** being able to adapt and change as situations change.

Funds of knowledge: Cultural qualities recognised as the language, values and beliefs, prevailing and accepted perceptions learnt in social relationships (Riojas-Cortez, 2001; Moll et al., 1992; Barron, 2014).

(Continued)

Play: Considered as the medium in which children mediate and develop new forms of thinking by combining their internal ideas and cultural dispositions with external realities in the process of learning.

Self-regulation: Refers to the ability to control behaviour and manage thoughts and emotions in appropriate ways.

Serve and return: The back-and-forth interactions between adults and children that support brain development; these can be both verbal and non-verbal and start in infancy.

Taxonomy: The development of a scheme of classification or categorising items.

INTRODUCTION

Throughout history, play has been at the heart of young children's learning and development. Montessori described play as 'the work of the child' (Montessori, 2017); Isaacs identified play as being essential to children's emotional and cognitive growth (cited in Leaton Gray, 2022); and Froebel described play as 'the highest expression of human development in childhood, for it alone is the free expression of what is in the child's soul' (Froebel Trust, 2024). It would be impossible to envisage an early childhood education without play. Yet when we seek to define what we mean when we talk about play our definitions and understandings are very much affected by the lens through which we view the world.

Defining play has been a topic of ongoing discussion among academics. According to Gray (2016), play is both objective and subjective, encompassing both qualities of observed behaviour and feelings experienced during play. Contemporary researchers such as Chesworth (2016) have explored the nature of play in the curriculum and whether taking into account their interests or *funds of knowledge* builds children's agency in the curriculum. Jarvis (2006) explores the role of rough and tumble play, which is often discouraged in group settings. Hughes (2002) developed a 'taxonomy of different play types'. There is still a discussion regarding what constitutes play and the circumstances in which it should take place. In addition, a child's definition of play and an adult's definition of play can differ considerably (McInnes et al., 2013). According to Eberle (2014, p. 214, quoted in Bradbury and Swailes, 2022), 'play consists of six elements: anticipation, surprise, pleasure, understanding, strength, and poise'. According to Eberle, play must be defined by children having fun. According to Bottrill (2018, p. 26), play is creativity and should be defined rather than provided with a definition. Play means many different things to different people.

Play has also been categorised into several types by many different academics and theorists in Early Years. In 1933, Margaret Parten described play in ways which we still use today when discussing the way babies and young children interact with their world and each other (Parten, 1933). She identified unoccupied, solitary, onlooker, parallel, associative and cooperative play as clearly defined stages through which children progress as they mature and adapt to being part of larger social groups. Jean Piaget identified four stages of cognitive development: sensorimotor, pre-operational, concrete operational and formal operational, and four types of play: functional, constructive, symbolic and games with rules (1962). Later, Bob Hughes identified 15 subcategories of play as part of his playworker's taxonomy, eventually expanding to 16 (Hughes and Melville, 2002). Hughes' taxonomy identifies symbolic, rough and tumble, socio-dramatic, social, creative, communication, exploratory, fantasy, imaginative, locomotor, mastery, object, role, deep, dramatic and recapitulative. The taxonomy was developed because of the difficulties in defining what is meant by play and the nebulous and esoteric nature of defining play as a concept. Hughes believed that by providing this taxonomy he could support those working with children to ensure that a range of playful opportunities, covering all types of play, were provided and that play was given status and value.

Typically, play is seen as a pleasurable, spontaneous and non-goal-oriented activity that involves anticipation, flow and surprise (Barnett and Owens, 2015). The fact that we cannot always understand play from the child's perspective, or all of the feelings they experience while playing, can lead to some anxieties among less experienced practitioners. In our high-stakes accountability system, how can we hold play to account?

The UN Committee on the Rights of the Child (UNCRC) (2013) explains that play is associated with children and is essential to their holistic growth, learning and development. Play is now a UNCRC right in itself.

Article 31 states:

> Children's play is any behaviour, activity or process initiated, controlled, and structured by children themselves: it takes place whenever and wherever opportunities arise.
>
> (UNCRC, 2013, Article 31)

It is through play that children construct a sense of meaning about the world around them. Children's autonomy and independence within play are the central pillars of play (Tovey, 2020). With so many different types of play, multiple definitions and understandings, it is easy to see why what we initially think of as a quite simple and straightforward concept suddenly becomes infinitely more complex.

PEDAGOGY AND PLAY

It is widely accepted that play is an integral part of strong Early Years pedagogy and practice; this is highlighted in the Early Years Foundation Stage Framework:

> Play is essential for children's development, building their confidence as they learn to explore, relate to others, set their own goals and solve problems.
>
> (DfE, 2023, p. 17)

However, activities which may be described as play by some practitioners might be viewed as *playful teaching* by others. *Playful learning* experiences and practices are valued differently by educators, depending on their understanding of the nature of play. Play can also be dismissed as frivolous and be misunderstood by those who view it as 'just play'. The non-goal-oriented nature of free play may seem at odds with our goals-based curriculum.

> For Froebel, play was not located in discourses of outcomes or accountability.
>
> (Flannery Quinn, 2017, p. 29)

However, our whole educational landscape is driven by outcomes and external accountability. This has led to some practitioners questioning their approaches to teaching and learning when working with young children. How do we align what we know about young children's development and the value of play with a system that demands pre-defined outcomes for every action?

REFLECTION 11.1

How do practitioners maintain an effective balance between the demands of the statutory Early Years curriculum and building on children's funds of knowledge to support their learning?

The place of play within Early Years pedagogy, though established over many years, is still widely discussed and contested by many in the wider education field. Those with considerable experience in Early Years understand the power and importance of play and its place within children's learning, but for some outside of the sector it can be viewed as frivolous and a waste of learning time. They also recognise the importance of providing a range of different play opportunities to meet the unique needs of children as they grow and develop. However, over the last decade, the growing influence of agencies such as Ofsted, the impact of ministers with pedagogical ideologies and their influence on initial teacher education and on teaching in general, have led to an increasing pressure to shift the balance away from play-based learning to pedagogy more suited to older children. The influence of teachers with limited or no experience of working with young children on government thinking from 2010 to 2024 has had considerable impact on the way play is viewed by many who work in the education sector, if not in early childhood.

WHERE ARE WE NOW?

Despite the widely recognised importance of play for children's wellbeing, social and cognitive development, over the last decade there has been a steady erosion of the value placed on play in English schools, particularly towards the end of the early childhood in Reception, Year 1 and Year 2 classes. The pressure to move to more formal learning earlier than ever before has been growing since the publication, by Ofsted, of *Bold Beginnings* in 2017, which stated;

> Some headteachers did not believe in the notion of free play. They viewed playing without boundaries as too rosy and unrealistic a view of childhood. They believed adults, including most parents, have always imposed limits on children's play, setting boundaries about when to be home and where children could go with friends.
>
> (Ofsted, 2017, p. 16)

The inclusion of this statement in Ofsted's report on the Reception curriculum seems to imply that the headteachers involved believed that the general consensus at the time of this report was that children should play without boundaries, yet the Early Years Statutory Framework (DfE, 2023) did not require such practice and this would not have been considered best practice by anyone with a strong understanding of effective pedagogy.

The report highlights several misconceptions about play, what it is and how it supports children's learning:

> Play, for example, was used primarily for developing children's personal, social, and emotional skills.
>
> (Ofsted, 2017, p. 16)

The report identifies that play is important, but seems to consider it a separate endeavour to teaching:

> Play was an important part of the curriculum in all of the schools visited. The headteachers knew which aspects of learning needed to be taught directly and which could be learned through play.
>
> (Ofsted, 2017, p. 5)

This is directly at odds with the definition of teaching in Early Years which Ofsted developed only two years before *Bold Beginnings*, and which is still present in the Ofsted *School Inspection Framework* (gov.uk, 2024b, paragraph 435) and the *Early Years Inspection Framework* (gov.uk, 2024a, paragraph 186). Ofsted define teaching as:

Teaching is a broad term that covers the many ways in which adults help young children learn. It includes their interactions with children during planned and child-initiated play and activities: communicating and modelling language; showing, explaining, demonstrating, exploring ideas; encouraging, questioning, recalling; providing a narrative for what they are doing; facilitating and setting challenges.

(gov.uk, 2024a, para 435a: 186b)

There is a lack of clarity and understanding around the role of play, expectations placed on practitioners regarding play and the impact and importance of play on young children's learning.

Certainly, it can be argued that Ofsted does not seem to place a great deal of importance on play in the Early Years. In both the school and Early Years inspection frameworks, play is barely mentioned. In the school framework the word 'play' appears once in the 'Good' descriptor for Early Years education, and it is within the context of physical development:

They [Teachers] teach children to take managed risks and challenges as they play and learn, supporting them to be active and develop physically.

(gov.uk, 2024b, para. 478)

In contrast, 'reading' appears seven times in the good descriptor, 'phonics' five times and 'curriculum' eight times. The word 'play' does not feature in the 'Outstanding' descriptor in the school framework, nor does it feature beyond the Foundation Stage; it seems play after the age of five is not important to Ofsted. Researchers such as Fisher (2020) have highlighted the importance of a play-based curriculum beyond Reception. Fisher highlights that the pressures faced by Early Educators and children in settings and schools are often a result of a perceived lack of alignment between the Early Years and primary curriculum, rather than the needs of the children. The *school readiness agenda* leads to pressure and play becomes a casualty of preparing for the next stage. Moreover, Bradbury (2024) argues play can be viewed as counter-discourse to an emerging formal curriculum.

However, the evidence suggests that Ofsted does not necessarily recognise the value and importance of play. Why does this matter? As the main arbiter of quality in education in the current system, the lack of focus on play in the Ofsted frameworks could lead to its further marginalisation at the expense of curriculum and phonics, which feature heavily in both frameworks. While these are important, they do not develop in isolation; indeed there is much research to show that play provides a wealth of opportunities to support children's learning across all domains.

Play provides the natural, imaginative and motivating contexts for children to learn about themselves, one another and the world around them. A single moment of sustained play can afford children many developmental experiences at once, covering multiple areas of learning.

(Ofsted, 2017, p. 8)

WHY IS PLAY IMPORTANT?

Bradbury and Swailes (2022) argue that early childhood education settings today are influenced by the theories and practices of child development theorists. Despite the differences between the theories of Froebel, McMillan, Vygotsky, Montessori and Piaget regarding the definition of learning for children, they all agree on the importance of play and that it is an innate and natural urge to explore and comprehend the world around them.

Neuroscience and research that supports these claims have identified that children demonstrate higher levels of motivation, self-esteem and engagement as well as higher levels of emotional wellbeing (McInnes et al., 2013). Goswami and Bryant (2007) also report evidence from neuroscience that learning depends on neural pathways developing across visual, auditory and kinaesthetic brain regions and that multisensory experiences and active learning are vital. Both freely chosen and guided play are crucial for facilitating both social and academic development. In addition to providing opportunities for children to learn to interact with the environment, adults and other children, play also promotes the development of responsive relationships. As a result of interactions through play, children can strengthen their connections between what they know and what they observe in the world around them.

In the brain, neural connections establish the basis for learning, as well as establishing the basis for thinking, knowledge, behaviour and general life skills. As a result of interactions within the environment or with other individuals, what is known as *serve and return interactions* are facilitated; these help to develop early brain architecture (Harvard, n.d.). The development of language, which the DfE identifies as underpinning all other areas of learning, relies heavily on this serve and return interaction. Stagnitti et al. (2016) investigated the impact of pretend play skills and oral language. The results suggested that, in addition to improving narrative language and play skills, a play-based curriculum had a positive impact on grammar acquisition. By interacting with their world, children can make sense of their world through experiences that are rich in learning patterns that support their development.

Play-based learning supports young children's development by providing them with a sense of agency in their own learning. By identifying and supporting children's individual interests, skilled practitioners can build on what children already know and understand, make links with their prior learning, and develop children's sense of themselves within the wider world. Derbyshire (2014) found that de-contextualised teaching content, which did not consider the life experiences and cultural values of the children, can lead to learning being inaccessible to the children and undermine their confidence. When children are playing, they draw upon their own experiences to help them to make sense of their world and incorporate new experiences into their knowledge. Thus, their understanding of the world, and their role within it grows. Campbell-Barr et al. (2023) state that an expressive curriculum values and builds on the child's autonomy and creates space for active and authentic participation. By valuing children's play we can support children to become active agents in their learning. Learning through play supports overall healthy development, acquisition of knowledge and learning to learn skills (e.g. planning, exploring, evaluating, reviewing) (Zosh et al., 2017).

Whitebread et al. (2007) identified that young children are born with the capacity to develop these skills, but need adult support through effective interaction to do so. They also highlighted the link between the development of self-regulation and executive function, and the development of language, which they stated was central to the entire process of developing these skills. They noted that young children were able to develop these skills in quite sophisticated ways when they were engaged in pretend play. A child can become more resilient through play when they can test out theories, take risks and solve problems in a safe environment without fear of failure.

GETTING THE BALANCE RIGHT

The misconceptions around play highlighted in the 'Bold Beginnings' report must be addressed if we are to ensure that play is given the status it deserves in the Early Years curriculum. Play is enshrined in the UNCRC (see Article 31, as shown on p. 131). As we have already established, there are many types of play, and many definitions of play. It is worth noting that the English statutory curriculum states:

> Children learn by leading their own play, and by taking part in play which is guided by adults.
>
> (DfE, 2023, p. 17)

It is important that there is an effective balance of child-led play, more structured and guided play, and playful learning activities. Practitioners need to decide on the correct balance based on their knowledge of the children they work with. This will vary from year to year and sometimes even change week to week, depending on the needs of the children.

Froebel presented children with 'gifts', which were open-ended resources to promote imagination and discover, as well as 'occupations' to support the development of life skills. The Froebelian principle of *freedom with guidance* (Froebel Trust, 2024) can be helpful when considering how to incorporate play effectively into our work with children and how to manage the balance between adult-led learning and child-initiated play.

Adults provide many types of guidance within the learning environment. The structure of the day, the way resources and furniture are organised, the questions and comments made when working with the children in the provision, and modelling how to use resources are all forms of guidance. Sometimes the *guidance* will resemble what our colleagues in primary schools might recognise in their own *teaching*. The challenge is to provide enough freedom to allow children to develop their sense of agency, to nurture their curiosity and critical thinking, to support the development of their resilience, motivation and engagement, while ensuring there is sufficient guidance to support children to make connections with their prior learning and deepen what they already know – to provide windows to the wider world and nurture their innate curiosity while retaining the joy and wonder of early childhood.

FIVE KEY TAKEAWAYS

1. Play must be at the heart of our early childhood curriculum; it should not have to fight for a place in the school day.
2. Rich, meaningful and playful opportunities that connect with young children's experiences and reflect their prior knowledge should be the basis for all curriculum development.
3. All adults who have influence on policy and practice in schools and settings must be supported to understand the power and importance of play in young children's development. Misconceptions about play must be addressed.
4. Play should be given more prominence within the Ofsted inspection framework in both the Early Years and the school handbooks.
5. Play provides a wealth of opportunities to develop vital skills in early childhood and needs to be valued in its own right; it should be included in teacher education programmes alongside early child development studies.

CONCLUSION

Children learn through play. It is the way in which they form friendships, how they formulate and test ideas, and how they make sense of their surroundings. There is a wealth of literature and research demonstrating how play facilitates learning. The provision of space for play, particularly in school settings where there is a tension between playful learning and the structure of most school curriculums, is vital. As adults we have the power and opportunity to facilitate high-quality spaces for play and to show that we value play as a significant part of our Early Years curriculum. By participating in play with children, providing time and space for play and advocating for a play-based curriculum, we send a clear message to the rest of the education sector that play matters – in fact, that it is vital for the next generation of learners. In order to promote a play-positive culture we must advocate for play, explain why play matters, ensure that we provide high-quality play opportunities and be open to challenge and discussion both within and beyond the sector.

REFERENCES

Barnett, L. and Owens, M. (2015). Does play have to be playful? In J. Johnson, S. Eberle, T. Henricks and D. Kuschner (eds), *The Handbook of the Study of Play*. Lanham: Rowan & Littlefield, pp. 453–9.

Barron, I. (2014). Finding a voice: a figured worlds approach to theorising young children's identities. *Journal of Early Childhood Research*, 12(3), 251–63.

Bottrill, G. (2018). *Can I Go and Play Now?* Thousand Oaks: Corwin.

Bradbury, A. (2024). The early years and play: the last bastion for democracy. *Research Intelligence*. BERA. 160. Available at: www.bera.ac.uk/publication/autumn-2024. Accessed 16 August 2024.

Bradbury, A. and Swailes, R. (2022). *Early Childhood Theories Today*. London: Learning Matters.

Campbell-Barr, V., Evans, K., Georgeson, J. and Tragenza, S. (2023). *Insights into a High Quality Early Years Curriculum*. Montessori Global Education/University of Plymouth. Available at: https://montessori-globaleducation.org/wp-content/uploads/2023/05/A-high-quality-early-years-curriculum.pdf. Accessed 12 July 2024.

Chesworth, L. (2016). A funds of knowledge approach to examining play interests: listening to children's and parents' perspectives. *International Journal of Early Years Education*, 24(3), 294–308.

Department for Education (DfE) (2023). *Statutory Framework for the Early Years Foundation Stage*. Available at: www.gov.uk/government/publications/early-years-foundation-stage-framework--2. Accessed 1 July 2024.

Derbyshire, N., Finn, B., Griggs, S. and Ford, C. (2014). An unsure start for young children in English urban primary schools. *Urban Review*, 46, 816–30.

Fisher, J. (2020). *Moving on to Key Stage One*. London: Open University Press.

Flannery Quinn, S. (2017) Locating play today. In T. Bruce, P. Hakkarainen and M. Bredikyte (eds), *The Routledge International Handbook of Early Childhood Play*. Abingdon: Routledge.

Froebel Trust (2024). *The Power of Play*. Available at: www.froebel.org.uk/about-us/the-power-of-play. Accessed 10 July 2024.

Goswami, U. and Bryant, P. (2007). *Children's Cognitive Development and Learning. Primary Review Research Survey 2/1a*. Cambridge: University of Cambridge Faculty of Education.

gov.uk (2024a). *Early Years Inspection Handbook*. Ofsted. Available at: www.gov.uk/government/publications/early-years-inspection-handbook-eif/early-years-inspection-handbook-for-ofsted-registered-provision-for-september-2023. Accessed 1 July 2024.

gov.uk (2024b). *Schools Inspection Handbook*. Ofsted. Available at: www.gov.uk/government/publications/school-inspection-handbook-eif. Accessed 1 July 2024.

Gray, P. (2016). Children's natural ways of learning still work: even for the three Rs. In D. C. Geary and D. B. Berch (eds), *Evolutionary Perspectives on Child Development and Education*. New York: Springer, pp. 63–93.

Harvard University (n.d.). *Brain Architecture*. Available at: https://developingchild.harvard.edu/science/key-concepts/brain-architecture/. Accessed 1 August 2024.

Hughes, B. (2002). *A Playworker's Taxonomy of Play Types*. 2nd edn. London: Playlink.

Hughes, B. and Melville, S. (2002). *A Playworker's Taxonomy of Play Types*. London: Playlink.

Jarvis, P. (2006). 'Rough and tumble' play: lessons in life. *Evolutionary Psychology*, 4(1), 147470490600400.

Leaton Gray, S. (2022). Phantasy and play: Susan Isaacs and child development. *London Review of Education*, 20(1), 40.

McInnes, K., Howard, J., Crowley, K. and Miles, G. (2013). The nature of adult–child interaction in the Early Years' classroom: implications for children's perceptions of play and subsequent learning behaviour. *European Early Childhood Education Research Journal*, 21(2), 268–82.

Moll, L. C., Amanti, C., Neff, D. and Gonzalez, N. (1992). Funds of knowledge for teaching: using a qualitative approach to connect homes and classrooms. *Theory into Practice*, 31(2), 132–41.

Montessori, M. (2017). *Maria Montessori Speaks to Parents: A Selection of Articles*. The Montessori Series, Vol. 21. Available at: www.amazon.com/Maria-Montessori-Speaks-Parents-Selection/dp/9079506362. Accessed 17 July 2024.

Ofsted (2017). *Reception Curriculum in Good and Outstanding Primary Schools: Bold Beginnings*. Available at: www.gov.uk/government/publications/reception-curriculum-in-good-and-outstanding-primary-schools-bold-beginnings. Accessed 4 July 2024.

Parten, M. B. (1933). Social play among preschool children. *Journal of Abnormal and Social Psychology*, 28(2), 136–47.

Piaget, J. (1962). *Play, Dreams, and Imitation in Childhood*. New York: Norton.

Riojas-Cortez, M. (2001). Preschoolers' funds of knowledge displayed through sociodramatic play episodes in a bilingual classroom. *Early Childhood Education Journal*, 29(1), 35–40.

Stagnitti, K., Bailey, A., Reynolds, E. H. and Kidd, E. (2016). An investigation into the effect of play based instruction on the development of play skills and oral language. *Journal of Early Childhood Research*, 14(4), 389–406.

Tovey, H. (2020). *Froebel's Principles and Practice Today*. Roehampton: Froebel Trust.

UN Committee on the Rights of the Child (UNCRC) (2013). *General comment no. 14 (2013) on the right of the child to have his or her best interests taken as primary consideration (art. 3, para. 1)*. Available at: https://digitallibrary.un.org/record/778523?ln=en. Accessed 1 July 2024.

Whitebread, D., Bingham, S., Grau, V., Pino Pasternak, D. and Sangster, C. (2007). Development of metacognition and self-regulated learning in young children: role of collaborative and peer assisted learning. *Journal of Cognitive Education and Psychology*, 6(3), 433–55.

Zosh, J. M., Hopkins, E. J., Jensen, H., Liu, C., Neale, D., Hirsh-Pasek, K., Solis, S. L. and Whitebread, D. (2017). *Learning Through Play: A Review of the Evidence*. Billund, Denmark: Lego Foundation.

12
SOCIAL CONTEXTS OF EARLY CHILDHOOD

Dr Sharon Colilles

KEY DEFINITIONS

Agency: An individual's ability or freedom to act in accordance with their own wishes regardless of social context.

Funds of knowledge: Cultural qualities recognised as the language, values and beliefs, prevailing and accepted perceptions learnt in social relationships (Riojas-Cortez, 2001; Moll et al., 1992; Barron, 2014).

Interaction: The social contexts within which practitioners and children engage which constitute and shape child development and learning.

Participatory approach: Learning associated with the co-construction of knowledge and skills stemming from a combination of adult-directed and child-enacted experiences.

Play: Considered as the medium in which children mediate and develop new forms of thinking by combining their internal ideas and cultural dispositions with external realities in the process of learning.

INTRODUCTION

Early childhood is a remarkable time in terms of the growth and development of cognition, language, social emotional and physical competence. It is recognised that this development occurs in different social contexts where issues relating to human diversity impact significantly on children's meaning-making and ways of being in the world. Understanding that children are unique individuals is perhaps the most important principle to grasp when thinking about the social contexts in which they develop. Besides physical and psychological differences, every one of us brings together our own individual combination of ethnicity, cultural and social background, not to mention protected characteristics of age, disability, gender, race, sex, religion or belief, sexual orientation (Equality Act, 2010). Correspondingly, early learning theories drawn from all over the world have researched and debated explanations about the nature and purpose of how children learn and develop – from debate surrounding nature, where thinking tends to consider learning as a *behaviour* in which both children and adults engage and learning occurs when the learner is taught and in some way responds to what is being taught, to *nurture* debate that presents the notion that learning behaviours have more to do with a construction and reconstruction by the learner through actions that make sense to the child alone, but which could be guided by the more experienced other.

It would be remiss not to consider the influence of policy and curriculums on children's learning and development where it could be arguably perceived that attention has been given to Vygotskian (1962) theorisations which view the adult as the co-constructor of higher conceptual learning, to more contemporary research that provides insight and understanding about children as having dispositions to learning (Wood, 2014). Principles that also appear to have influenced the design of curriculum learning outcomes stem from notions that see children through the lens of Piagetian (1971) thinking, ideologies that suggest children construct learning through participation. In addition, perspectives drawn from neuroscience have had a highly significant impact in shaping understanding about children being 'natural seekers after pattern and hence meaning' (Moyles, 2005, p. 7), so practices should relate directly to them and involve first-hand experiences as a basis for lasting learning. Taken together, these insights can be seen to have significantly informed both policy and the pedagogical approaches seen in the 21st century.

This chapter, however, attempts to take as its focus social contexts that may serve to reshape attitudes surrounding child development, learning and ways of behaviour for 21st-century Britain. It recognises that sociology is a complex area as it is a subject that studies human societies. However, it seems timely to look back, reset and make a wish for the future for social contexts in early childhood.

THE PROBLEMATIC NATURE OF EARLY CHILDHOOD EDUCATION

The history of early childhood policy and curriculums reform in England is highly significant when considering contexts that have had a societal impact. Until recently, changes in statutory Early Years curriculum development (DCSF, 2008, to DfE, 2023) appear to have placed limited focus in guidance to address social inequities for disadvantaged groupings of children and their families. Witnessed is a distinct top-down nature of policy development, one in which a prescriptive and assessment-driven Early Years agenda exists. Over a decade ago, Ang (2010) recognised that monitoring, measuring and assessing children's learning are increasingly significant factors in Early Years practice in the UK. Coupled with the dominance of a *school readiness* rhetoric and government preoccupation with early education as a preparation for later schooling, this gives rise for concern about the role of early education and, more significantly, the agency of Early Years professionals.

Demonstration of professional agency is closely related or intertwined with social settings and with other people (Vähäsantanen, 2014). At an individual level, agency can be likened to the teacher's professional identity, competencies and work experiences, whereas notions at a social level suggest agency relates to the management culture of the organisation (early childhood provision) and teachers' professional relationships. Of course, issues surrounding the professionalisation of the Early Years workforce are important for supporting comprehension about the problematic nature of pedagogy and practice.

Research concerns associated with qualifications and professionalising the Early Years workforce to deliver high-quality experiences were raised well over a decade ago in the *Foundations for Quality* report (Nutbrown, 2012). It must be acknowledged that government did endeavour to address some of the recommendations made in the report in the *Early Years Workforce Strategy* (DfE, 2017); nonetheless, efforts to 'shift' attitudes towards developing professional practice based on incorporating knowledge of child development and learning rather than a dominance towards care routines remain problematic in the present day.

CHANGING VIEWS OF THE DEVELOPMENTAL CHILD

Correspondingly, contexts that also appear to have influenced curriculum design and curriculum learning outcomes still appear to stem from notions that see children through the lens of Piagetian (1971) thinking – particularly an established discourse that views the child as a passive recipient of learning from the knowledge of the adult. For me, traditional theories that propose stages and ages of development as well as always assuming distinct universal features applicable to all children, and in all societies, can no longer be applied to descriptions about the developmental child of today. Judgements using these descriptions appear contextually limited if they choose to ignore social and cultural influences (Dahlberg et al., 2007) as these judgements and approaches serve to invalidate and influence children's agentic ways of being. It therefore seems somewhat timely to reshape notions of deficit and seeing children as passive learners to one which situates children as being competent, creative and capable participants in educational processes – conceptions where the child is enabled to demonstrate strong behaviours of mind and are driven by habits to socially interact and connect with those around them. Co-creating conditions where the child can connect with the environment as educator and facilitator of learning (Rinaldi, 2006) is congruent with supporting the child of today. This chapter seeks movement towards a lens that informs new ways of knowing, one which enhances and transforms principal models of pedagogical understanding about how children can be involved more actively in educational processes.

SOCIAL CONTEXTS – NEW WAYS OF KNOWING: EARLY CHILDHOOD INTO THE FUTURE

Acknowledging that educational contexts can mean different things to different individuals, enduring perspectives in scholarly debate position a discourse of teaching for social justice; respecting and valuing difference and similarity in early childhood education; and raising critical consciousness (Freire, 1970). Inspired by strategies for raising consciousness, approaches of empowerment and the development of self-efficacy for children (as well as practitioners) present convincing perspectives for early childhood contexts. Embracing the view that pedagogy-in-participation exercises consciousness, Formosinho and Pascal (2016) reason:

> democracy develops in a context of respect for human rights … and of identity development for children and professionals which is also an educative process of self-identity development of themselves and others as learners.

(2016, p. 30)

From birth, children make active spontaneous attempts to understand and interpret their 'world'. Insights from research suggest children's social attitudes are communicated, shaped and shared in the social contexts in which they are situated. Synthesising philosophies associated with rights to participate (UNCRC, 1989) and young children's capacity for sharing knowledge highlight young children will bring rich cultural knowledge into their play and learning repertoires, usually acquired from shared experiences in the home and wider community. Defined as *funds of knowledge* (FOK) these cultural qualities are recognised as the language, values and beliefs, prevailing and accepted perceptions learnt in social relationships (Barron, 2014; Riojas-Cortez, 2001; Moll et al., 1992). It is this essential component of children's knowledge, along with the vehicle of play, that brings the cultural dispositions of the child into learning processes.

Utilising children's internalised cultural knowledge in planned experiences should be the cornerstone for facilitating interaction between the educator and child in early childhood education practices. For me, the process of learning new things such as using a knife and fork are fundamentally the same as processes associated with learning social attitudes. Arguably, children learn not only what to do but how things are seen from the lens of the significant adults surrounding them. While doing so they are also constructing for themselves a description of the world. Additionally, the way in which children make sense of the world around them can be seen through observation of their play repertoires, where they will revisit and reconstruct lived experiences that have been previously internalised. Positioning a focus on play is therefore paramount for providing insights about the social contexts in which children learn and develop.

THE CENTRALITY OF PLAY

Articulated in research is the importance of play as an invaluable vehicle for supporting young children's learning and development. Credible arguments focused on promoting the benefits of play in education and child development can be found in many historic bodies of work. Erikson (1963), for example, considered the historic meaning of pretend play rituals and its potential for giving children power and control of emotions from early childhood and throughout life. Piagetian (1971) theorisations relating to stages of play development differentiated play from processes of imitation to processes of assimilation, where, it was considered, children use play to construct knowledge of the world by trying to connect new experiences to their existing cognitive schema. Similarly, seen in Vygotskyian (1962) theorisation are thoughts about internalisation processes and how they constitute the law of transformation of the external into the internal. In support with this theorisation, Broadhead and Burt (2012) suggest Vygotsky's theorisations provide a lens for understanding that play is a process in which children mediate and develop new forms of thinking, where they combine internal ideas with external realities.

While not always in agreement about its status and form, early pioneers such as Froebel, Montessori, McMillan and Issacs all identified and promoted play as an essential element of children's learning. Their theorisation and philosophies informed our understanding about the need for rich and stimulating environments (particularly the outdoors), and that through imaginative play children learn at the highest level. Scholarly debate also informs perspectives about play being essential for emotional and cognitive development. Pioneers such as Bruce and Hughes continue to provide insight for pedagogy and practice about features of free flow play, choice and types of play for supporting children's learning.

While there may be differences between rhetoric and reality about definitions of what play is, there does appear to be a consensus that children will draw from and re-engage with experiences as a means of understanding their social worlds, where their use of play can be seen as an accommodating tool for mediation in interactions between peers and practitioners.

Understanding how children shape their sense of self in social contexts is key for shaping the confident and competent learner of the future. I also contend that consideration should be given to those children who may not experience play as defined in traditional scholarly theorisation. It is important to recognise that some young learners may not know how to play or what being playful is. Children who could need the support of peers and practitioners may be those facing the trauma of war, or those in need of protection from harm, as well as the post-pandemic child. Developing slow knowledge and an unhurried approach to learning (Clark, 2023) via creative alternative experiences and making effective use of an enabling play-based pedagogical approach (Colilles, 2020) will be an essential component for ensuring children's varying developmental needs are met.

In continuing to build a case for the use of play I turn to the *characteristics of effective learning* (CoEL) in an endeavour to make clear how play can provide outcomes to emerge associated with a child's many ways of being in learning processes. Defined by the statutory framework (DfE, 2023, 1.13) as:

- *playing and exploring* – children investigate and experience things and 'have a go'
- *active learning* – children concentrate and keep on trying even if they encounter difficulties and enjoy achievements
- *creating and thinking critically* – children have and develop their own ideas, make links between ideas, and develop strategies for doing things.

Moylett (2024) helpfully guides the educator to understand that CoEL are 'universal lifelong learning skills' where all three can be observed in everyday practice. What is significant when contemplating social contexts in early childhood education is the need to recognise that these learning behaviours not only underpin all areas of learning in the Early Years Foundation Stage (EYFS), but also relate to behaviours that characterise how children learn in their play endeavours. Offered for deliberation is a proposal that play and playful learning is the best preparation for more formalised and structured processes in later learning, but what is most beneficial for supporting a child's disposition to learn is a love of learning itself.

In concluding this section, it can be questionably positioned that children have the right to use this medium as a form of expression and communication in their learning because there is compelling evidence in educational research to suggest (in its many forms of expression) play belongs to the child; indeed, the young learner is a master of play. Play can therefore act as a significant vehicle for tuning in to and engaging with the thoughts of our youngest learners. Indeed, play is the *work* of children.

ENABLING ENVIRONMENTS

Social contexts in early childhood cannot be considered without positioning the value of an enabling environment. The importance of social and environmental influences on children's learning and development can be seen in Vygotskyian insights (1962) which placed an emphasis on activity as the basis for children's learning and for the development of thinking. This chapter previously contended young children's disposition to learn and develop stem from their active attempts to interact and make meaning of the world around them. Encounters and experiences in their inhabited worlds create for children inner dialogues that form the process of mental self-regulation. Sociocultural debate provides evidence that within these social situations children learn 'names' and 'labels' in interactions with significant others (family, peers and educators) within their immediate environment. For me, the enabling learning environment in modern-day learning environments in England must offer opportunities for the diverse learner to reconnect with an ethnic/racial identity, heritage, traditions and customs to meet the cultural needs of children. When play and culturally appropriate materials become central and embedded in the learning environment children are afforded opportunities to take things that they already know and combine them with new ways of knowing so that their understanding deepens. A responsive and value-based environment creates contexts in which equity of outcomes prevail, particularly where the environment and the resources utilised within it create contexts for exploration, imagination, creativity and participation for *all* children. An enabling environment will also consider contexts that support young children to connect home-setting cultures. Here an affordance for deep explorations in play, time and space in a slow play-based pedagogical approach is highly beneficial for all children, but even more so when the child can see themselves in the educational process. Essentially, the central role of the early childhood educator is to establish a learning environment which listens to, hears and responds to young children.

A RIGHTS-BASED APPROACH

When reflecting on children's right to participate, the UNCRC (1989) has made an important contribution towards perceptions of children as citizens with rights and has changed the landscape for early childhood education and care. At a policy level EYFS principles do acknowledge that 'every child is unique' (DfE, 2023, p. 7), as well as setting the legal requirement that:

> early years providers must guide the development of children's capabilities to help ensure that children in their care will fully benefit from future opportunities.
>
> (DfE, 2023, p. 8)

No one can argue that educational rights (priorities and goals) are related to children's right to participate in decisions that affect them. However, principled approaches in practice should mean adapting approaches to give voice to those children who may be silenced in the process of 'education'. Aligned with this perspective the influence of global and national research has significantly shaped awareness about the many ways that young children can and do express their opinions – from Malaguzzi's (1993) 100 languages, Rinaldi's (2006) concept of a pedagogy of listening, Clark and Moss's (2001) mosaic approach for listening to young children and Pascal and Bertram's (2009) thought-provoking perceptions about listening to the voices of young children that are silenced in the production of knowledge and understandings about their lives.

A rights-based approach is not one that is solely dependent on the dominance of top-down, target-driven methods, where achievement is solely seen in terms of achieving curricular goals. An early childhood teaching approach should not be solely premised on preparation of children for future stages of learning. Key features of a participatory approach should involve learning associated with the co-construction of knowledge and skills formulated in rich dialogic conversations with children that stem from a combination of adult-directed and child-enacted experiences, together with space for opportunities for play in accordance with curriculum goals.

PARTICIPATION AND THE ONGOING NEED FOR REFLECTION IN AND ON PRACTICE

This chapter has provided sound evidence to suggest why play should feature as a plausible approach within the early education framework (DfE, 2023). Children's capacities for agency incorporate their ability to create their own social and cultural worlds in their play repertoires (Colilles, 2020). Indeed, there is evidence in scholarly debate to show children's agency can be linked to the demonstration of skills and knowledge, as well as being a 'testing ground for whose freedom, power and control can be exercised' (Wood, 2014, p. 9). When questioning perceptions about 'power', consideration still appears to have been limited to the nature and purpose of adult intervention only in the EYFS (DfE, 2023). I believe that fostering children's engagement in a child-centric approach, alongside planned developmental play strategies, is needed to help children to manage socially complex situations such as enacting their right to participate in decision-making processes. In planning for and guiding learning it is imperative that early childhood educators have a clear understanding that children may have differing cultural understandings about what might be being shared. In these instances, it may be necessary to acknowledge and adapt participatory approaches in the planning of learning experiences. CoEL helpfully explain that characteristics are a myriad of ways of learning not a *sequence of progression* which it is recognised can be delayed. It is about understanding that some children may require different types of support than others. It is about validating the contributions that all children bring into the classroom and listening and responding to contributions (FOK) whether that meets the expected level of learning or not. Here I make the call for a slowing of pedagogy, for the creation of curriculums where the unhurried child (Clark, 2023) prevails – thus creating an affordance to enable reflection on and time for truly understanding the needs of the unique child.

Freire's suggestion that human activity consists of action and reflection is helpful for thinking about the role of reflective and reflexive practitioner. Contended are thoughts that 'if they [I interpret this to mean practitioners] are truly committed to liberation their action and reflection cannot proceed without the action and reflection of others [children]' (1970, p. 99). Educators who can reflect on their own values and attitudes in facilitating learning recognise the importance of planning for and implementing effective early childhood programmes that provide children with first-hand experiences to promote construction of knowledge that values cultural similarities and, more significantly, differences in children's learning capacities. I offer the perspective that construction of knowledge between educator and learner requires opportunities where children can lay stake to their perspectives, where co-creation in the process of learning provides opportunities for new ways of knowing and understanding to emerge. Principled, reflective and inclusive practitioners affirm cultural and linguistic identities and backgrounds. Acknowledged, however, is the reality that in practice this may be a problematic and complex concept, especially when adult interpretations and conceptions of rights, reflection on and action in practice may differ. Correspondingly, it is also acknowledged that children's agency to participate in the context of participation in planned curriculum experiences is complex.

FIVE KEY TAKEAWAYS

1. Children's rights to participate in decisions that affect them: principled approaches in pedagogical strategies.
2. Developing understanding about how social experiences constitute and shape child development and learning.
3. Positioning new ways of imagining early childhood into the future for the developmental child.
4. Raising awareness about the ongoing need for reflection in and on practice.
5. Promotion of the enduring importance of play as an invaluable vehicle for supporting young children's learning and development.

CONCLUSION

Among scholarly debate is the common goal of trying to understand how social experiences constitute and shape child development and learning. Whatever lens is chosen to reflect on social contexts in early childhood it is understood that different contexts and opportunities for social interaction determine the kinds of knowledge and meanings (Vygotsky, 1962) that young children will develop. When thinking about children's capacities and dispositions to engage as co-constructors of learning, plausible interpretations in this chapter view agency as an individual's ability or freedom to act in accordance with their own wishes regardless of social context. Other descriptions can be seen to view agency as being limited or in some way reduced when dominated by social structures. Whatever individualistic stance is chosen these explanations are significant when exploring notions about what children's agency and the Early Years professional influence on children's learning experiences looks like while implementing Early Years curriculum programmes. The power of the practitioner cannot be underestimated because they truly can take control of the process of schooling to drive forward what, for me, is the real purpose of Early Years education. I pause momentarily to acknowledge that many early childhood educators are deeply knowledgeable, resilient and care about outcomes for young children, but I also advocate for the educator who is courageous enough to seek a change of direction, is confident to develop their own knowledge and awareness about a participatory pedagogical approach that is inclusive of all children in their endeavours to seek social change. If I was afforded a magic wand the best outcomes for children would be that processes of schooling would be more significantly concerned with: promoting children's positive sense of self; facilitating children's confidence in who they are and how they fit in the world; structures where agency and rights of children to influence and shape their own learning trajectory are visible; and an early childhood education framework where a real positive love of learning through the vehicle of play is realised!

REFERENCES

Ang, L. (2010). Critical perspectives on cultural diversity in early childhood: building an inclusive curriculum and provision, Early Years. *International Research Journal*, *30*(1), 41–52.

Barron, I. (2014). Finding a voice: a figured worlds approach to theorising young children's identities. *Journal of Early Childhood Research*, *12*(3), 251–63.

Broadhead, P. and Burt, A. (2012). *Understanding Young Children's Learning Through Play: Building Playful Pedagogies*. London: Routledge.

Clark, A. (2023). *Slow Knowledge and the Unhurried Child: Time for Slow Pedagogies in Early Childhood Education*. London: Routledge.

Clark, A. and Moss, P. (2001). *Listening to Young Children: The Mosaic Approach*. London: National Children's Bureau and Joseph Rowntree Foundation.

Colilles, S. (2020). Exploring how play-based pedagogies support mixed ethnic identity formation. PhD, Bristol City University. Available at: www.open-access.bcu.ac.uk/id/eprint/11679. Accessed 16 October 2024.

Dahlberg, G., Moss, P. and Pence, A. (2007). *Beyond Quality in Early Childhood Education and Care: Languages of Evaluation*, 2nd ed. London: Falmer Press.

Department for Children Schools and Families (DCSF) (2008). *Statutory Framework for the Early Years Foundation Stage*. Available at: https://dera.ioe.ac.uk/id/eprint/6413/7/statutory-framework_Redacted.pdf. Accessed 1 July 2024.

Department for Education (DfE) (2017). *Early Years Workforce Strategy*. London: Crown copyright.

DfE (2023). *Statutory Framework for the Early Years Foundation Stage: Setting the Standards for Learning Development and Care for Children from Birth to Five*. Available at: https://assets.publishing.service.gov.uk/media/670fa42a30536cb92748328f/EYFS_statutory_framework_for_group_and_school_-_based_providers.pdf. Accessed 16 October 2024.

Early Years Coalition (2021). *Birth to 5 Matters: Non-Statutory Guidance for the Early Years Foundation Stage*. Available at: https://birthto5matters.org.uk/wp-content/uploads/2021/04/Birthto5Matters-download.pdf. Accessed 16 October 2024.

Equality Act (2010). London: HMSO.

Erikson, E. H. (1963). *Childhood and Society*. 2nd edn. New York: Norton.

Formosinho, J. and Pascal, C. (eds) (2016). *Assessment and Evaluation for Transformation in Early Childhood*. London: Routledge.

Freire, P. (1970). *Pedagogy of the Oppressed*. London: Continuum.

Malaguzzi, L. (1993). History idea and basic philosophy. In C. Edwards, L. Gandinin and G. Forman (eds), *The Hundred Languages of Children*. Norwood, NJ: Ablex.

Moll, L. C., Amanti, C., Neff, D. and Gonzalez, N. (1992). Funds of knowledge for teaching: using a qualitative approach to connect homes and classrooms. *Theory into Practice*, *31*(2),132–41.

Moyles, J. (2005). *The Excellence of Play*, 2nd ed. Maidenhead: Open University Press.

Moylett, H. (2024). Everything to play for: the characteristics of effective learning (CoEL). *Nursery World*, 2, 18–21.

Nutbrown, C. (2012). *Foundations for Quality: The Independent Review of Early Education and Childcare Qualifications (Nutbrown Review)*. Available at: www.gov.uk/government/uploads/system/uploads/attachment_data/file/175463/Nutbrown-Review.pdf. Accessed 16 October 2024.

Pascal, C. and Bertram, A. (2009). Listening to young citizens: the struggle to make real a participatory paradigm in research with young children. *European Early Childhood Education Research Journal*, *17*(2), 249–62.

Piaget, J. (1971). The theory of the stages in cognitive development. In L. Carmichael (ed.), *Carmichael's Manual of Child Psychology*. Vol. *1*. New York: Wiley, pp. 703–32.

Rinaldi, C. (2006.) *In Dialogue with Reggio Emilia*. London: Routledge.

Riojas-Cortez, M. (2001). Preschoolers' funds of knowledge displayed through sociodramatic play episodes in a bilingual classroom. *Early Childhood Education Journal*, *29*(1), 35–40.

UNCRC (1989). *United Nations Convention on the Rights of the Child*. Available at: www.2.ohchr.org/english/law/crc.htm. Accessed 24 June 2024.

Vähäsantanen, K. (2014). Professional agency in the steam of change: understanding educational change and teachers' professional identities. *Teaching and Teacher Education*, *47*, 1–12.

Vygotsky, L. S. (1962). *Thought and Language*. Cambridge, MA: MIT Press.

Wood, E. A. (2014). Free choice and free play in early childhood education: troubling the discourse. *International Journal of Early Years Education*, *22*(1), 4–18.

13
KEEPING CHILDREN SAFE IN A CHANGING WORLD

Professor Eunice Lumsden

> **KEY DEFINITIONS**
>
> **Safeguarding:** This is an umbrella term used to cover all aspects of child safety including health and safety and child abuse.
>
> **Child protection:** This includes legislation, policy, procedures and services to protect and support children from child abuse.
>
> **Child abuse:** This term is a generic term for all forms of abuse on children, including physical and emotional abuse, neglect, domestic violence and internet abuse.
>
> **Family support:** This embraces all the services available to support families in their parenting role.
>
> **Children's workforce:** This is a broad term that encompasses all the practitioners and professions for health, social care, education and Early Years that work with children and their families.

INTRODUCTION

In today's rapidly evolving world, the challenges and threats to safeguarding children from harm are more complex and multifaceted than ever before. In addition to the ongoing issues of child abuse, trauma and adverse experiences, children's safety is further compromised by digital technology, shifting social norms, economic fluctuations and environmental changes. Furthermore, the impact of social disadvantage on children cannot be ignored. This chapter explores the importance of a holistic approach to keeping children safe in a changing world. Three key themes will be explored, providing a framework for understanding the challenges and approaches to promote change. Firstly, there is a focus on the complex factors that impede keeping young children safe. Despite legislation, policy, professional training and family support, child abuse is still a major issue nationally and globally. The discussion will then explore intervention and support for families and the vital importance of a highly trained workforce that can work collaboratively to create lasting change.

UNDERSTANDING THE PROBLEM

I start this section by offering you two quotes which drive my work and help keep me focused when the challenges of keeping children safe from harm feels insurmountable. The first comes from the final work of Bronfenbrenner (2005). He was critical of governments for not providing resources to address the increasing challenges children were facing. As he argued 'the prospects for the future are hardly rosey' (Bronfenbrenner, 2005, p. 192). He challenged us to do something about this and, drawing on the words of Shakespeare, he states 'I offer to the prologue now, in advance, in the hope that others too may be moved to get into the act. "The play's the thing"' (Bronfenbrenner, 2005, p. 124). For me, this quote reinforces that our knowledge and understanding of human development and the factors that affect 'normal' development will always be an ongoing learning process. As he argues, our development continues to be impacted across the life course by the immediate environment people interact with and the interaction of these environments with the larger systems of society in which they are embedded. These can then be impacted by *chaos*, where different traumatic events such as abuse, war or natural disasters impact the life course through the under-researched *chaotic system*.

Arguably, this system has an important role in understanding the challenges that affect keeping children safe in a changing world, including the rapid rise in young children's engagement with online media. In 2023, Ofcom reported that 87 per cent of three- to four-year-olds in the UK used the internet, mainly to watch videos (Ofcom, 2023). It is also a system that allows us to explore the knowledge, skills and attributes those working in early childhood need and the support, guidance and information parents and carers need to keep their children safe. Ensuring that practitioners understand the issues and dangers of social media is crucial and so is supporting parents and carers on how they can enable their young children to use the internet safely. For example, parents and carers need to be aware of the risk of bullying, exposure to inappropriate content and the potential for children to be abused online. A recent report by the Internet Watch Foundation (IWF) (2023) found that child sexual abuse material available online was increasing, including self-generated pictures and an increase in photographs of primary school children.

The second quote is an important reminder that an appreciation of the impact of trauma, abuse and the effect of social disadvantage is not new:

> Though much remains to be learned about how to lay necessary foundations during the pre-school years, which will enable children to achieve eventually the fullest measure of their potential, yet enough is known to take some action now ... promoting optimal emotional, social and intellectual development; preventing neglect and deprivation; and, most difficult of all, for breaking into the vicious circle of the emotional or intellectually deprived children of today becoming tomorrow's parents of yet another generation of deprived children.
>
> (Pringle and Naidoo, 1975, p. 169)

Pringle and Naidoo were writing in 1975, yet their message is as relevant today as it was then. The difference now is that we do have research about human development and how adversity in early childhood can impact across the life course, yet the intergenerational cycle continues.

It also reinforces how difficult it is to ensure we keep all children safe and the crucial importance of focusing on prevention. In fact, the *Nurturing Care Framework* (WHO, 2018) clearly articulates that investing in early childhood, especially from birth to the age of three, is transformational for society and enables all infants and young children to flourish and achieve their full potential. However, the reality is that the youngest citizens in the world continue to be impacted by a whole raft of issues, including poverty, poor nutrition, housing, adverse experiences and trauma. Their safety is further compromised by the fast pace of technological change, the impact of social media and more recently the potential challenges that artificial intelligence brings.

If data from WHO (2022) is considered, around 300 million children between three and four years old globally experience physical or emotional abuse by their parents or carers. Data also emphasises that infants under one year old are most vulnerable to harm that leads to serious harm or death. For example, in England 36 per cent (142) of the 393 of the Serious Incident Notifications between 2022 and 2023 involved infants under the age of one (Child Safeguarding Review Panel, 2024). A further 16 per cent (63) were aged one to five, therefore over half of children killed or seriously harmed were under five years of age.

Key contributing factors to emerge for the under-one age group were:

- practitioners' challenges in recognising when babies were vulnerable
- how practitioners worked together in the same organisations and
- the perennial issues that impede interagency working.

These are important areas that are continually highlighted in Child Safeguarding Reviews (formerly Serious Case Reviews – see Sidebotham et al., 2016).

However, it is important to note that capturing the true extent of maltreatment globally is impossible. Definitions of what constitutes abuse and how data is collected are country specific. Importantly, maltreatment in early childhood can also be hidden as it often occurs in the privacy of the family home by parents, carers or family members who should be providing a safe environment. Even when it is detected, it does not mean that infants and young children are protected; the role of the state in intervening in family life is also country specific.

In England, legislation, policy and procedures exist to keep children safe, yet we know that actually protecting children is complex; even when services are working with families, children can still be harmed. As the Child Safeguarding Review Panel (2024) reported, many families involved in Serious Incident Notifications were already known to children's social care services, with neglect and domestic violence being significant contributing factors.

Young children's safety can also be compromised in the communities where they live and in the settings they attend. In England, the case of Genevieve Meehan, who died following being strapped face down in a bean bag reminds us of the vulnerability of young children, especially if settings lack appropriate leadership (Greater Manchester Police, 2024).

For some children, their safety is increasingly affected by war, conflict and migration, with the number affected rising exponentially since the 1990s. Around one in five children are impacted on by living with conflict and face long-term psychological harm as well as having to manage the life-changing consequences of being injured. In fact, children in the early childhood period are more likely to have long-term damage from blast injuries than any other age (Save the Children, 2023).

In summary, keeping young children safe is and will always be a work in progress. As well as the ongoing challenges of abuse, trauma and adverse experiences, young children continue to experience the impact of child poverty, war and displacement. They also have to contend with new threats that the digital world and global warming bring. It is in this context that the systems that support families, communities and practitioners need to be responsive to the shifting sands of keeping children safe.

ENABLING FAMILIES

If we are to ensure the safety and wellbeing of our children within their families and communities, we need to support families appropriately, especially with the ever-changing demands of parenting in a complex world. As the Children's Commissioner in England argues, the family has an important protective role by providing:

> emotional connection: love and joy; Shared experiences of family life; Strong, positive, and enduring relationships and the ability to depend on one another for practical and emotional support.
>
> (Children's Commissioner, 2022a, p. 48)

The *Family Review* she undertook (Children's Commissioner, 2022a, 2022b) indicated that families wanted to:

- get along and love one another;
- support themselves and each other;
- spend quality time together;
- trust and rely on each other.

> (Children's Commissioner, 2022b, p. 7)

Parents participating in the review articulated the importance of clear advice and guidance. They wanted practitioners to understand that parenting was challenging and did not want to be told how to parent or be judged, as parenting is hard.

However, providing timely and supportive services for families is, like keeping children safe, a work in progress. While there is a wider debate about what is meant by the term 'family support' (Featherstone, 2004; Frost et al., 2015), evidence clearly shows that families want and need multifaceted support that involves preventive measures, education and targeted interventions. In other words, services need to be provided that strengthen the family and the communities in which they reside. Formal support systems are also needed when more structured interventions are required. Moreover, the support offered needs to be research-informed and recognise that children's outcomes are improved if their home environments are sensitive and responsive to children's developmental needs (Melhuish and Gardiner, 2020).

Globally, the approaches to these areas will reflect political and policy priorities and the different perspectives on state involvement in family life. If we consider the UK, all four nations have different approaches to supporting the family. These are susceptible to political change and financial challenge. In Scotland and Wales, there is currently a strong focus on trauma-informed approaches to all aspects of work with children and families and workforce training (ACE Hub Wales, 2022; Scottish Government, 2022).

In England, there has been a more recent focus on the extensive research into the importance of the first 1,001 days of a baby's life, conception to the age of two, to improve outcomes for children across the life course (Early Years Healthy Development). This review and the subsequent *Best Start for Life* policy development (HM Government, 2021) was the first time a government had focused on this area in England. However, like all policy initiatives it is subject to political change and while there was cross-party agreement for this policy initiative there is no guarantee it will continue or indeed extend to all areas of England. (At the time of writing this chapter the UK has a new government and only time will tell what the direction of travel will be.)

Despite the volatile space family policy locates, there is no doubt that research reinforces the importance of enabling families through timely and appropriate support. The Early Years Healthy Development Review and a subsequent report from UNICEF (2022) highlighted that we must and can do better for families at the start of their journey to parenthood and beyond. We cannot meet the needs of our youngest citizens if parents do not know what support is available for them or where to access services. Both reports evidenced the national inconsistency of the quality and availability of services, with variations in maternity support, health visiting services and early childhood education and care provision.

It is important to note here that our maternity and health visiting services are crucial universal services for supporting new parents, the early identification of issues and safeguarding babies and young children. Yet these services have been eroded with huge regional variations. For example, one of the important measures for monitoring a baby's development is weight gain, yet the 'drop-in' weekly clinics have become eroded. These clinics have historically provided an important service for new parents, not only to make sure their baby is thriving but to get immediate answers to questions they may have. They also provided opportunities to meet other new parents and to intervene early if there were any concerns.

Early intervention, whether informally or formally, can make a huge difference in keeping children safe and providing families with the support they need. However, research by the Institute of Health Visiting (2024) provides a stark insight into the complex situation families in the UK are experiencing. When health visitors were asked about families being able to access services if they had a problem, only 7 per cent felt they would be able to. There was also considerable concern about the capacity of other services to support families, with 86 per cent indicating challenges of other services being able to accept referrals. Moreover, the health visitors who responded were clear that the assistance they could provide families was influenced by the geographical area they worked in rather than being driven by the needs of the family.

This section has just touched the tip of the iceberg in relation to the complexities of enabling families so that they have the knowledge and skills to keep their children safe. However, the key message is clear, to keep children safe their families need timely and appropriate support that starts at the beginning of their journey to become parents. The way this is provided varies globally, but if we consider the UK as an example, there is no consistency across the four nations. There is an ongoing decline in universal as well as more targeted support services, with a postcode rather than needs-led approach to services. Furthermore, family policy is susceptible to political change and while England has recognised the importance of investing in the first 1,001 days of life through *Best Start for Life* (HM Government, 2021), this is still in its infancy and there are no guarantees it will exist in its current format.

THE WORKFORCE MATTERS

In 2013, when I was part of the consultation process for the Sustainable Development Goals (SDGs) (UN, 2015), I was asked to produce one sentence of what I thought the early childhood workforce should look like. What I wrote then is still valid today:

> All children have the right to experience a professionalised early years workforce that supports, challenges and inspires those working within it, works in partnership with others and draws on inter-disciplinary knowledge to address inequality and promote all aspects of children's care, health, development and learning.
>
> (Lumsden, 2016)

In short, those working with families need the right knowledge and skills to meet the holistic developmental needs of children and support their families. However, I can often be found on top of an imaginary mountain shouting very loudly about the workforce working with young children and their families, the lack of investment and recognition of their vital role in keeping children safe. For decades I have shouted even more loudly about the lack of joined-up working between health, social care and early childhood education and care.

Early childhood is a flexible space occupied by diverse services, professionals and practitioners who should work together to ensure children are safe. Unfortunately, discrepancies in pay, working conditions and the power imbalances between different professional groups present real barriers to our collective responsibility to keep children safe. Time after time, Child Safeguarding Reviews highlight the systemic failings of agencies working together to protect children from harm. These challenges can be found elsewhere in the services for families; lack of interdisciplinary training and high caseloads were highlighted as barriers to working with families by the Early Years Healthy Development Review (HM Government, 2021).

If we are going to keep children safe in the complex and changing society in which they live we need the right team around the child. They need the right knowledge, understanding, attributes and skills to work in the *zone of integrated working* (Lumsden, 2018). At a minimum, these need to reflect the following:

(i) a sound knowledge and understanding in their own specific area of expertise;

(ii) to recognise the importance of integrated working;

(iii) know how to work in inter-disciplinary and multi-professional teams;

(iv) understand what it means to be inter-professional.

(Lumsden, 2018, p. 55)

While there is a plethora of professions that work in the flexible space of early childhood, it is important to point out here that there is not a distinct *early childhood profession*. For me, this is an important missing piece in the team supporting families. Since my doctoral research into workforce reform in early childhood (Lumsden, 2012) I have argued that we need a new early childhood profession, with professional standards that embrace the knowledge and skills embedded in the Quality Assurance Agency (QAA) *Early Childhood Studies Subject Benchmark Statement* (QAA, 2022).

I see this new profession as working alongside families and other professions in a range of contexts to promote early childhood development. Part of this role is working directly with new parents and carers, supporting them to develop their knowledge and understanding of child development and how they can support their children. Through empowering families with the knowledge and skills they need, we support them in keeping their children safe and are able to intervene early when there are difficulties.

EARLY CHILDHOOD INTO THE FUTURE

We know that keeping children safe is a complex task, compounded by the multifaceted challenges experienced in and outside the family. However, we have compelling research evidence that if we invest in early childhood development we can make a difference across the life course. Despite this we continually fail to invest fully in this vital period of human development. We have short-term policy initiatives that are susceptible to political change. This needs to change; we need investment that lasts beyond the term of a government, and we need to invest in a workforce to ensure that it is equipped with the knowledge and skills needed. It is also crucial to acknowledge that the systems in place to protect children do not always work effectively and embrace the fact that we need to change them. As Buckminster Fuller (1895–1983) states, 'You never change things by fighting the existing reality. To change something, build a new model that makes the existing model obsolete' (cited in Sieden, 2011, p. 358).

FIVE KEY TAKEAWAYS

1. Keeping children safe in a changing world will always be a work in progress.
2. Families need non-judgemental services to support them in their parenting role; however, there are huge international variations in how safeguarding children and supporting families is undertaken.
3. The four nations that make up the UK all have different approaches to family support and services increasingly appear to be postcode- rather than needs-led.

4. The flexible space of early childhood is occupied by a plethora of professions and professionals. However, there is not a distinct early childhood profession. For me, this is a missing piece in the jigsaw in keeping children safe. We need to develop a new professional who is steeped in knowledge and understanding of holistic child development; is able to provide appropriate, non-judgemental support and advice to their families; and has the skills to advocate for children across professional boundaries.
5. Children have the right to a graduate-led professionalised workforce to work with them.

CONCLUSION

The message embedded in this chapter is that keeping children safe in a changing world will always be a work in progress. The factors that lead to children being unsafe are complex and not just to do with experiences within their families. War, natural disasters, global warming and the ever-evolving online world bring new challenges for us all to navigate.

Enabling families to develop the knowledge and skills to keep their children safe must continue to be of paramount importance. They need timely, high-quality, non-judgemental support. This needs to be provided by a workforce equipped for the job. However, research and inquiries into safeguarding incidents in the UK inform us that we still have challenges working multi-professionally; we must and can do better. For me, part of the solution is addressing what I see as the missing piece for families, a professional steeped in holistic child development who can collaborate with parents and carers, empowering them to keep their children safe in the shifting global landscape.

REFERENCES

ACE Hub Wales (2022). *Trauma-informed Wales: A Societal Approach to Understanding, Preventing and Supporting the Impacts of Trauma and Adversity*. Available at: https://traumaframeworkcymru.com/wp-content/uploads/2022/07/Trauma-Informed-Wales-Framework.pdf. Accessed 18 June 2024.

Bronfenbrenner, U. (ed.) (2005). *Making Human Beings Human: Bioecological Perspectives on Human Development*. London: Sage.

Child Safeguarding Review Panel (2024). *Annual Report 2022/23: Patterns in practice, key messages and 2023/24 work programme*. Available at: https://assets.publishing.service.gov.

uk/media/65bce1df7042820013752116/Child_Safeguarding_Review_Panel_annual_report_2022_to_2023.pdf. Accessed 28 May 2024.

Children's Commissioner (2022a). *Family and its Protective Effect: Part 1 of the Independent Family Review*. Available at: www.childrenscommissioner.gov.uk/resource/family-and-its-protective-effect-part-1-of-the-independent-family-review/. Accessed 18 June 2024.

Children's Commissioner (2022b). *A Positive Approach to Parenting: Part 2 of the Independent Family Review*. Available at: www.childrenscommissioner.gov.uk/resource/a-positive-approach-to-parenting-part-2-of-the-independent-family-review/. Accessed 18 June 2024.

Featherstone, B. (2004). *Family Life and Family Support: A Feminist Analysis*. Basingstoke: Palgrave Macmillan.

Frost, P. N., Abbott, S. and Race, T. (2015). *Family Support: Prevention, Early Intervention and Early Help*. London: Polity Press.

Greater Manchester Police (2024). *Nursery Worker Jailed for Manslughter of 9-month-old Baby Genevieve*. Available at: www.gmp.police.uk/news/greater-manchester/news/news/2024/may/nursery-worker-jailed-for-the-manslaughter-of-9-month-old-baby-genevieve/. Accessed 16 October 2024.

HM Government (2021). *The Best Start in Life: A Vision for the 1,001 Critical Days*. Available at: https://assets.publishing.service.gov.uk/media/605c572b8fa8f545d23f8a73/Early_Years_Report.pdf. Accessed 17 October 2024.

Institute of Health Visiting (2024). *State of Health Visiting. UK Survey Report: Millions Supported as Others Miss Out*. Available at: https://mcusercontent.com/6d0ffa0c0970ad395fc6324ad/files/58826862-c0d8-d7a4-a792-a5556667d8b8/State_of_Health_Visiting_Report_2023_FINAL_VERSION_16.01.24.pdf. Accessed 16 October 2024.

Internet Watch Foundation (IWF) (2023). *Self-generated Child Sexual Abuse*. Available at: www.iwf.org.uk/annual-report-2023/trends-and-data/self-generated-child-sex-abuse/#:~:text=Of%20the%20275%2C652%20webpages%20actioned,were%20'self%2Dgenerated'. Accessed 16 October 2024.

Lumsden, E. (2012). The Early Years professional: a new professional or a missed opportunity? PhD thesis, University of Northampton.

Lumsden, E. (2016). *Workforce Issues*. University of Nottingham. Available at: https://pure.northampton.ac.uk/files/6258414/Lumsden_Eunice_2016_Workforce_Issues.pdf. Accessed 29 October 2024.

Lumsden, E. (2018) *Child Protection in the Early Years: A Practical Guide*. London: Jessica Kingsley.

Melhuish, E. C. and Gardiner, J. (2020). *Study of Early Education and Development (SEED): Impact Study on Early Education use and Child Outcomes up to Age Five Years*. London: Departent of Education. Available at: https://assets.publishing.service.gov.uk/media/5e4e5c10e90e074dcd5bd213/SEED_AGE_5_REPORT_FEB.pdf. Accessed 29 May 2024.

Ofcom (2023). *Children and Parents: Media Use and Attitudes*. Available at: https://www.ofcom.org.uk/__data/assets/pdf_file/0027/255852/childrens-media-use-and-attitudes-report-2023.pdf. Accessed 29 May 2024.

Pringle, M. and Naidoo, S. (1975). *Early Child Care in Britain*. London: Gordon and Breach.

Quality Assurance Agency (QAA) (2022). *Early Childhood Studies Subject Benchmark Statement*. Available at: www.qaa.ac.uk/the-quality-code/subject-benchmark-statements/early-childhood-studies. Accessed 2 July 2024.

Save the Children (2023). *Annual Report 2022*. Available at: www.savethechildren.org.uk/content/dam/gb/reports/annual-report-2022-save-the-children.pdf. Accessed 31 May 2024.

Scottish Government (2022). *Getting it Right for Every Child*. Available at: www.gov.scot/policies/girfec/. Accessed 29 May 2024.

Sidebotham, P., Brandon, M., Bailey, S., Belderson, P., Dodsworth, J., Garstang, J., Harrison, E., Retzer, A. and Sorensen, P. (2016). *Pathways to Harm, Pathways to Protection: A Triennial Analysis of Serious Case Reviews 2011 to 2014 Final Report*. Available at: https://assets.publishing.service.gov.uk/media/5a803010e5274a2e8ab4eb1f/Triennial_Analysis_of_SCRs_2011-2014_-__Pathways_to_harm_and_protection.pdf. Accessed 2 July 2024.

Sieden, L. S. (2011). *A Fuller View: Buckminster Fuller's Vision of Hope and Abundance for All*. Nederland, CO: Divine Arts Media.

World Health Organization (WHO) (2018). *The Nurturing Care Framework for Early Childhood Development: A Framework for Helping Children Survive and Thrive to Transform Health and Human Potential*. Available at: https://iris.who.int/bitstream/handle/10665/272603/9789241514064-eng.pdf. Accessed 28 May 2024.

WHO (2022). *Child Maltreatment*. Available at: www.who.int/news-room/fact-sheets/detail/child-maltreatment. Accessed 28 May 2024.

UNICEF (2022). *Early Moments Matter: Guaranteeing the Best Start for Life for Every Toddler and Baby in England*. Available at: www.unicef.org.uk/wp-content/uploads/2022/10/EarlyMomentsMatter_UNICEFUK_2022_PolicyReport.pdf. Accessed 16 June 2024.

United Nations (UN) (2015). *Sustainable Development*. Available at: https://sdgs.un.org/goals. Accessed 1 July 2024.

14

INCLUSION, SPECIAL EDUCATIONAL NEEDS AND DISABILITIES

Gary Coffey and Lynsey Wigfull

> **KEY DEFINITIONS**
>
> **SEND:** 'Special educational needs and disabilities' (SEND) is a term used to describe learning difficulties or disabilities that make it harder for a child or young person to learn compared to children of the same age (Sense, 2024).
>
> **Disability:** A physical or mental impairment where the impairment has a substantial and long-term adverse effect on their ability to carry out normal day-to-day activities (Equality Act, 2010).
>
> **Anti-discriminatory practices:** Continually challenging racism, sexism and other stereotypes in everything that we do. This involves challenging our own beliefs as well as those of other people.

Inclusion: Children must actively belong to, be welcomed by and participate in a setting and community – that is, they should be fully included (Farrell, 2001, p. 7).

Equality and equity: *Equality* has to do with giving everyone the exact same resources, whereas *equity* involves distributing resources based on the needs of the child.

Key person: Their role is to help ensure that every child's care is tailored to meet their individual needs, to help the child become familiar with the setting, offer a settled relationship for the child and build a relationship with their parents and/or carers. They should also help families engage with more specialist support if appropriate (DfE, 2023).

INTRODUCTION

'Inclusion' is a word that is widely used in society, particularly in reference to work with children and young people, and is something that most professionals feel strongly that they achieve. Bound up in statute and law such as the Equality Act (2010), in its simplest form, *being inclusive* means ensuring that every person feels that they belong and as a result can participate fully and achieve or succeed at the best level they can. Described in this way, it sounds like something that anyone who works with young children could reasonably be expected to naturally have at the very core of their purpose, passion and practice. However, to assume this would be to over-simplify what genuine inclusion is and should be, and might lead to a light-touch, tokenistic approach to inclusive practice which does not actually fully serve our children, or indeed their families, in the way the spirit of inclusion intends.

In this chapter, we will consider what inclusion is and how this relates to our work with children. We will explore the links between inclusive practice and early childhood and the way in which each supports the other, along with the important role that adults can play in reducing and removing barriers. Controversially, perhaps, we will also suggest that true inclusion might not ever be possible; we look at the factors that might influence success. Finally, we will think about the potential impact that developing inclusive practice in childhood and getting it right in the earliest years could have not just on the children themselves, but also on the community, on society, on the wider world and in the future. Inclusion isn't really a 'thing' or an action to be done. It is a *mindset* which involves believing that every single person has the right to be involved, to feel a sense of belonging and has something special and unique to offer, no matter how big or small.

It is subjective and it involves the perception of the person being 'included' about the extent to which they feel they belong. For this reason, it is true to say that no matter the actions being taken to include, these only succeed if the person themselves truly *feels* that they *are* included. When viewed in this way, a person may always feel they could belong to a greater extent. We should always be striving to improve how included someone is and be relentless in reviewing and addressing any new barriers or challenges that arise, no matter how big or small. It is for this reason that inclusion could be considered as being fluid, never static, and therefore something which is never truly achieved. Although this sounds like a negative, it is actually incredibly positive and requires us to continually examine our practice and the way in which we enact our beliefs. *Birth to 5 Matters* (Early Years Coalition, 2021, p. 9) states that we should all be 'anticipating, paying attention, responding to and reflecting on the needs and interests of all children'. It is through this ongoing practice that we create opportunities to ensure that relevant information is gathered and used to offer appropriate support and to adapt our delivery.

MODELS OF DISABILITY

In order to support a shared understanding of terminology, it's important to understand the term 'disability'. It is complex within itself and can be interpreted by different people in all manner of ways – be that their lived experience, internal bias or perceptions of society. There are two models of disability – the *social model* and the *medical model*.

The medical model of disability states that 'people are disabled by their impairments or differences. These impairments or differences should be "fixed" or changed by medical and other treatments' (Disability Nottinghamshire, 2020). This can have negative connotations as it often focuses on what a person cannot do, which leads to lower self-esteem and independence.

In 1983, Mike Oliver first coined the term 'social model of disability' (Oliver, 2004). Prior to this the only definition could be found within medical paperwork and the specialist fields. In the mid-20th century society began to clearly understand the experiences of people with a disability, who were able to share that they felt excluded from aspects of society. In 2013, Mike Oliver wrote an article reflecting on the successes of the model in improving inclusion and rights (Oliver, 2013). The social model of disability can be described as 'understanding that disability is something that is created by society' (Sense, 2024). There are barriers to disabled people being able to engage (physical, social and attitudinal) and the social model focuses on removing these barriers – linking to the work of inclusion and equity.

BELONGING, PARTICIPATION AND ACHIEVEMENT

We all thrive when we feel a sense of belonging, participation and achievement. The very same is true for our children. In order to create a real sense of inclusion, we must ensure that our practice is truly adaptive and focused on every child's ability to flourish. Hunt (2022) states within her work that:

> it's about belonging and being a part of a community and further reinforces the importance of recognising and appreciating the uniqueness of every child and their community and culture.
>
> (p. 29)

Within the *Early Years Foundation Stage Statutory Framework* (DfE, 2023, Section 5) it is made clear that the overarching principles of good provision include taking into account the *unique child, enabling environments* and *positive relationships*. These are the bedrock of what we should be offering and, when delivered well, support all children to learn, grow and achieve. Belonging is more than just making everyone feel welcome; it is ensuring that they know that they are important and have an integral part to play each day. The children, families and colleagues should see themselves and their reality represented in the environment and be respected by others.

However, it isn't a case of completing a reflective study or discussion within the setting once a year and claiming to be inclusive. In order to be secure within our own judgements of this, we need to ensure that inclusion is embedded deeply within day-to-day practice. It will constantly evolve based on the needs of the children and the skills and knowledge of professionals. We should be working on the understanding that inclusion is never truly achieved and further work can be done to support everyone. Fisher (2024) refers to the importance of educators offering 'experiences that allow [children] to continue believing in themselves as competent, and that allow them to show us, every day, their strengths and what they enjoy' (p. 11).

Again, this draws on our ability to see success in all forms, not just the achievement of an Early Learning Goal (ELG). You may want to consider the questions below and share these with colleagues in your setting.

- How do we measure success for each child?
- How do we celebrate this in a meaningful way?
- How do we make them feel valued?
- What does *participation in learning* look like for individual children?
- How does each child show joy and respond to positive experiences?
- Am I aware of how an identified SEND may impact all of the above?

THE IMPORTANCE OF THE ADULT'S MINDSET

As mentioned in the section above, the adults working with children have a pivotal role to play in securing the very best provision. Not only must we constantly reflect on the success of the child's learning and personal development, but we must also reflect on our own knowledge too. We must establish a mindset of what inclusion and SEND mean within settings. In a 2018 study, Collett (2018) identified that although a lot of developments have been made within the inclusion of disabled children within early education, often an identified disability can present as an 'issue' or a 'problem' to many practitioners. The national context shows that there has been a rapid increase since 2010 in the number of children born with a disability, who will be accessing Early Years provision (gov.uk, 2020). Therefore, there is a moral imperative to 'get it right' for all children and in adapting our practice to the changing needs.

The relationships that adults develop with children are integral to success. Bradbury and Grimmer (2024) state that:

> through relationships we learn empathy, social etiquette, how to relate to others and how to be a good friend.
>
> (p. 90)

For children with SEND, these relationships are paramount to support this. Often, the adult might initiate communication or use gestural or physical prompts to engage a child in their learning. Children must feel secure in these relationships and in the support that they are receiving. As important role models and communication partners, adults must adapt their practice frequently to meet the needs of every child – which will vary from group to group, day to day and year to year. The practice we offer now will likely be very different to our experiences only a couple of years ago. The expectation of the Early Years Foundation Stage Framework is that every child is allocated a key person who is responsible for ensuring that individual needs are met and to offer a secure relationship. This adult (key person) is best placed to be the advocate for ensuring that further training and professional development are aligned to any emerging SEND and child-specific need.

The key person's relationship with the child can only be successful when the child's family and caregivers are involved. This is true for all children, but it is critical when supporting children with SEND. Families and carers will be attuned to their child's specific needs and will have a deep-rooted understanding of how their child communicates, their preferences and how to support their participation and promote achievement. Dowling (2010) states that:

> practitioners recognise that the development of close links between the home and the setting is above all else in the interest of the child.
>
> (p. 34)

Bakopoulou (2022, p. 648) recently completed a study into the impact of transitions on children with SEND and found that 'visits to school were seen as important in building relationships, enabling the [adults] to observe and spend time with the child'. This was further enhanced through discussions with families, who could share rich and meaningful information too. Settings should be mindful of the transitions into and out of the provision and how this time is successfully utilised to build relationships with families and caregivers. Dunlop and Fabian (2007) introduce the concept of *transition models*, which encourage practitioners to focus on the different aspects of a child's transition between settings and the 'formality' of these. It is these opportunities that practitioners should be using to ensure that the relevant information is gathered and used to inform the appropriate support within the setting and that this is identified quickly.

Within this section we have focused on the role of practitioners to develop positive relationships with children and their families. However, we must acknowledge the importance of self-awareness too. As professionals within Early Years, we must understand our own practice and be encouraged to recognise our biases – be they conscious or unconscious. For example, the language we use when talking about an individual child with SEND to their family or a work colleague may unintentionally lead to upset or a misunderstanding. Daniel (2023) states that:

> we have to acknowledge that our best intentions for every child in our setting can be undermined by this kind of implicit bias which leads us to form quick decisions about a situation or a person without necessarily being consciously aware of it.
>
> (p. 67)

We must have professional regard and curiosity for our own practice to ensure that we are not limiting our expectations of children's abilities or using 'labels' and diagnoses to make predictions about their future success. Wall (2006, p. 96) refers to the negative impact that labelling can have and states that this 'may inadvertently place unrealistic expectations on the child or simply assume that they will demonstrate unacceptable behaviours and wait for it to happen'. Good professional development and ongoing training will help to ensure that we are continuing to learn about newly identified needs and will help to prevent these situations from occurring. Practitioners must be eager to engage in this process and Borkett (2021) references the importance of this by stating that it is vital that practitioners are trained appropriately when supporting all children, but especially those who have SEND. Children may have medical issues whereby staff are required to put in place interventions which can be obtrusive and difficult to administer. Further support for settings can be found through collaborative working with families, but also external agencies including local health teams such as speech and language therapists, physiotherapists and community nurses.

EARLY CHILDHOOD: A MEANS FOR AFFECTING REAL CHANGE

Good Early Years education provides children with a secure and strong start in life. The greatest support that practitioners can offer is that of early identification of potential barriers to health and learning and to make appropriate adaptations as soon as possible. This may also include referral onwards to health and/or social care, but it's important to note that a formal diagnosis is only one part of the inclusion agenda; how we use this on an individual basis to shape our provision and develop the positive relationships is crucial, as mentioned previously. Lansing Cameron and Thygesen (2015) state that:

> the increasing influence of the social model over the last several decades represents an historical transition in the field of special education that is closely tied to the movement towards inclusive education in general.
>
> (p. 9)

Best practice can be identified as that where the child is at the centre of every decision made and this aligns with the UNCRC (1989) which Musgrave (2017) states 'was the start of a global initiative to recognise children as individuals in society' (2017, p. 34). Our drive to discover what children can do, as opposed to what they can't, reinforces the notion of the social model of disability as set out earlier in this chapter. Practitioners who start their work from a strengths-based perspective rather than applying a deficit model will help to build the self-esteem of each child and this will undoubtedly have a positive impact on outcomes and success. Dowling (2010) acknowledges this and states:

> one of the most important gifts we can offer young children is a positive view of themselves. Without this gift they will flounder throughout life and be constantly seeking reassurance from others as they cannot seek it from within.
>
> (p. 15)

This early support and development will have a lasting impact into later childhood and, in turn, adulthood. By getting the offer right early on, we can ensure that children are given positive strategies to help them be successful.

High-quality and effective Early Years settings can help to raise the expectations for school-based education too. Well-trained and skilled Early Years practitioners will be able to transfer a wealth of knowledge about individual children and how their learning may be affected by an identified need onto their next phase of education. In order for settings to be able to effectively include children with SEND into their individual transition pathway, it is important to develop a strategy. Ravenscroft et al. (2017) recommend that all professionals develop a transition strategy document with clear procedures, timelines, relevant agencies, target groups and indicators for success. It is imperative that families are involved within this document too as their understanding and lived experience is extremely useful. The information shared will help to ensure that other professionals, including those within schools, are able to build on effective strategies for all children.

Ultimately, we should strive for a culture where diversity is normalised, leading to differences being celebrated and welcomed by all. We know that children are naturally curious about the world around them, including each other, and the Early Years are ideal as a time to ensure that this is carried out through a positive lens and one that values everybody equally. We can reduce fears and increase acceptance of difference through shared experiences. Daniel (2023, p. 130) states that we should 'never give up on trying to do better for the children in our care', which includes those from different backgrounds, genders and with a range of disabilities. It may be helpful to consider the questions below when considering the wider impact of your work and anti-discriminatory practice.

- How do you promote a sense of positive inclusion with the children you work with?
- Are your resources reflective of the needs and experiences of all children?
- Is your practice starting from a strengths-based model?
- What transitional arrangements do you have in place to ensure that the information for the 'whole child' can be shared?

EARLY CHILDHOOD INTO THE FUTURE

Although there has been a significant change towards greater inclusion in recent years, there is still much work to do be done to ensure that this is applied equally across all settings and stages of education. The following points highlight a number of key areas that are important for future development within Early Years specifically.

CURRICULUM

Following an increase in the number of children with a SEND now accessing Early Years, it is important to consider the curriculum being offered. It is not possible for *one* curriculum model to effectively meet the needs of all children, especially those with additional needs. Goodwin (2023) states that:

> developmentally sequenced curriculums are typically based on normative child development sequences and do not consider the complexity of multiple disabilities that pervasively impact and which alter a pupil's developmental trajectory.
>
> (p. 24)

The Early Years curriculum of the future must be one which recognises this and provides greater scope for practitioners to be brave and to make relevant changes to the provision, in order for every child to succeed. Greater recognition and celebration of achievement at all levels should be aligned to the strengths-based approach for what a child *can* achieve, as opposed to the goals that they haven't. Currently, the framework and measures of success are too narrow in facilitating this and practitioners may not feel that they have the support to be able to do so.

Lacey (2011) explains that success is achieved when practitioners understand that they are teaching fundamental skills which are often mastered by typically developing children in their formative years. It is important for practitioners to be confident in their own knowledge of a child's development through their knowledge of the child via observations and other assessment. Crutchley (2018) draws attention to the issue of the national frameworks for Early Years assessment for children with SEND as having:

> limited usefulness for practitioners wishing to know how to support children with SEND who may be operating at a level below the expected level of attainment.
>
> (p. 51)

The curriculum should be reflective of the needs of the child and, in turn, focused on the here and now and informed and adapted based on the child's immediate preferences and skills base. If settings try to work towards unachievable and unattainable goals set by those who do not know the child, then the *true* progress and steps of success are at risk of being lost within a system that was not designed for every child.

FUNDING

Early Years settings and practitioners must be funded at a level which recognises the important work that takes place in the formative years. A respected, well-skilled, appreciated and well-paid workforce would ensure that all of these discussion points were implemented effectively. However, funding also relates to the prominence given to developing practice and continuing professional development. There must be greater access to responsive training which better meets all children's needs. This could be in partnership with local specialist providers and services and funded from a local level. Often, individual settings are having to buy in additional support, which should be available as a universal service. This can lead to a lack of joined-up thinking and action between services – often to the detriment of the child. Burrows and Cowie (2022) state that:

> multi-agency discussions can provide a valuable perspective due to the opportunities they have had of getting to know families and their children over a significant period of time.
>
> (p. 348)

FIVE KEY TAKEAWAYS

1. Good provision for children with SEND is good provision for *all* children.
2. Adults are key and a focus on training, delivery and ongoing development is important, alongside collaborative partnerships with families and caregivers.
3. Inclusion is ongoing and we must be truly reflective at all times to ensure that we are working towards equity for all.
4. Curriculum and assessment should be entirely focused on meeting the needs of each child.
5. Early identification of additional needs and suitable interventions have a positive impact on children's futures. Therefore, investment in interagency support and quick access to relevant professionals should be a priority.

CONCLUSION

This chapter has focused on the key elements of effective inclusion for children with SEND. However, there is so much more to consider and, as mentioned, it is our responsibility as practitioners to ensure that we are further seeking out new information and engaging in meaningful professional development. To summarise the key concepts covered within, the simple diagram shown in Figure 14.1 represents the identified strategies to consider within every setting.

By following the strategies above, we will be able to ensure that they build on the successes for inclusion. Fails-Nelson (2004) suggests that successful settings are those that have spent time building home school community partnerships and ensure that these support families, local settings and the wider community too.

There must be an increased awareness of how the environment and other adults can impact a child's life experiences, which incorporates inclusion at the centre. Linked to this is the importance of the key person in ensuring that they have a secure understanding of the child's experiences, skills and needs and that they learn from the child too. This reciprocal relationship cannot be underestimated; Patel (2000) argues that children must feel safe and secure in order to continue to develop, and for children to feel a sense of belonging a homely, stable environment must be provided. This supports the cause for practitioners to focus on getting *inclusion* right for each child and for developing a nurturing environment from the start.

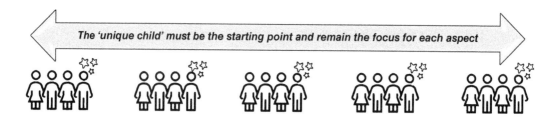
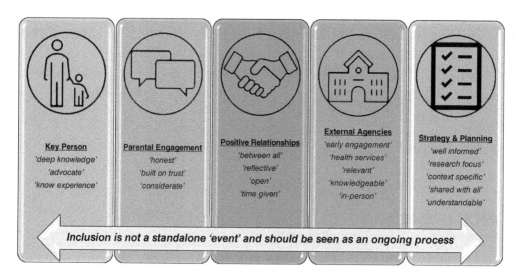

Figure 14.1 Strategies for inclusion

REFERENCES

Bakopoulou, I. (2022). The impact of the COVID-19 pandemic on Early Years transition to school in the UK context. *Education 3–13, 52*(5), 648–61.

Borkett, P. (2021). *Special Educational Needs in the Early Years: A Guide to Inclusive Practice*. London: Sage.

Bradbury, A. and Grimmer, T. (2024). *Love and Nurture in the Early Years*. London: Sage.

Burrows, P. and Cowie, J. (2022). *Health Visiting*. 3rd edn. London: Elsevier.

Collett, C. (2018). *Disability and Inclusion in Early Years Education*. London: Routledge.

Crutchley, R. (2018). *Special Needs in the Early Years*. London: Sage.

Daniel, V. (2023). *Anti-racist Practice in the Early Years: A Holistic Framework for the Wellbeing of All Children*. London: Routledge.

Department for Education (DfE) (2023). *Early Years Foundation Stage Statutory Framework*. Available at: https://assets.publishing.service.gov.uk/media/65aa5e42ed27ca001327b2c7/EYFS_statutory_framework_for_group_and_school_based_providers.pdf. Accessed 8 September 2024.

Disability Nottinghamshire (2020). *Social Model VS Medical Model of Disability.* Available at: www.disabilitynottinghamshire.org.uk/index.php/about/social-model-vs-medical-model-of-disability/. Accessed 8 September 2024.

Dowling, M. (2010). *Young Children's Personal, Social and Emotional Development.* 3rd edn. London: Sage.

Dunlop, A. and Fabian, H. (2007). *Informing Transitions in the Early Years: Research, Policy and Practice.* 1st edn. Maidenhead: McGraw-Hill/Open University Press.

Early Years Coalition (2021). *Birth to 5 Matters: Non-statutory Guidance for the Early Years Foundation Stage.* Available at https://birthto5matters.org.uk/wp-content/uploads/2021/04/Birthto5Matters-download.pdf. Accessed 8 September 2024.

Equality Act (2010). London: HMSO.

Fails-Nelson, R. (2004). The transition to kindergarten. *Early Childhood Education Journal, 32*(3), 187–90. Available at: https://link.springer.com/article/10.1023/B:ECEJ.0000048971.21662.01#citeas. Accessed 8 September 2024.

Farrell, P. (2001). Special education in the last twenty years: have things really got better? *British Journal of Special Education, 28*(1), 7.

Fisher, J. (2024). *Starting from the Child?* 5th edn. Maidenhead: McGraw-Hill Education.

Goodwin, M. (2023). Let the pupil lead the learning! *PMLD Link, 35*(105).

gov.uk (2020). *Research and Analysis, Chapter 1: Education and Children's Social Care.* Available at: www.gov.uk/government/publications/people-with-learning-disabilities-in-england/chapter-1-education-and-childrens-social-care-updates. Accessed 8 September 2024.

Hunt, M. (2022). *Helping Every Child to Thrive in the Early Years: How to Overcome the Effect of Disadvantage.* London: Routledge.

Lacey, P. (2011). Developing a curriculum for pupils with PMLD. *The SLD Experience, 61*(1), 5, 6.

Lansing Cameron, D. and Thygesen, R. (2015). *Transitions in the Field of Special Education.* Munster: Waxmann.

Musgrave, J. (2017). *Supporting Children's Health and Wellbeing.* London: Sage.

Oliver, M. (2004). The social model in action: if I had a hammer. In C. Barnes and G. Mercer (eds), *Implementing the Social Model of Disability: Theory and Research.* Leeds: Disability Press.

Oliver, M. (2013). The social model of disability: thirty years on. *Disability and Society, 28*(7), 1024–6.

Patel, A. (2000). Supporting transitions in the Early Years. *Teach Early Years.* Available at: www.teachearlyyears.com/a-unique-child/view/supporting-transitions-in-the-early-years. Accessed 8 September 2024.

Ravenscroft, J., Wazny, K. and Davis, J. (2017). Factors associated with successful transition among children with disabilities in eight European countries. *PLOS ONE, 12*(6), e0179904. Available at: https://journals.plos.org/plosone/article?id=10.1371/journal.pone.0179904. Accessed 8 September 2024.

Sense (2024). *The Social Model of Disability.* Available at: www.sense.org.uk/about-us/the-social-model-of-disability/#:~:text=The%20medical%20model%20suggests%20that,barriers%20they%20experience%20in%20society. Accessed 8 September 2024.

UNCRC (1989). *United Nations Convention on the Rights of the Child.* Available at: www.2.ohchr.org/english/law/crc.htm. Accessed 17 October 2024.

Wall, K. (2006). *Special Needs and Early Years: A Practitioner's Guide.* 2nd edn. London: Sage.

INDEX

The 2030 Agenda for Sustainable Development (UNESCO), 27–28

Academy of Medical Sciences Report, 54
active learning, 146
adult's mindset, importance of, 167–169
adverse childhood experiences (ACEs), 41
advocacy, 9
agency, 10, 27, 72, 112–114, 129
Alexander, E., 76
Ang, L., 143
antenatal care, 50
antibiotics, discovery of, 49
anti-discriminatory practices, 164, 171
apprenticeship, 123
Arlemalm-Hagser, E., 29
Aslan, Z., 87, 88
assessment, and curriculum, 172
Association for the Professional Development of Early Years Educators, 98
attachment, 41, 44
auto-education, 64
Aynsley-Green, A., 19

babies and children's health and wellbeing, 48–58
Bakopoulou, I., 168
Belonging, Being and Becoming: The Early Years Learning Framework for Australia (2009), 87
belonging, importance of, 84, 87–88, 166–167
Bertram, A., 148
Bessell, S., 78
Best Start for Life policy development, 3, 11, 40, 74, 157–159
Birth to 5 Matters document, 18–19, 86, 112, 114, 166
Bold Beginnings (Ofsted), 133
Borkett, P., 77, 169
Bottrill, G., 130
Bradbury, A., 102–103, 134, 135, 168
Broadhead, P., 145
Bronfenbrenner, U., 26, 154
Bryant, P., 135
Building Great Britons (2015), 3, 11
Burrows, P., 172
Burt, A., 145

Cameron, C., 17, 111
Campbell-Barr, V., 65, 66, 136
change, manifesto for, 79
characteristics of effective learning (CoEL), 146
Chesworth, E. A., 66
Chesworth, L., 130
child abuse, 153, 155
Childcare Act (2006), 2, 98

childhoodnature, 114
Child Poverty Action Group (CPAG), 1
child protection, 153
children
   access to play, 109–110
   agency, 112–114
   anxiety, 40
   apprenticeship into digital literacy, 123–124
   changing views of developmental child, 143–144
   emotional literacy in, 42–43
   as experts in their own lives, 110–114
   forced displacement on, 84–85
   funds of knowledge, 66, 85, 112, 130
   health and wellbeing, 48–58
      contemporary health issues, 53–54
      early childhood education and care settings, 54–57
      factors influencing, 50–53
      helping the family (case study), 54–55
      historical perspective, 49–50
      promoting, 56–57
   inclusion of technology in play, 125
   listening to voices of young, 148
   locus of control, 113
   participation of, 107, 111–112
   play, 131
   in poverty, 1, 49, 54
   refugee and migrant, 84–90
   rights, 107, 108–110
   safe internet use for young, 155
   safety, in changing world, 153–161
   See also early childhood; *specific entries*
   with SEND, 168, 172
   voices, 107, 110–111
   workforce, 153
   working theories, 66
Children's Alliance, 12–13
Child Safeguarding Review Panel, 156, 159
child's bio-system, revised module of, 26
Choice for Parents, the Best Start for Children (HM Treasury, 2004), 2
chronic health condition, 48
Clarke, A., 88
cognitive behavioural therapy (CBT), 38, 42
cognitive development, stages of, 131
cognitive flexibility, 129
Collett, C., 168
communicable diseases, 53
community, 72, 75
conduct disorders, interventions for, 42

contextual curriculum, 61, 66
continual professional development (CPD), 103
Contreras, M. J., 116
converged play, 122
'coping with our kids' programme, 41
coproduction, 73, 76, 77
Cottle, M., 76
Cowie, J., 172
creative and critical learning, with technologies through play, 122–123
critically reflective technology use, in early childhood, 120–121
Crutchley, R., 172
culture, importance of, 29
curriculums, 54, 57, 61–69, 171–172

Daniel, V., 169, 171
Davis, J., 26
Delfin, A. B., 122
Derbyshire, N., 135
developmental child, changing views of, 143–144
Development Matters (DfE), 18
digital devices, in early childhood, 118–126
digital literacy, children's apprenticeship into, 123–124
digital play, 124
digital technology, 118
Dillon, J. T., 62
disability, 164, 166
Dowling, M., 168, 170
Dunlop, A., 169

early childhood
  as academic discipline, 15
  agency, 27
  critically reflective technology use in, 120–121
  curriculums, 54, 57, 61–69
  degrees, 101
  Education Health Promotion Toolkit, 57
  and education settings, 95
  into the future, 39–40
    children's rights, 114–115
    curriculums, 67–68, 171–172
    funding, 172
    keeping children safe, 160
    social contexts, 144–145
    sustainable pedagogy and wisdom shepherds, 28–34
  global dynamics of, 83–91
  graduates, 96–97
  harnessing the potential of digital devices in, 118–126
  learnt from the workforce, 100–102
  maltreatment in, 156
  means for affecting real change, 169–171
  physical and emotional environments, 113
  play and pedagogy, 129–138
  positioning of parents in, 75–77
  into post-digital future, 125
  qualifications, 97–100
  quality of, 97
  refocusing and working towards strategy, 102–103
  and relevance of educational sustainable development, 25
  social contexts of, 141–150
  sustainable pedagogy, 23–35
  workforce, 159
    development, 94–104
early childhood education and care (ECEC), 15
  children's rights, voice and participation in, 108
  graduate-led workforce in, 101
  health promotion in, 56–57
  role of, 54–56
  welcoming practices to support belonging in, 83–91

An Early Childhood Education for Sustainability Resource (Boyd), 34
Early Childhood Manifesto (ECSDN), 12, 13–14
early childhood policy
  academics and research, 16–17
  advocating for change, 3–4, 9–20
  child-centred approach, 12–14
  opportunities for advocacy, 18–19
  overview, 10–11
  potential of research, 14–16
  role of early childhood professional, 19–20
  setting, 10
  Sure Start initiative, 15–16
early childhood professional
  role in policy development, 10, 19–20
Early Childhood Studies Degrees Network (ECSDN), 12, 13–14, 100
early education, as split system, 95
Early Intervention: The Next Steps – Allen Report (2011), 2
Early Learning Goals (ELGs), 63, 65, 167
Early Years, 15
Early Years Coalition, 18
Early Years educator (EYE) role, 98
Early Years Foundation Stage (EYFS), 2, 25, 42, 54, 63, 65, 98, 109, 146, 168
Early Years Foundation Stage Statutory Framework, 167
Early Years Healthy Development Review, 158, 159
Early Years initial teacher training (EYITT), 102
Early Years Inspection Framework, 133
Early Years pioneers, 63–65
Early Years professional status (EYPS), 101–102
Early Years teacher (graduate) role, 98
Early Years teacher status (EYTS), 102
Early Years Workforce Strategy, 143
ecological systems theory, 26, 87
education for sustainable development (ESD), 24, 25
Education Health Promotion Toolkit, 57
educators, 118
Eisenstadt, E., 14
Elliott, S., 26, 29
emergent curriculum, 61, 66
emotional literacy, 39, 42–43
empowerment, 25, 29, 144
Equality Act (2010), 165
equality and equity, 165
Erikson, E. H., 145
Every Child Matters agenda, 2, 102
Evidence-based Early Years Intervention (2018), 3, 11
executive function, 129
expressive curriculum, 61, 66, 136

Fabian, H., 169
Facetime, 121
Fails-Nelson, R., 173
family
  role in child wellbeing and safety, 156–159
  support, 153, 157
First 1000 Days of Life (2019), 3, 11
Fisher, J., 134, 167
Fleming, K., 77
forced displacement, 83, 84–85
Formosinho, J., 144
Foundations for Quality report, 143
freedom with guidance, 136
Free Nursery education for two-year-olds (2010), 2
Froebel, F., 64, 65
Fuller, B., 160

funding, 172
funds of knowledge (FOK), 66, 85, 112, 129, 130, 144

Gaywood, D., 85, 86, 88
Goodwin, M., 171
Goswami, U., 135
government policy, 9
Graduate Practitioner Competencies (GPCs), 27, 78–79, 94, 96, 99
Gray, P., 130
Green Paper – Every Child Matters (DfES, 2003), 2
Grimmer, T., 168
guided participation, 123
Günther, J., 30

Hakyemez-Paul, S., 76
Hasan, A., 1
Hawkes, J., 78
Hayes, N., 111
health, 48
health promotion, in early childhood education and care settings, 56–57
Healthy Child Programme (PHE), 39
Hedges, H., 66
Hevey, D., 101
hidden curriculum, 61, 68
Hoffman, E., 88
home-from-home learning environment, with curriculum, 65
Huber, B., 122
Hughes, B., 130, 131
Hultcrantz, E., 85
Hunt, M., 167

impulse control, 129
inclusion, 165, 168, 173
    strategies for, 174
Inclusive Education Toolkit, 84
Incredible Years™ programme, 42
infant health, 38, 41
infant mortality, 49
in-groups, 87
Insights into a High Quality Early Years Curriculum project, 65–66, 67
Institute for Economics and Peace, 84
Institute of Health Visiting, 158
intent participation, 123
interaction, 141
intercultural sensitivity, promoting, 89–90
Internet Watch Foundation (IWF), 155
Ipsos MORI (2020), 3, 11
Isaacs, S., 64, 65
It's a No-Money Day (Milner), 34

Jarvis, P., 130

key person, 165, 168, 173
Key Stage 1, of national curriculum, 63
kindness tree, 88–89
Kjørholt, A. T., 75, 78

Lacey, P., 172
Lansing Cameron, D., 170
lobbying, 9
local policy, 9
locus of control, 113
Lumsden, E., 101

Malaguzzi, L., 64, 148
Malone, K., 114

A Manifesto for Babies (Parent Infant Foundation), 12, 13
Marmot, M., 39
Marsh, J., 124
maternal health, 38
McMillan, M., 49, 64, 65
medical model of disability, 166
mental health, 40–41, 48
mental self-regulation, 147
models (medical/social), of disability, 166, 170
Moll, L. C., 85
Montessori, M., 64, 65
More Affordable Childcare (2013), 3
More Great Childcare (2013), 3
Mosaic approach, 111
Moss, P., 17, 29, 111
motherhood and early childhood workforce, 100–101
Moylett, H., 146
multi-agency collaboration, 38
Murray, J., 110
Musgrave, J., 101, 170

Naidoo, S., 155
National Childcare Strategy (DFEE, 1998), 2
neoliberalism, 10, 17, 26, 73
non-communicable diseases, 53
Nuffield Foundation, 101
Nurturing Care Framework, 155
Nutbrown, C., 95, 97–98, 102

Ofcom, 154
Ofsted, 132, 133
Oliver, M., 166
Organization for Economic Co-operation and Development (OECD), 97
Ortega, Y., 85
out-groups, 87
Oxford, R., 85

Parent Infant Foundation, 12, 13
parenting, 41–42, 156–157
parents, 72
    positioning, in early childhood, 75–77
Paris Agreement, 27–28
Parten, M., 131
participation, children's, 72, 107, 111–112, 166–167
participatory approach, 141
partnership with parents and caregivers, 79
Pascal, C., 144, 148
Patel, A., 173
pedagogy
    and play, 131–132
    See also sustainable pedagogy
Penn, H., 75
Pestalozzi, H., 64
Peterson, L., 43
physical/emotional abuse, 155
Piaget, J., 131
play, 130, 141
    access to, 109–110
    associated with children, 131
    balance of child-led, 136
    centrality of, 145–146
    across childhood, 12–13
    creative and critical learning with technologies through, 122–123
    in curriculum, 130, 134
    defining, 130
    importance of, 135–136

inclusion of technology in, 125
learning through, 136
misconceptions about, 133
pedagogy and, 131–132
playful learning and, 146
six elements of, 130
subcategories of, 131
teaching and, 133
types of, 131
as work of children, 146
on young children's learning, 134
playful learning experiences, 132
Plowman, L., 123, 124
policy, 9
post-digital, 118, 119–120
posthuman theories, 114
The Power of Play: Building a Creative Britain (Children's Alliance), 12–13
Pringle, M., 155
problematic nature of early childhood education, 143
problem-solving, 43–44
professional, 72
Prosser, J., 116
proximal and distal interaction, 123
psychiatric disorders, 41
psychotic disorders, 41

qualifications, in early childhood sector, 97–100
qualified teacher (QT), 98
qualified teacher status (QTS), 102
Quality Assurance Agency (QAA)
　Early Childhood Studies Subject Benchmark Statement, 160

Ravenscroft, J., 170
research and reports, across early childhood networks, 15
resignation syndrome, 85
rights, 107
rights-based approach, 147–148
rights-based pedagogy, 23
Rinaldi, C., 148
Rousseau, J. J., 64
Royal College of Paediatricians and Child Health (RCPCH), 49–50
Rwanda Bill, 84

safeguarding, 153
School Inspection Framework, 133
school nurse
　transforming the role, to meet health needs of young children, 38–45
school readiness, 74, 134, 143
Scott, F., 124
screen time, 119
Seker, B. D., 87, 88
self-esteem, 170
self-regulation, 130
self, sense of, 87, 89
serve and return interactions, 130, 135
Skype, 121
social and cultural sustainability, through coproduction, 77–78
social cohesion, 74, 75
social contexts of early childhood, 141–150
　centrality of play, 145–146
　changing views of developmental child, 143–144
　enabling environments, 147
　new ways of knowing, 144–145
　participation and ongoing need for reflection in and on practice, 148–149
　problematic nature of early childhood education, 143
　rights-based approach, 147–148

social identity theory, 87
social media risks, addressing, 155
social model of disability, 166, 170
social sustainability, 27, 29
special educational needs and disabilities (SEND), 164, 168, 172
Stagnitti, K., 135
Stop, Think, Act, Reflect programme, 44
Strekalova-Hughes, E., 89
suicide rate, 43
Sure Start initiative
　short- and medium-term impacts of, 15–16
sustainability
　in Brundtland report, 25
　early childhood education for, 31
　environmental pillar of, 30
　foundations of, 25–26
　key components for, 25
　relating to early childhood, 25
　three pillars of, 24, 30–31
Sustainability and Climate Change Strategy (DfE), 24, 28
Sustainability Matters in Early Childhood (Boyd), 27
Sustainable Development Goals (SDGs), 23, 24, 27–28, 52, 159
sustainable ethos (case study), 31–33
sustainable pedagogy, 23, 27, 34
　and wisdom shepherds, 28–34
Swailes, R., 135
symbolic play, with pretend technologies, 122

Tackling Disadvantage in the Early Years (2019), 3t, 11
Tajfel, H., 87
taxonomy, 130
teaching, defining, 134
Thompson P., 76
three pillars of sustainability, 24, 30–31
Thygesen, R., 170
Transforming Early Childhood Education in England (Moss and Cameron), 17
transition models, 169
transitions, 84, 86–87
Turner, J. C., 87

United Nation High Commission for Refugees (UNHCR), 84
United Nations Convention on the Rights of the Child (UNCRC), 52, 109, 110, 112, 114, 115, 131, 136, 147, 170
Urban, M., 73, 74

Vandenbroeck, M., 17
voices, children's, 107, 110–111
von Knorring, A., 85
Vulnerable Children Resettlement Scheme, 84
Vulnerable Persons Resettlement Scheme, 84

Wagner, J. T., 74
Wall, K., 108, 110–111, 169
Wang, W., 122
Wang, X. C., 89
welcoming practices, 84, 88–90
wellbeing, 48
Whitebread, D., 136
wisdom keepers, 30
wisdom shepherds, 23, 30
Wood, E., 66
workforce
　early childhood, 100–102, 159–160
　strategy, 94
working memory, 129

Zoom, 121